PSYCHOLOGY PRACTITIONER GUIDEBOOKS

EDITORS

Arnold P. Goldstein, Syracuse University
Leonard Krasner, Stanford University & SUNY at Stony Brook
Sol L. Garfield, Washington University in St. Louis

COGNITIVE-BEHAVIORAL INTERVENTIONS WITH YOUNG OFFENDERS

Pergamon Titles of Related Interest

Related Journals
(Free sample copies available upon request)

COGNITIVE-BEHAVIORAL INTERVENTIONS WITH YOUNG OFFENDERS

CLIVE R. HOLLIN
University of Leicester

PERGAMON PRESS
Member of Maxwell Macmillan Pergamon Publishing Corporation
New York • Oxford • Beijing • Frankfurt
São Paulo • Sydney • Tokyo • Toronto

Pergamon Press Offices:

U.S.A.	Pergamon Press, Inc., Maxwell House, Fairview Park, Elmsford, New York 10523, U.S.A.
U.K.	Pergamon Press plc, Headington Hill Hall, Oxford OX3 0BW, England
PEOPLE'S REPUBLIC OF CHINA	Pergamon Press, Room 4037, Qianmen Hotel, Beijing, People's Republic of China
FEDERAL REPUBLIC OF GERMANY	Pergamon Press GmbH, Hammerweg 6, D-6242 Kronberg, Federal Republic of Germany
BRAZIL	Pergamon Editora Ltda, Rua Eca de Queiros, 346, CEP 04011, São Paulo, Brazil
AUSTRALIA	Pergamon Press Australia Pty Ltd., P.O. Box 544, Potts Point, NSW 2011, Australia
JAPAN	Pergamon Press, 8th Floor, Matsuoka Central Building, 1-7-1 Nishishinjuku, Shinjuku-ku, Tokyo 160, Japan
CANADA	Pergamon Press Canada Ltd., Suite 271, 253 College Street, Toronto, Ontario M5T 1R5, Canada

---

Library of Congress Cataloging in Publication Data

Hollin, Clive R.
  Cognitive-behavioral interventions with young offenders / Clive R. Hollin.
    p. cm. -- (Psychology practitioner guidebooks)
  Includes index.
  ISBN 0-08-035870-5 :   ISBN 0-08-035871-3 (soft)
  1. Rehabilitation of juvenile delinquents. 2. Social work with delinquents and criminals. 3. Juvenile delinquents--Counseling of. 4. Behavior modification. I. Title. II. Series.
    [DNLM: 1. Behavior Therapy--methods. 2. Criminal Psychology. 3. Juvenile Delinquency--rehabilitation. HV 9069 H741c]
  HV9069.H67   1989
  364.3'6--dc19   89-2946
                                                                         CIP

Printed in the United States of America

The paper used in this publication meets the minimum requirements of American National Standard for Information Sciences -- Permanence of Paper for Printed Library Materials, ANSI Z39.48-1984

For Kate

Contents

Preface

When embarking on any piece of writing one never quite knows what will happen on route to the final manuscript: Some books and papers turn into demons possessed with a spirit of their own, others refuse to come to life; some make one's life a misery, others become a pleasing experience. This book has been a pleasure to write, the material flowing easily and each chapter forming itself quickly without those dreadful pauses sometimes encountered as one waits for a structure to appear. On reflection the relative ease of the writing is perhaps not too surprising, as the topic of clinical criminology is one I have been concerned with for the past decade in the various roles of clinician, researcher, and teacher.

Working with young offenders gave me some harsh lessons in the realities of institutions in which some young offenders, like some of the staff, want nothing to do with you or your interventions. One quickly discovers the difficulties, the petty bureaucracies and politics, of delivering a service even to those young offenders who reject what you have to offer. Yet further, there is the realization that criminal behavior is not the same as other behaviors with which clinicians are more familiar: In the real world there are genuine rewards for criminal behavior—What can a clinician possibly offer to compete with the financial and social gains offered to the successful offender? I recall one particular conversation with an articulate young offender who was perfectly able to defend his brand of crime—theft from business premises—both morally and politically. My only defense against the charge of my being a "mug," i.e., someone being unwittingly used by the system, was that at the end of the day I could go home and he was locked inside.

Such rational arguments gave me occasion to wonder whether the answer to crime lies, as many administrators and politicians would have us believe, in rational responses in the form of harsh regimes to deter would-be offenders. As sometimes happens, a personal experience convinced me that this abstract notion of simple deterrence is not satisfactory.

In the young offender institution in which I worked there was a set of cells, known as "the block," which served to contain and to punish any young person who offended seriously against institutional rules by, say, committing acts of aggression or attempting to abscond. The young offenders with whom the psychologists were familiar were among those who were likely to spend some time "down the block." We psychologists would periodically receive a telephone call saying that "one of ours" was heading for the block, and we would make our way down to do what little we could. The block was, at least at the times I visited it, always calm: There might be no more than two or three young people there, so that there was none of the noise one associates with institutions containing large numbers of people. There were perhaps a dozen cells, all painted light green and with high ceilings, which were long and narrow with one small, barred window set high up from the floor allowing a little natural light but no view of the world. The bed was taken out during the day, leaving only a slightly raised concrete platform on the floor to break the uniformity of the cell: No books, newspapers, or radios were allowed.

On this particular occasion I was in the central area of the block, a clear open space with cells leading off from either side, talking with a young offender who in a fit of temper had hit another offender and was serving 2 weeks in the block as punishment. A prison officer was at hand, and when the offender and I had finished talking, I thanked the officer for allowing me access to the young person. "Okay, son," he said, without any particular emotion, to the offender. The boy, aged perhaps 16, stood up and walked uncomplainingly into the bare cell, the door was shut, and the lock turned. Just an ordinary everyday minor social exchange that had happened hundreds of times before, but as I left the block, I realized what I had seen: two human beings who accepted, without bitterness or rancor on either side, that it was normal to lock someone up for hours in such a bare, featureless environment. A prison officer who turned a key impassively, not for revenge or with glee, but simply as a part of his job; a young person who walked so matter-of-factly into a cell because that was the way his world worked.

I recall that incident so vividly because it frightened me. Was it possible that I might one day come to accept such a system, to argue that it's not so bad and, anyway, they all deserve it? Is this poverty of action really the best that we can come up with as an answer to young people who commit acts of which we disapprove? What have we done to create a system that crushes the life from all those caught within it? Any behaviorist knows the power of the environment, and so after 4 years I left for a new environment, a university post training professional staff committed to a clinical approach to working with disturbed young people, including young offenders. Since completing my doctorate I had carried out research and had been published and so was committed to using the literature to inform practice, and to an empirical, experimental approach to clinical work, so the new academic demands were not daunting. The entry into teaching came as something of a shock: It's not until you have to stand up and say it out loud that you realize exactly what you know and what you don't. Teaching forces one to read carefully and to marshal facts and arguments succinctly and precisely. Not to be prepared for the following day's teaching is to know a sleepless night.

Thus on reflection perhaps it's not too surprising that this book went well in the writing. On both political and humanitarian grounds I believe strongly in a clinical approach with young offenders; I hold strong opinions about the quality of research and treatment delivery in this area; I am convinced of the force of behavioral theory and practice; and I know the literature, at least to a reasonable degree. In writing I discovered I was simply faced with the task of putting this down on paper. I have tried hard not to preach or to express my own theoretical (or political) views and opinions too strongly, if at all.

In gathering the material I was also aware that I was writing a guidebook to be used by those from a variety of professions, not a practice manual or a "cookbook." While a guidebook must to a certain degree include notes on practice, I think it should go further in considering wider issues. I have tried to reflect this broader concern by attempting to guide the reader through issues such as institutional factors in clinical work, alternatives to one-to-one work, and pointers for research. Although of direct relevance to those clinicians who work with young offenders, the material should prove of interest to researchers and administrators alike. I have drawn on a reasonably wide range of literature, without claiming to be exhaustive, which should make the text a source for further study, a point teachers might like to note.

Finally, I would like to say that my own thinking and development have not occurred in a vacuum, and a number of friends and colleagues have been of influence: Monika Henderson was one of my first partners in crime; Graham Huff persuaded me that I am a behaviorist; Kevin Howells tries to persuade me that I am not. I admire greatly the work of all those clinicians and researchers who have persevered despite the unpopularity, both academically and politically, of clinical intervention with young offenders; the writings of Robert Ross are for me a model of a steadfast, committed professional approach to clinical work with offenders. For assistance in the preparation of the book I would like to thank Sheila Wesson who word-processed the first draft of the manuscript, including the references, the typist's nightmare. My partner in life, Felicity Schofield, was as always a source of support; our children, Gregory and Kate, are too young to care one way or the other, thereby allowing me some sense of perspective in thinking about those other young people we've elected to call offenders.

Clive Hollin
October 1988

One

Young People and Crime

The aim of this opening chapter is threefold: to define the present use of the term *young offender*, to introduce cognitive-behavioral theories of offending, and to discuss the merits of a clinically oriented approach with young offenders. The starting point therefore is concerned with a definition: What is a young offender?

JUVENILE CRIME

One way of defining crime is to take a legal standpoint: Williams (1975) gives the much quoted view that "a crime is an act that is capable of being followed by criminal proceedings." This definition raises two issues of immediate concern: first, that to be criminal an act must be defined in criminal law, and second, that the individual must be capable of being dealt with under criminal law. Following the first point leads to the distinction between antisocial and criminal behavior. It is important to note that the former does not necessarily equate with the latter. For example, most people would agree that theft is antisocial, and this is reflected in criminal law; it might equally be argued that, say, video piracy and computer fraud are also antisocial acts, but these are less clearly defined in criminal law. One reason for this is, of course, that definitions of "antisocial" change with time: In recent times abortion, suicide, and certain homosexual acts have all been removed from the criminal law domain. On the other side of the coin, in the United States it was legal to own and sell marijuana until federal law was amended in 1937. Similarly, recent changes in English law have made it illegal to sell certain solvents to children. However, although there are acts that pass in and out of criminal law, there are others that are almost universally deemed wrong or bad in themselves. Such acts include those that inflict harm on another person, such as assault, murder, and rape, or that damage or interfere with another's property, such as malicious damage, theft, and criminal trespass.

This then gives the first part of the working definition of a young offender—an individual who has committed an act that is capable of being dealt with by criminal proceedings—and so excludes antisocial behavior of any other sort such as noncompliance with parental demands, disruptive behavior in school, and so on. This latter type of behavior is best viewed as "conduct-disordered" and so kept quite separate conceptually from criminal behavior.

The second definitional point refers to the suitability of the individual to be dealt with under criminal law. There are a number of reasons why, having committed an act defined as criminal by law, criminal proceedings may not follow. The person involved may not be of an age to be held legally responsible for his or her actions and so cannot be tried under criminal law. The age of criminal responsibility varies from country to country but is usually about 10 years of age. (The transition from young offender to adult offender similarly varies but generally occurs at about 18 years of age.) The presence of mental disorder is another reason for not progressing with criminal proceedings. As with age, different legal systems have different definitions of *mental disorder*, although the term can generally be taken to include those diagnosed as mentally ill, usually with schizophrenia and depression, and those with a significant mental handicap (Gunn, 1977; Monahan & Steadman, 1983). The mentally disordered offender poses management and treatment issues beyond the scope of this book.

In total this allows a more refined definition of the term *young offender* for the present purpose: *A young offender is a person within prescribed age limits and not suffering from mental disorder who commits an act capable of being followed by criminal proceedings.* A final point concerns the word *capable:* Young lawbreakers do not necessarily have to be caught to be considered offenders; it is sufficient that they commit the act deemed to be criminal. This does, however, raise the issue, as exemplified by self-report studies, of possible differences between apprehended and non-apprehended young offenders.

Self-report Studies

In order to study the "dark figure"—the gap between official crime statistics and the real crime rate—self-report studies have been widely employed. A typical study on young people and theft was reported by Belson (1975). A sample of 1,445 boys, aged from 13 to 16 years, was randomly selected from a large sample of households in London. Confidential interviews with the boys revealed that approximately 70% had stolen from a shop, and about 17% had stolen from private premises. Similarly, West (1982), with a sample of 405 boys 14 years old, found relatively high rates for minor offenses such as breaking windows in derelict property (68.9%), but lower rates for more serious offenses such as using weapons in fights (12.1%). The picture is broadly the same in the United States (Dunford & Elliott, 1984).

Although there are methodological concerns with self-report studies, principally in regard to the reliability and validity of the data they generate, verification studies allow some confidence in the general conclusions from such studies (Hindelang, Hirschi, & Weis, 1981; Huizinga & Elliott, 1986). It can be stated that most young people will, at some time in their early life, commit a criminal act. However, only a very small number of these criminal acts will result in a court appearance, with the type and seriousness of the act being a major determinant of whether a court appearance occurs. Thus crimes such as car theft and breaking and entering are significantly more likely to result in a court appearance than petty vandalism and minor theft (West & Farrington, 1977). It is the young people who pass through the courts who become the "official" young offenders.

A number of studies have addressed the issue of whether official young offenders differ in any way from the general population of "unofficial" young offenders who never appear before the courts. The most obvious distinguishing characteristic is offense seriousness. As noted above, most offenses are trivial, and it follows that only a minority of young people are "at risk" of legal intervention because of their criminal activity. In addition there is the suggestion that the amount of offending by convicted young offenders is greater than that of nonapprehended young offenders (Shapland, 1978). However, the differences extend beyond the type and volume of criminal acts. As shown in Table 1.1, West (1982) reports a range of individual, family, social, and economic differences that characterize "official" young offenders. It is also known that those apprehended early in their criminal careers are significantly more likely to be criminals as adults. In summarizing the position regarding official and unofficial young offenders, Rutter and Giller (1983) are forceful and to the point: "The view that everyone is somewhat delinquent and that there are no meaningful differences between those who are slightly so and those who are markedly so can be firmly rejected" (p. 29).

It is important to note that Rutter and Giller (1983) are not stating that differences of the type noted in Table 1.1 are necessarily the cause of criminal behavior. The relationship among offender characteristics, the legal system, and economic, social, and political systems is too complex to allow such an inference to be made. Indeed, the complex interplay

Table 1.1.   Adverse Features Associated with Young Offenders
(after West, 1982)

Adverse Feature	Convicted Young Offenders[a]
"Troublesome" at primary school	44.6
Low family income	33.3
Large family size	32.3
Criminal parent	37.9
Unsatisfactory child rearing	32.3
Lower quartile of IQ	31.3

[a] Percentage of sample (N = 84).

among these various factors partly defines the discipline of criminology, and it is to theories of crime that attention is now turned.

PSYCHOLOGICAL THEORIES OF OFFENDING

As noted above, the study of crime is a speciality in its own right, although it draws on the knowledge base of a number of disciplines such as sociology, psychology, economics, and jurisprudence. This multidisciplinary interest has produced a wealth of theories of crime causation: Siegal (1986), for example, reviews classical and neoclassical theories, biological theories, psychological theories, social structure theories, social process theories, and social conflict theories. Further, nested within each broad class of theory there are a number of more specific theories, at times complementary and at times competing. It is, of course, beyond the scope of this book to review theories of crime—for that the reader is referred to a criminology text such as Siegal (1986). The particular field of criminological psychology has been reviewed by Hollin (1989). The present focus is on the application of one specific psychological perspective, the cognitive-behavioral model, to both the understanding and management of juvenile offending.

For many years the preferred model in psychology was behaviorism, a way of understanding human behavior based primarily on learning theory and in which the emphasis was on observable behavior. More recently, psychology has been said to have undergone a "cognitive revolution" (Baars, 1986) in which the pendulum of psychological interest has swung back from observable behavior to the psychological world "within the skin." It is possible to outline two opposite positions. The radical-behavioral position, which although not neglecting cognitions, emotions, and so on, suggests that the emphasis should be on environmental influences on behavior. This approach maintains that the patterns of environmental reinforcement and punishment must be understood in order to predict and change behavior. Skinner (1986a) summarizes the radical-behaviorist position:

> In a given episode the environment acts upon the organism, something happens inside, the organism then acts upon the environment, and certain consequences follow. The first, third, and fourth of these is the field of a science of behavior, which undertakes to discover how they are related to each other. What happens inside is another part of the story (p. 716).

The *cognitive* position is, following Skinner's sequence, related to the second part of the scheme. It maintains that in order to understand human behavior it is necessary to look to thoughts, memory, language, beliefs, and so on. The emphasis is clearly on inner rather than environmental determinants of behavior.

The *cognitive-behavioral* position represents an uneasy middle ground between these two schools of thought. It acknowledges the importance of environmental influences while seeking to incorporate the role of cognitions in understanding behavior. Thus cognitions may be given some mediational role between the outside world and overt behavior such that cognitions are seen as determining what environmental influences are attended to, how they are perceived, and whether they might affect future behavior.

These three psychological viewpoints have all at various times been applied to the study of crime. The following discussion of this application serves a number of functions: It will introduce the models themselves, illustrate the contrast and complementarity in the behavioral and cognitive perspectives, and raise some important points concerning the nature of crime.

Learning Theories

Differential Association Theory. Although categorized in some texts as a sociological theory, differential association theory has such clear links with learning theory that it merits a place in any discussion of this nature. The basis of differential association theory was first proposed by Sutherland (1924), who later modified it (Sutherland, 1947), and further refinements were made by Sutherland and Cressey (1970, 1974). The strength of the theory is that not only is it concerned with the *social* conditions associated with crime but it also attempts to explain the processes by which the *individual* becomes criminal. Crime itself is viewed as being politically defined by those within society who hold power over legislation. However, whereas some people behave in accordance with these definitions, others act outside them. This latter group of people are criminal in the sense that their favored definitions of acceptable behavior are seen as deviant by the powerful law makers. The means by which an individual acquires the definitions conducive to a life of crime are described in detail. Sutherland (1947) states nine postulates to account for the process of acquisition:

a. Criminal behavior is learned.
b. The learning occurs through association with other people.
c. The main part of the learning takes place within close personal groups.
d. The learning includes techniques for executing particular crimes and also specific attitudes, drives, and motives conducive toward committing crimes.
e. The direction of the drives and motives is learned from perception of the law as either favorable or unfavorable.
f. People become criminals when their definitions favorable to breaking the law outweigh their definitions favorable to nonviolation.
g. The learning experiences—differential associations—vary in frequency, intensity, and importance for each individual.
h. The process of learning criminal behavior is no different from the learning of any other behavior.
i. Although criminal behavior is an expression of needs and values, crime cannot be explained in terms of these needs and values. (For example, it is not the need for money that causes crime, rather the means used to acquire the money; the means themselves are learned.)

Differential association theory is therefore an explanation of offending in terms of learning, and social learning at that. It proposes that through contact with other people who hold favorable definitions toward crime the individual acquires similar definitions. It is important to note that the theory does *not* propose that learning has to occur through association with criminals, but rather through association with people who hold definitions favorable to crime. Parents who steadfastly tell their children it is wrong to steal may, nevertheless, show examples of dishonesty such as not informing a salesperson if they are given too much change. Further, varying definitions can coexist: An individual might argue that it is perfectly reasonable to falsify his or her tax return but would steadfastly define burglary as a crime.

Despite various attempts at empirical validation there are problems with the theory in its original form, such as problems with the meaning of the term *definition* and a lack of detail as to why, given similar conditions, some individuals adopt criminal definitions while others do not.

Sutherland and Cressey (1974) respond to the criticism in two ways: The first, as noted, is to dispel various misconceptions such as the idea that crime is learned through association with criminals; the second is to point out that shortcomings, such as lack of knowledge of the role of individual differences, point to areas for further research rather than refute the theory. Indeed, since the formulation of differential association theory, great advances have been made in the study of learning, making it possible to place some flesh on the bones of Sutherland's theory.

Operant Learning. Skinner's (1938, 1953) formulation of the principles of operant learning, leading to the emergence and growth of behaviorism, has been a major influence in contemporary psychology, although not without fierce debate and controversy (Modgil & Modgil, 1987; Zuriff, 1985). At the heart of operant theory is the principle that the individual's behavior is related to the environmental consequences it produces. Behavior that results in desirable consequences (desirable to the individual concerned, that is) may increase in frequency, in which case it is said to have been _reinforced;_ behavior that produces aversive consequences may decrease in frequency, in which case it is said to have been _punished._ In other words, behavior _operates_ on the environment to produce changes that may be reinforcing or punishing. The pattern of reinforcement and punishment in turn relates to the probability of future occurrences of the particular behavior. Most behavior—driving a car, writing a letter, talking to a friend, setting fire to a house—is _operant_ behavior. Further, operant behavior does not occur at random; environmental cues signal when certain behaviors are liable to be reinforced or punished. These three elements combine to give the concept of the _three-term contingency:_ The Antecedent conditions are the signal for Behavior that in turn produces environmental Consequences—the A:B:C of behavioral theory. The operant behavior of answering the telephone provides a simple example: The ringing tone is the antecedent to the operant behavior of lifting the receiver, which in turn results in the consequences of speaking to the person at the other end of the line. We do not _have to_ answer the telephone. The ringing signals that a certain behavior—answering the telephone—will produce consequences which have been previously reinforced.

There are two types of reinforcement contingencies: With _positive_ reinforcement the behavior produces a rewarding consequence; with _negative_ reinforcement the behavior has the consequence of _avoiding_ an aversive consequence. It should be emphasized that both types of consequences increase or maintain the behavior. Similarly there are two punishment contingencies: With positive punishment the consequences of the behavior are aversive; with negative punishment the behavior leads to the removal of something desirable. In both cases the consequences reduce the frequency of the behavior. To summarize, if a behavior is being maintained or is increasing in frequency, it is being reinforced; if a behavior is decreasing in frequency, it is being punished.

The force of this position is that as the consequences of an individual's behavior are delivered by the environment in which the behavior occurs, then the principal causes or determinants of behavior are to be found *outside* the person. Thus while the potential for learning, Skinner suggests, is principally a matter of genetic constitution, the acquisition of behavior must be accounted for in terms of the individual's learning history via environmental reinforcement and punishment.

Following Sutherland's inclusion of learning in theories of crime, Jeffery (1965) offered a refinement of the notion of differential association by incorporating operant principles into the original theory. Jeffery suggests that criminal behavior can be seen as operant behavior. In other words, crime is maintained by the environmental consequences it produces for the offender. It follows that to understand crime it is necessary to understand the consequences of the act for the individual concerned. Many crimes are concerned with stealing in which the consequences are material and financial gain: The gains may be positively reinforcing the stealing as the proceeds are rewarding in themselves; alternatively, the gains may be negatively reinforcing the stealing as they enable the individual to avoid the unpleasant experience of financial hardship. The rewarding consequences of crime can be social as well as material gain. For example, within delinquent groups repeated misconduct is rewarded with social approval and a position of leadership. Other crimes can be similarly explained. Violence, for example, may be positively reinforced by the consequences it produces, or negatively reinforced by removing some unwanted event. Theft becomes simpler if the victim's resistance is removed by the use of force as in armed robbery. The theft is positively reinforced by the financial gain; the violence is negatively reinforced as it avoids resistance from the victim. As well as reinforcing outcomes, crime can also have aversive outcomes—being arrested, being sent to prison, having a probation officer, family problems, and so on—which might have a punishing effect on the criminal behavior (punishing in the operant sense of decreasing the frequency of the behavior). As Jeffery notes,

> The theory of differential reinforcement states that a criminal act occurs in an environment in which in the past the actor has been reinforced for behaving in this manner, and the aversive consequences attached to the behavior have been of such a nature that they do not control or prevent the response (p. 295).

In the final analysis it is the balance of reinforcement and punishment in an individual's learning history that dictates the presence or absence of criminal behavior. The important point is that each act must be considered in its own right for each individual. Some individuals will have been rewarded for criminal acts, and others will have suffered aversive consequences. In addition the pattern of reinforcement and punishment is unlikely to have been constant over time, leading to a complex learning history in terms of both antecedents to crime and reinforcement schedules (the rate at which reinforcement occurs—not every act is successful). Similarly, even within broadly similar social groups or subcultures differences will exist at an individual level in peer group interactions, family processes, schooling, official policies toward crime, and so on. This complex, individually based analysis offers a means of explaining why even within apparently similar environments there are some people who offend although others do not.

Whereas operant learning stresses the importance of environmental consequences on behavior, later theoretical developments led to a form of learning theory that seeks to expand upon the role of the person, rather than the environment, in learning. The more recently formulated *social learning theory* has also been applied to the understanding of offending.

Social Learning Theory. Although formulated by Rotter (1954), social learning theory is more generally associated with the American psychologist Albert Bandura. As Bandura (1977) makes clear, social learning theory is in part an extension of operant principles, although there are differences, mainly concerned with the role of cognition. Whereas operant theory maintains that behavior is acquired principally through the direct experience of reinforcement and punishment from the environment, social learning theory holds that behavior can also be learned through observing the behavior of other people. Bandura (1977) describes various stages in the process of observational learning. The first stage is *attention* to the model's behavior, followed by *retention* of the information at a cognitive level and finally by *motor reproduction* of the observed behavior. Once the behavior is carried out it can be reinforced or punished by its consequences just like any operant behavior. Another extension of operant theory comes with the concept of *motivation*. Bandura (1977) suggests that there are three aspects of motivation—*external reinforcement* (as in operant theory), *vicarious reinforcement*, and *self-reinforcement*. Vicarious reinforcement is the observation of other people's behavior being reinforced or punished. This observation then motivates the observer to behave in a similar manner when the opportunity arises. Self-reinforcement refers to a sense of pride, achievement, or meeting one's own behavior standards and motivates the individual to behave similarly in the future.

In total, social learning theory suggests that through observation—especially if the model is someone regarded as successful or of high status—we learn at a cognitive level how to perform the observed behavior. Given the opportunity, the behavior may be practiced and refined; the behavior is then reinforced or punished both internally and externally, so motivating future behavior. In addition, if a certain behavior has been reinforced in the past, this creates an *expectancy* that the same behavior will be reinforced in the future. The inclusion of cognition as a means of learning, the notion of internal as well as external reinforcement, and the introduction of concepts such as motivation and expectancy in explaining behavior mark clear divergencies from operant theory.

The applicability of social learning theory to understanding offending was seen by both psychologists (Bandura, 1973; Nietzel, 1979) and sociologists (Akers, 1977; Krohn, Massey, & Skinner, 1987). The social learning approach to offending suggests that the observational learning that leads to criminal behavior takes place primarily in three contexts: in the family, in the prevalent subculture, and through cultural symbols—television, books, and so on—that form part of the social environment. Explanations for offending are therefore found, in part at least, in the behavior modeled within families, by peer groups, and on television, in films, and so forth. The reinforcement for offending comes from both internal and external sources such as tangible rewards, social acclaim, and increased self-esteem.

Thus Sutherland's initial inclusion of learning in explaining offending has led to refined theories of criminal behavior incorporating principles from both operant and social learning theories. To a greater or less extent, the theories discussed thus far give some emphasis to the environment in which the offender lives. Another line of theoretical development moves away from such an emphasis to a much greater concern with what occurs inside the person.

Cognitive Theories

The "Criminal Mind." The term *cognition* is used in different ways by different authors. In general terms it refers to concepts such as memory, imagery, intelligence, and reasoning, although perhaps it is most widely used as a synonym for thinking. In explanations of offending, cognition is implicit in the theories of a number of writers who suggest that various styles of thinking, such as "impulsive" and "concrete," are characteristic of offender populations (Ausubel, 1958; Glueck & Glueck, 1950). More recently the claim was made by Yochelson and Samenow (1976) that, on the basis of in-depth interviews with male offenders, it is possible to describe the "criminal thinking patterns" common to all offenders. They describe over 50 styles and errors of thinking which they claim define the criminal mind. These thinking patterns include concrete thinking, fragmentation, failure to empathize with others, a lack of any perspective of time, irresponsible decision making, and perceiving themselves as victims.

Although there is much of interest in this work, there are a number of methodological criticisms. The sample interviewed by Yochelson and Samenow consisted of 240 persistent offenders, many of whom had been judged not guilty by reason of insanity. It is questionable just how far it is possible to generalize findings from such a sample to the remainder of the offender population. Similarly, their conclusion that all offenders share similar thinking patterns must be treated with caution. As the research design did not include a nonoffender control group, it is not well established that the thinking patterns they describe are peculiar to criminal populations. The interview method of data gathering, while a rich source of material, should when used as a research strategy be standardized and include a check for reliability and validity, which was not the case. It is unfortunate that the shortcomings of this work, which have led to considerable controversy, have detracted from a potentially valuable contribution to clinical criminology.

Social Cognition. The approach taken by Yochelson and Samenow (1976) is not that adopted by all investigators. Although the distinction may not be an exact one, Ross and Fabiano (1985) distinguish between *imper*sonal cognition and *inter*personal cognition. The former is that aspect of cognition that "deals with the physical world"; the latter is concerned with "understanding people and their actions"—sometimes called social cognition. While impersonal cognition may be a factor in the development of criminal behavior—for example, as indicated by research pointing to the role of intelligence in offending (e.g., Andrew, 1977)— Ross and Fabiano argue that interpersonal cognition may well be more important in understanding crime. In reviewing studies on social cognition with criminal populations, Ross and Fabiano describe a variety of types or styles of cognition that characterize offender populations.

Impulsivity is defined by Ross and Fabiano as the omission of thought between impulse and action. This lack of reflection may be due to a variety of causes: a failure to learn to stop and think, a failure to learn "effective thinking," or a failure to generate alternative responses. The empirical evidence is mixed regarding impulsivity in offender populations: Some studies find offenders more impulsive than nonoffenders (e.g., Rotenberg & Nachshon, 1979), whereas others fail to show this distinction (e.g., Saunders, Reppucci, & Sarata, 1973). These seemingly conflicting findings may, as is the case with a great deal of the research in this field generally, reflect differing definitions and measures (of impulsivity in this case) and the heterogeneity of the offender population (Arbuthnot, Gordon, & Jurkovic, 1987).

Locus of control refers to the degree to which individuals perceive their behavior to be under their own *internal* control, as opposed to being controlled by *external* agents such as luck or authority figures (Rotter, 1966). A number of studies have shown that offenders tend toward external control; that is, they explain their behavior as determined by influences outside their personal control (Kumchy & Sayer, 1980). Not all studies are in agreement: Some have failed to show any difference between offenders and nonoffenders (Groh & Goldenberg, 1976), and one study found that offenders were more *internally* controlled than nonoffenders (Lefcourt & Ladwig, 1965). As with impulsivity, these discrepant findings may be explained by the multidimensionality of locus of control and variations across offender groups such that, for example, violent young offenders tend toward greater external control than nonviolent young offenders (Hollin & Wheeler, 1982).

Role taking refers to the ability to see things from the other person's point of view. Chandler (1973) reported significant differences between young offenders and nonoffenders on a role-taking task, with the nonoffenders giving less egocentric responses. Similar findings have been reported in other studies (e.g., Rotenberg, 1974), although Kaplan and Arbuthnot (1985) suggest a refinement in noting that the difference between young offenders and nonoffenders may be in terms of affective empathy rather than cognitive role taking. In other words, it is not the ability simply to see things from the other's point of view that is important, but rather the capacity to care at an emotional level about what is perceived.

Social problem solving involves the ability, in a given social situation, to call upon a range of cognitive skills such as generating feasible courses of action, considering the various alternatives that would follow, and planning how to achieve the desired outcome (Spivack, Platt & Shure, 1976). A number of studies have suggested that young offenders show significant disabilities in social problem-solving skills (Higgins & Thies, 1981). In a typical study Freedman, Rosenthal, Donahue, Schlundt, and McFall (1978) found that young offenders gave less competent responses than nonoffenders to a series of social problems. The findings of Hains and Ryan (1983) further suggest that the age of the young offender may also be important when considering problem-solving ability.

Moral reasoning is another dimension of social cognition that may differentiate young offenders from nonoffenders. A body of experimental study, for which several reviews are available (Blasi, 1980; Jennings, Kil-

kenny, & Kohlberg, 1983; Jurkovic, 1980), has compared the moral judg-
ments of young offenders and nonoffenders. Although not all studies
have found differences (e.g., Hains & Ryan, 1983), there are indications
that young offenders use less mature moral reasoning than nonoffenders. However, this difference is attenuated by variables such as personality, type of offense, and type of moral problem. In addition, even
though research has focused on the *content* of the offender's moral code,
that is, knowledge, beliefs, and attitudes, this contextual aspect can be
contrasted with the *process* of moral reasoning. It is an assumption that
process is related to content. Although developmental delay may be the
cause of an antisocial moral code, it is also possible that, as Ross and
Fabiano suggest, "One can argue eloquently and convincingly about so-
cial/moral issues yet have a personal set of values which are entirely
self-serving, hedonistic or anti-social" (p. 169).

The "Reasoning Criminal." The beginnings of this particular cognitive
view of offending stem from studies focusing on the environment rather
than on the individual. Following the suggestion that increases in crime
can be related to increased opportunity, Cohen and Felson (1979) describe the offender as someone who decides to take advantage of the
opportunity for criminal behavior. Thus as more family members go out
to work, leaving homes empty for longer periods of time, so the opportunity for burglary is increased. The recent rise in the number of bur-
glaries reflects the decision of greater numbers of individuals (or perhaps more decisions by the same number of individuals) to take
advantage of these opportunities. Following the lead given by studies
on cognitive information processing, offending can therefore be seen as
the end point of a rational decision-making process centering on the
risks, costs, and benefits of the crime. In a refinement of this broad position, Cornish and Clarke (1986a) make the distinction between criminal
involvement and criminal *events*. The former is the process by which an
individual chooses to become involved in crime, while the latter refers
to the short-term immediate decisions in a given set of circumstances.
Involvement may be related to social factors such as type of upbringing;
event decisions may be based on considerations such as the presence of
a dog or burglar alarm in the case of housebreaking. The individual's
growing involvement in crime may in turn be associated with a sense
of "professionalism" as an offender and changes in life-style and peer
group (Taylor, 1984).

Developmental Considerations. An emerging line of research, especially
important with regard to young offenders, has pointed to the importance of developmental variables in criminal careers. Studies on the de-

velopment of criminal careers have employed longitudinal research designs in which a large sample of individuals are selected and followed for a lengthy period of time. The Cambridge (England) Study in Delinquent Development, for example, commenced in 1961, beginning with a sample of over 400 males aged 8 years and ending in 1980 when the youngest person was 25 years of age. Such longitudinal studies give a wealth of data, from variables associated with offending such as sex, socioeconomic class, income, parenting, and race, to variations in type of crime shown by those who become offenders. Over the past 5 years or so a number of longitudinal studies have been concluded in both England (West, 1982) and the United States (Wolfgang, Thornberry, & Figlio, 1987) which have presented some revealing data concerning age and crime. Farrington (1983), reviewing offending from 10 to 25 years of age, made four firm conclusions: (a) The peak ages for most offenses is 16–17 years; (b) juvenile and adult crime are closely related; (c) as the number of convictions increases beyond six, so the probability of further convictions becomes greater; (d) juveniles convicted at the earliest ages (10–12 years) become the most persistent offenders.

The first finding, that offending peaks at about 16–17 years of age, has been taken to suggest that there is a "life span" for most delinquent activity (see Figure 1.1). As Farrington (1986) notes, "Typically the crime rate increases from the minimum age of criminal responsibility to reach a peak in the teenage years; it then declines, at first quickly, but gradually more slowly" (p. 189). Importantly, it appears that the peak in offending is caused by a rise in *prevalence* rather than *incidence*. In other words, there are more nonoffenders committing offenses, rather than existing offenders committing more offenses as they grow older. Wolfgang et al. (1987) are in agreement with this point, noting the consistency of the number of offenses per offender, which varied from an average of 1.2 to 1.8 offenses per year. They conclude that the peak at about 16–17 years of age "is due almost entirely to an increase in the number of active offenders and not to an increase in their annual 'productivity'" (p. 44).

Farrington's first point appears to reflect a general developmental trend, whereas the latter three points may give some indication of who will remain set in a criminal career. As noted previously, West (1982) suggests that low-income families, convicted parents, and poor parenting are strong predictors of an early onset of criminal activity. Similarly, Blumstein, Farrington, and Moitra (1985) suggest that a convicted sibling, being "troublesome," and poor school performance at about 8–10 years are good predictors of chronic offending. Reflecting on this pattern of results, West (1982) argues that although the importance of attachment between parents and child cannot be neglected, this in itself

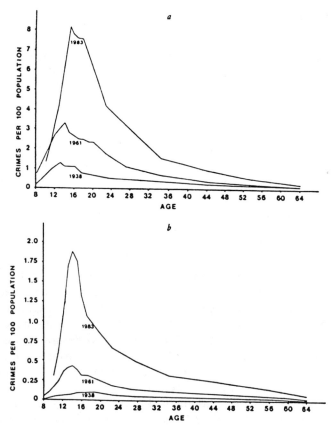

FIGURE 1.1. The relationship between age and crime for English males (graph a) and English females (graph b). From D. P. Farrington, Age and crime. In *Crime and Justice: An Annual Review of Research* (Vol. 7, p. 192) edited by M. Tonry and N. Morris, 1986, Chicago: University of Chicago Press. Reprinted by permission of The University of Chicago Press.

will not prevent persistent offending unless adequate social learning has taken place. As discussed above, understanding of social learning is reasonably well advanced, although there are a number of theoretical points that require consideration before moving to a broader discussion of cognitive-behavioral theories of criminal behavior.

THEORETICAL ISSUES

It is as well to begin with the popular misconception that operant theory ignores or denies the existence of thoughts, feelings, emotions, and other "private events." Skinner (1974) has explored this issue in full, and Blackman (1981) expresses the position with perfect clarity:

Contemporary behaviorists adopt a philosophical position which does not commit them to the assertion that people are no more than puppets, pushed and pulled by forces beyond their control and unable to enjoy or suffer private experiences. Instead they adopt a way of looking at behavioral phenomena which emphasizes the functional importance of environmental influences on what we do, which seeks to find an appropriate way of incorporating private experiences, and which sets these elements within a dynamic and interactive system (p. 15).

The precise role of private events in the behavioral sequence is a matter of debate, although as Blackman (1981) makes plain, cognitions are not to be afforded the status of autonomous causes of behavior. As Skinner has observed, if someone kicks us and makes us angry enough to kick back, it is not the anger that causes the retaliation but that we were kicked in the first place. However, it is a criticism of operant research that it has neglected the role and function of private events, although recent studies are beginning to redress the balance (Lowe, 1983; Lowe & Higson, 1981).

The role and status of cognition are important issues, reflecting the long-debated issue of free will versus determinism that has vexed philosophers for centuries and played an important part in criminological discussions (Glaser, 1977; Schafer, 1977). It may be the case, as Ross and Fabiano (1985) suggest, that "social cognitive skills are *learned* skills; their acquisition is very strongly influenced by environmental factors" (p. 143). However, once acquired what happens then? Do cognitions change and modify themselves to create new forms and new content? Do cognitions control and guide behavior, as some cognitive and social learning theorists might claim? Or are cognitions better viewed as an integrated part of human functioning, acting within a system rather than as separate from it? Obviously there are no right or wrong answers to these questions, and it seems highly unlikely that they will be resolved in the near future. Nevertheless, it is advantageous to have a working model, and it is the cognitive-behavioral model that has been selected here. The model, as shown in Figure 1.2, suggests that a person can be seen as a complex interplay of biological, private, and motor behaviors. The term *private* refers to activities within the skin, such as cognition and emotion. A person does not exist in a vacuum. The functioning of the human system is related to previous events including, for example, biological insult, type of upbringing, level of education, and so forth. Current functioning is related to the available reinforcement and punishment in the environment. This can be viewed from a "micro level" such as current living circumstances, to a "macro level" including cultural and economic factors.

This cognitive-behavioral model incorporates all the factors noted

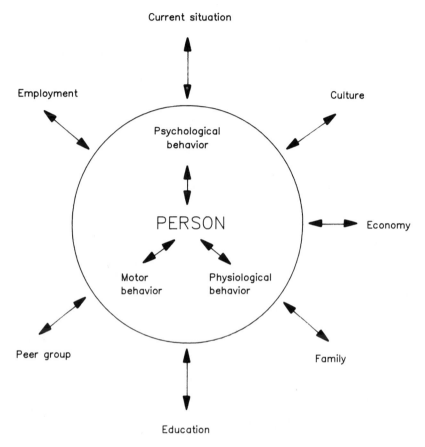

FIGURE 1.2. Schematic representation of factors in person-environment interaction.

above as distinctive of offender populations. It includes social behavior, cognition, and moral processes, as well as social processes such as family upbringing and levels of employment. Cognition is not afforded an autonomous, independent role as it is in some cognitive theories; rather it is viewed as an integral, if covert, aspect of human behavior having a reciprocal relationship to overt behavior. As shown in Figure 1.3, Clarke (1977) has set these factors within a system that includes a variety of elements thought to be related to crime.

When viewed in this light, what explanatory powers does a cognitive-behavioral theory have in explaining offending? Again this is a matter of debate. It would be an error to omit psychological variables from an analysis of offending, yet it would equally be an error to place all the

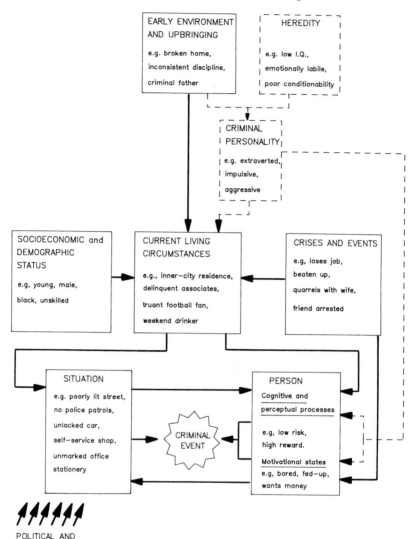

FIGURE 1.3. Elements contributing to the occurrence of a criminal event. The examples within each box have significance only with respect to particular types of crimes. From "Psychology and Crime" by R. V. G. Clarke, 1977, *Bulletin of the British Psychological Society, 30,* p. 281. Reprinted by permission of The British Psychological Society.

emphasis on the environment at the expense of the individual. One of the strengths of any behavioral model is that it should force consideration of the interaction between a person and his or her environment. The strength of behavioral theories may, in fact, be greater than even its proponents suggest.

Criticisms and Responses

There are a number of criticisms of cognitive-behavioral theories that merit attention. Nietzel (1979) comments that "behavioral theories do not explain why people who commit the same acts, who perform the same violations of law are treated differently" (p. 111) and suggests that social labeling theory might provide a better answer to issues of this type. However, taking this a step further, the question becomes, If social labeling occurs, then how does this labeling process occur? A behavioral answer might be formulated by analyzing the behavior of people— for example, law makers, magistrates, school teachers—who apply the labels and so define some individuals as criminal. Such a behavioral analysis would direct attention to the various discriminative stimuli— such as the offender's race, sex, and social class—functioning as antecedents in the labeling process; would illuminate the beliefs and cognitions of the labelers; and would describe the consequences of the labeling for those concerned. There is a wealth of research findings that might contribute in some way to such an analysis. Incorporating this knowledge into a behavioral framework might well inform our understanding of the social processes associated with crime.

Nietzel also comments that "we are all quite aware of the potentially rewarding consequences of property offences; however, few of us steal" (pp. 110–111); and he makes the same observation for exposure to television violence and the relatively low levels of personal violence. There are two points to be made: First, as crime surveys reveal, more than "a few of us" appear to be stealing. And second, cognitive-behavioral theory does offer explanations for the suppression of behavior: Vicarious punishment—seeing others suffer the consequences of being caught— is one ready explanation. In addition some of the control theories present a detailed account of *learning* not to offend (e.g., Eysenck, 1987).

Rutter and Giller (1983) also voice a number of reservations. They suggest that behavioral theories avoid problems of sex differences, age changes, and developmental factors. This is debatable: Herbert (1987), for example, details the way in which these individual and developmental factors must play an integral part in any behavioral assessment and theory. Rutter and Giller also suggest that learning theories lack specificity on the acquisition of antisocial behavior and on the issue of individual differences. These are curious statements, as the theories go into great detail to attempt to account for the way *all* behavior is learned. Behavioral theories are also at great pains to stress that individual differences in behavior result from both unique biological factors and unique learning histories. Finally, Rutter and Giller suggest that there is an unresolved problem with behavioral theory in "accounting for the observation that punishment is less effective with antisocial children and may actually *increase* their antisocial behaviors" (p. 253). On examination, however, there is no problem with this observation; it is the use of terminology that poses the problem. It will be recalled that the behavioral definition of punishment is a contingency in which the consequence of a behavior is followed by a decrease in frequency of the behavior. This specific terminology is different from the common use of the word *punishment* which usually means something physically aversive. In behavioral terms, however, punishment cannot be more or less effective with any particular group, nor can it increase behavior. It appears that Rutter and Giller are *assuming* that certain consequences will be punishing for *all* children, but have observed that these unpleasant consequences do not decrease behavior for *some* children. This observation is in accord with behavioral theory: Experimental evidence has demonstrated that continual exposure to aversive stimuli can produce a high tolerance level, so that unpleasant consequences that might be predicted to have a punishing effect on behavior actually have no effect at all or might even act as a reinforcer (e.g., Miller, 1960).

At a theoretical level, behavioral models are capable of providing adequate responses to problems of the type put forward by Nietzel and by Rutter and Giller. The real challenge to any model of human behavior is at a philosophical level where the model itself is questioned (Mogdil & Mogdil, 1987) or at least revised (Zuriff, 1985).

Offending and Cognitive-Behavioral Theory

If the cognitive-behavioral model is accepted, it follows that criminal behavior is seen as a function of the individual in interaction with his or her environment. The "person" part of the interaction is where psychologists might claim some knowledge, as psychology has for most of its short history been primarily concerned with the study of the individual (although biological factors are the province of geneticists, physiologists, and so on). The "environment" side of the interaction is altogether less certain: The environment contains social forces, the province of sociologists; political forces, best understood by political theorists; legal forces as studied by criminologists; and a myriad of other forces as hinted at in Clarke's (1977) analysis shown in Figure 1.3. A meaningful behavioral analysis must strive to take all these forces into consideration in seeking to account for any behavior. In practice this rarely, if ever, happens. A behavioral analysis considers the individual in detail, perhaps even including biological factors; analysis of the environment, on the other hand, is usually restricted to the immediate social environment, such as family or peer group, but seldom progresses to political, economic, and sociological levels.

Although there have been attempts at behavioral analysis on a grand social scale (Skinner, 1986b), this is not commonplace in clinical practice. This is not to say that a comprehensive behavioral analysis would not illuminate many of the reasons why problems occur at an individual level. Beyond doubt it would. Rather, a restricted analysis reflects the clinician's sphere of influence: A clinician may be able to influence a client's biological, cognitive, and behavioral functioning and may even be able to influence family functioning and classroom or workplace functioning; but political, legal, and economic change are beyond the scope of clinical intervention. If offending is a product of all the forces noted in Figure 1.3, can there be any place for clinical methods based on psychological theories in attempts to change criminal behavior?

THE CLINICAL APPROACH TO
CRIMINAL BEHAVIOR

In seeking to affirm the potential of clinical approaches to criminology West (1980) suggests that "the crucial importance of economic, social and political factors in the definition and incidence of crime is undeniable, as is the need for socio-political change, but the part played by individual characteristics in determining who becomes labelled a criminal should not be neglected" (p. 619). The inherent danger, as West acknowledges, is that in concentrating upon the individual, environmental factors are forgotten. Indeed, the criticism can be made that a clinical approach colludes with the system, placing the spotlight of responsibility and blame exclusively on the individual to the exclusion of environmental factors (Goff, 1986). However, such a criticism is more applicable to dated psychoanalytic theories than to contemporary cognitive-behavioral explanations which seek to emphasize the importance of environmental factors.

It has been my own experience, and I'm sure that of many others in this field, that one is accused of being a "do-gooder," and that a clinical approach is instrumental in the offender being treated lightly and the victim neglected. In replying to such criticisms I think it is important to make the point that one's personal preference is to be a do-gooder rather than a "do-badder." The exchange of letters in a local newspaper shown

Table 1.2.   Differing Views on Clinical Utility

When will they think of the victim?

AFTER reading the comments of Leicester University lecturer, Dr. Clive Hollin, who advocates the supply of drink to young offenders with drink problems while in detention, I have one or two other suggestions to make.

How about arranging a supply of grannies for professional muggers, or a willing child or two for the sexual deviant? The scope is endless for offenders who have anti-social habits.

Hopefully, one of these days the eminent professionals will lend a sympathetic ear to the victims of this sickening breed, who are growing in number each week.

PRISON OFFICER.

Dr. Hollin suggested that drink should be available in special units and given in a

controlled clinical environment to teach youngsters how to control their drinking and behaviour. He is a psychologist and his views were supported by a psychologist at the Glen Parva custody centre.

— EDITOR.

LEICESTER MERCURY, WEDNESDAY, AUGUST 17, 1983

Prison doesn't deter them

In relation to my suggestions for the treatment of drink problems in young offenders your Prison Officer correspondent asks "When will they think of the victim?"

I think your reader has not understood my position. My argument for treating drink problems in young offenders is in large part based on consideration for future victims.

If a young offender's criminal behaviour is related to his drinking (as my research indicates it is in a number of cases) then curing the excessive drinking may well eliminate future crime. Potential victims may then be spared from further drunken criminal behaviour.

I can assure Prison Officer that I, and many others, are as concerned as the next person about the effects of crime (I bear the scars of a criminal attack).

However, from reconviction figures it is obvious that imprisonment does not deter young people from crime. My suggestion is based on a wish to prevent young people from returning to crime when they leave detention, so reducing the number of victims and helping the young person return to society.

Surely, then, the Prison Officer and I have the same aims?

DR. CLIVE R. HOLLIN
Tutor, Department of Psychology, The University, Leicester.

LEICESTER MERCURY, THURSDAY, AUGUST 25, 1983

in Table 1.2 illustrates my point. These comments followed a newspaper report on research findings suggesting that alcohol abuse may be a contributing factor in some juvenile crime and that controlled drinking programs might be considered as a means of intervention in such cases (Hollin, 1983). I would argue further that the administration of harsh physical retribution to young offenders makes matters worse, not better. Many young offenders come from environments in which, for whatever reason, aggression, physical violence, and emotional deprivation are the order of the day. For society to respond to transgressions with more of the same is simply to confirm to the offender that this is an acceptable means of solving problems—the way the world prefers to function. At an empirical level there is little evidence that harsh regimes have any effect on recidivism (Thornton, Curran, Grayson, & Holloway, 1984).

That victim support schemes are sadly lacking is hardly the fault of the clinician. If the social and political will were there, financing for the necessary work would be forthcoming. Although a clinician working with an offender cannot undo the damage to the victim, the point remains that effective clinical work may prevent the suffering of future victims. In an ideal world prevention programs would spare all victims, and although there is a growth in such programs (Burchard & Burchard, 1987; Johnson, 1987), the majority of young offenders are first seen after the commission of an offense. Indeed, the clinician often makes initial contact with the offender only after legal or penal intervention—that may well have created problems of an individual and social nature for the offender. Overall, even though there is a strong case for both reform of the system and for intervention with the individual, there is no reason why social reform and clinical intervention should be incompatible.

In summary, it would be foolish to suggest that clinical intervention, of any type, is a remedy for crime. Crime is a multidimensional concept, and its amelioration will require changes across a range of factors—some concerned with the individual, others with the environment. It is also true that not every offender will be suited to clinical intervention. The decision as to whether clinical work is appropriate rests on an understanding of the individual concerned, and it is to the process of assessment that attention is now turned.

Two

Assessment

Assessment should be the starting point in any clinical intervention, although the method and focus of intervention of course varies for different therapeutic approaches. Cognitive-behavioral assessment follows a number of procedures, using a range of assessment methods, in order to arrive at an understanding of an individual's behavior and so to devise methods of change. Ideally the process of assessment should begin before any intervention is started, although it is recognized that this is not always possible: Behavior that is a danger to the self or to others may have to be tackled immediately. In such instances the clinician is forced to rely upon experience, advice, and the relevant literature. However, with many offenders, time is available to complete an assessment. The major difficulty may well be deciding where to start.

PLANNING THE ASSESSMENT

Reid (1982) notes seven classes of problem behavior typically found in young offenders. As detailed in Table 2.1, this categorization moves from major offense behaviors, to minor offenses, and on to behavioral deficits and excesses. The clinician faced with a young offender must first set a list of priorities for intervention. The priorities might be determined by the seriousness of the behavior, so that it is deemed more important to assess fire setting than verbal abuse. Alternatively, the priorities may be determined by the immediate contingencies: Self-mutilation may demand immediate attention, and institutional problems may need to be resolved before any work with offending behaviors can be undertaken.

Regardless of the focus, it is helpful to commence by planning what will be required to achieve the best possible assessment. A number of decisions need to be made: What method(s) of assessment are feasible? What resources are available or will be required? And what time scale

Table 2.1.   Target Behaviors in Clinical Work with Young Offenders

1. Major offence behaviours Murder Manslaughter Armed Robbery Sexual Assaults Arson	5. Behavioural excesses Physical violence (persons and property) Self-mutilations (head banging, wrist slashing, overdoses) Verbal violence
2. Minor offence behaviours Theft Take and drive away Burglary Prostitution	6. Institutional problem behaviours Hostages Sit in/barricades Sexual behaviour Violence Attempted escapes
3. 'Clinical' problems Obessional rituals (e.g., washing, dressing, thoughts) Enuresis Faecal smearing Anxiety	7. Problems of generalization Self-help skills Job skills—interview behaviour, work skills, etc. Family conflicts Deviant peer-group influences Abscondings
4. Behavioural deficits Limited intellectual ability Lack of educational attainment Lack of social skills (verbal and non-verbal) Lack of survival skills (e.g., self- help, budgeting, etc.)	

Note: From *Developments in the Study of Criminal Behavior* (Vol. 1., p. 86) edited by M.P. Feldman, 1982, Chichester, England: Wiley.
Reprinted by permission of John Wiley & Sons, Ltd.

will be allowed to complete the assessment? The aim of this chapter is to discuss the range of assessment methods, their relative merits and pitfalls, the various parameters of assessment, and the mechanics of collecting assessment information. However, although these are all necessary conditions for assessment, the real art in behavioral analysis lies in interpretation of the information supplied via the assessment techniques.

ANALYZING BEHAVIOR

The goal in behavioral assessment is to understand the *function* of the behavior for the individual concerned. Assessment can generate a vast amount of data, but it is the skill of the behavior analyst that makes sense of this information. The clinician will be concerned with questions such as the following. Which particular consequences are reinforcing the behavior? What previous history of punishment has suppressed behavior? Is a behavior being carried out to achieve a certain consequence or to avoid others? How do the clients' own explanations of their actions fit in with these hypotheses? The answers to these and other questions will inform the practitioner's understanding of the client's behavior. Armed with this understanding it should be possible to begin to pinpoint targets for intervention.

It is ironic that one of the many criticisms of behavior analysis is that it is mechanical, rigid, and inflexible. The truth could not be more different: Making sense of a set of data, the product of the assessment, is a highly individual undertaking. As all practitioners have different learning histories, so their interpretations, hypotheses, and analyses will differ even within a common cognitive-behavioral framework. That there is no "correct" or "incorrect" behavioral analysis is a fact that many students are slow to grasp. However, as the analysis generates hypotheses about behavior, it becomes possible to test the validity of these hypotheses. In a traditional experimental analysis this is achieved by the manipulation of antecedents and consequences and attendant monitoring of changes in behavior. In clinical practice the testing of hypotheses is achieved by intervening to change either some part of the individual's behavior or some aspect of the environment. This, however, is reaching ahead. The immediate concern is with assessment and the formal model used to conduct this assessment.

Functional Analysis

As the name implies, a functional analysis is concerned with understanding what function, what payoffs, the behavior has for the individual concerned. The guiding framework for a functional analysis is the A:B:C sequence based on Skinner's three-term contingency. Thus behavioral assessment is concerned with discovering as much as possible about the antecedents of a particular behavior, the behavior itself, and the consequences it produces in order to suggest the exact nature of the relationships between antecedents, consequences, and the behavior in question.

Antecedents. Antecedents are those environmental events that precede any given behavior or sequence of behaviors—in other words, the individual's entire learning history to date. This is obviously something that is beyond any reasonable assessment, and to assist practice writers such as Herbert (1987) have drawn a distinction between *distal* and *proximal* antecedent events. Herbert distinguishes between the two, such that distal antecedents "refer to the more distant (historical) events in the client's life" (p. 56), whereas proximal antecedents "are close in time to the actual behavior" (p. 56). It is not clear where distal ends and proximal begins, but as a rule of thumb I find it helpful to assume that proximal is the point at which the formal process of assessment commences.

In assessment it is neither possible nor desirable to glean every last historical detail in pursuit of distal antecedents. Details will be lost or forgotten, or will have changed over time as they are told and retold by the individual or recorded by the written word. It is also doubtful how illuminating they will be in a functional analysis and in subsequent planning of an intervention. Nonetheless, it would be a mistake to omit them entirely. Knowledge of distal antecedents may indicate which situations might precipitate the behavior in the future and, indeed, give some clues as to which proximal antecedents should be monitored. In addition, many clients seek an explanation for their behavior, and they may find it helpful to relate present behavior to past events.

The main concern is with proximal antecedents—events that occur immediately before the behavior itself. These antecedents or "setting conditions" can be any aspect of the environment: a particular type of *situation* such as an argument; a certain *place* such as a classroom; a particular *time* of day such as a mealtime; or the appearance, words, or actions of a particular *person* or *group of people*. Further, the *physical* aspects of the environment should not be ignored. There is strong evidence, for example, that aversive conditions such as high temperatures and air pollution are antecedents of aggressive behavior (Rotton & Frey, 1985). It may well be that there is not one specific, well-defined antecedent. There may be a more subtle, complex cue to behavior, such as a certain person, in a given setting, at a particular time of day.

Behavior. The word *behavior* is perhaps most commonly used to refer to motor behaviors that are publically observable. We talk about good behavior, appropriate behavior, and deviant behavior, in each case referring to actions upon which we can express judgment. However, for the social learning theorist, *behavior* takes on a much wider meaning in that it refers to *all* of a person's behavior. Although observable behavior certainly occurs, there is a great deal more behavior taking place that is not open to public observation. This, of course, is the behavior taking place in the world within the skin. This private behavior can be classified in various ways, such as cognitive, emotional, and physiological, although each is composed of a variety of elements. Physiology, for example, includes the integrated functioning of the central and autonomic nervous systems, the influence of genetic material, the endocrine system, and so on. Although the structure of the physiological system can be described in this way because it can be opened to public inspection, the same cannot be said for other private behaviors. Therefore even though it is possible to construct theoretical cognitive systems such as short-term memory, long-term memory, personal constructs, beliefs, and so on, these cannot, given the present limitations of science, be shown to exist and function in the same way as, say, the hypothalamus can be shown to exist and function. This is not to say that hypothesized cognitive systems are not important or are to be dismissed, rather that their understanding must always be restricted by the limits on observation and scientific experimentation. It is commonly held that private behaviors can have only a single observer, the person himself or herself. Even this, however, may not always be the case. There is ample evidence, both experimental and experiential, that some private behavior takes place outside of self-perception and self-awareness. Subliminal perception, the "cocktail party effect," and dreaming are all commonplace examples. There is also evidence that anxious people selectively attend to anxiety-producing cues without being aware that this is taking place (Mathews & MacLeod, 1986). With regard to assessment, as Shepherd (1984) points out, if some aspects of private functioning are not open to inspection by the individual, then how are measures of cognition to be formulated?

If *behavior* is used as a generic term for all aspects of human functioning, what is the exact nature of the relationships among the various aspects of behavior? Novaco (1978) suggests that there may be a reciprocal relationship between cognition and emotion. Thus particular cognitions may induce anger, and experiencing anger leads to aggressive thoughts. Similar reciprocal relationships may function between cognition and motor behavior, and between emotion and motor behavior. Until the primacy of one system over the others is firmly established, it is safest to take the position suggested by Novaco—that observable and private behaviors function in a reciprocal fashion.

Consequences. An individual's actions will produce some effect on the environment, and it is this effect, the consequences of behavior, that is the third concern of functional analysis. As with antecedents, it is possible to distinguish between proximal and distal outcomes. Proximal outcomes are the immediately observed outcomes following a specified behavior; distal outcomes are those outcomes that will occur after a period of time. Whereas reasonably clear statements can be made about proximal outcomes, only probability statements can be made about distal outcomes. For example, it can be readily seen that successfully stealing a car will result in a quicker journey time than walking; it can be suggested, with some confidence but not with certainty, that if enough cars are stolen on enough occasions the person will be caught and legally punished.

There are a variety of consequences that flow from a behavioral act: The consequences may be social in the sense that the behavior evokes a reaction from another person or group of people; alternatively the consequences may be physical in that they cause some environmental change—vandalism of property is a relevant example. These are all consequences in which some event take place, an event that the individual concerned may experience as either desirable or aversive. Alternatively the behavior may be intended to avoid a particular outcome: Claustrophobic people take the stairs rather than the elevator not because they enjoy walking, but to avoid panic should they go into the closed environment of the elevator.

There are a number of points to be made about consequences. The first is that behavior does not always produce an immediate consequence; the consequence may be delayed either until a requisite number of behaviors have been performed or until some period of time has elapsed. The relationship between behavior and the delivery of its consequences is referred to as the *schedule* of reinforcement (or punishment). Although the schedule will affect the frequency of behavior, it also appears that the way in which individuals describe to themselves their behavior and its consequences is important in mediating the effects of the environmental consequences (Lowe, 1983). The second point to note is that the picture is not static. The individual's behavior produces consequences, and these consequences influence behavior to produce a new situation which, in turn, demands a fresh response. Further, the sequence is interactive in that if another person is involved, there is a pattern of exchange in which one person's behavior is the antecedent of another's behavior; the second person's behavior acts as a consequence for the first person but also creates a new situation to which a further response is required. Thus, far from being static, the interaction between individual and environment, particularly the social environment, is a rich, dynamic process constantly shifting and changing.

BEHAVIORAL ASSESSMENT

Finds

Having selected the target behaviors on the basis of the preliminary assessment, the next step may be to gather information in greater detail over a period of time. The first decision concerns the dimensions of the behavior to be assessed. Herbert (1987) has coined the acronym FINDS to assist in recall of the five basic dimensions of behavioral recording. The first is *frequency,* a count of the number of times a behavior occurs within a given time interval. The *intensity* of the behavior may be thought of as how long the particular behavior lasts: An aggressive outburst lasting 5 min is of greater intensity than a similar outburst lasting 2 min. Another way to judge intensity is in terms of severity rather than duration. This may involve self-ratings or observer ratings on a scale designed for this purpose, as is often seen in self-ratings of anxiety or staff ratings of institutional behavior. The third dimension is *number*, a count of the number of behaviors that are of concern and are to be assessed. The fourth aspect is *duration*; again this can be looked at from two directions. The first, as with intensity, is to measure how long an episode of the particular behavior lasts; the second is to estimate how long the behavior has been part of the individual's repertoire. The final part of the FINDS sequence is *sense*, the individual's own understanding and explanation for his or her behavior. In some instances the person will present an accurate account of his or her behavior, but in other cases the individual may be confused or devise elaborate, erroneous explanations.

The frequency, intensity, and duration of a behavior are usually recorded numerically for each of the individual behaviors that give the total (i.e., number). The individual's explanation (sense) of the behavior is generally recorded as qualitative information. It is good assessment practice to measure repeatedly over time the frequency, duration, and intensity of the behavior before treatment. This *baseline*, often referred to as the *A phase* of the intervention, serves a number of purposes. First, it aids comprehension by reducing the chances of recording an extreme sample of behavior, as might be the case if only one recording were made. Second, any fluctuations in behavior may be informative if it is possible to determine what is happening to cause the changes. Third, the baseline gives a standard against which to estimate the effects of the treatment program—the *B phase* of the intervention. Indeed, program design for studying behavior change has reached a considerable level of sophistication (Barlow & Hersen, 1984).

There are a number of practical points to be made with respect to baselines. The first is a question of length: How long—in terms of either time or data points—should a baseline be? The most favored recommendation is that baseline measurement be continued until the behavior is stable according to the particular assessment measure. However, in clinical practice this is not always possible or even desirable. There may be limitations on the time an individual can be seen—a point that applies particularly to those in institutional settings. In addition, the individual, or indeed any others concerned, may weary of an extended period of assessment and the concomitant withholding of treatment. As hinted above, stability may not occur: If there are regularly changing reinforcement contingencies, then there may be a regular cycle of behavior change over the baseline period. Finally, the phenomenon of *reactivity* may militate against a stable baseline over long periods. The individual may shift his or her criteria for self-report, observers may "drift" in their ratings, or knowledge of the assessment findings as time progresses may cause rater behavior to change. Given this, it is difficult to say how long a baseline should be. What can be stated, however, is how short it should be: "A minimum of three separate observation points, plotted on the graph, during this baseline phase are required to establish a trend in the data" (Barlow & Hersen, 1973, p. 320).

Assessment Methods

There are a range of texts available that provide detailed reviews of behavioral assessment techniques (e.g., Bellack & Hersen, 1988; Ciminero, Calhoun, & Adams, 1986). The focus here is on a brief summary of the methods, followed by particular note of behavioral assessment with young offenders.

Regardless of the reasons for assessment the practitioner is concerned with three types of behavior: private behavior, motor behavior, and physiological behavior. In order to assess these behaviors the practitioner has available two basic strategies: These are *indirect* measures of behavior and *direct* measures of behavior. Bellack and Hersen (1988) distinguish indirect and direct methods by means of the temporal proximity of the behavior and its assessment:

> The further removed an assessment of a problem response is from the time and place of its natural occurrence, the more indirect is the method of measurement. . . . Assessment procedures that call for little passage of time between the monitoring of a client's performance and the recording of said observations are considered direct methods (pp. 22–23).

The assessment methods of interviewing and self-report are examples of indirect measures; self-observation and role-play are examples of direct measures.

As well as the directness of the assessment, there is also the question of authenticity. The physiological response of heart rate can be measured in a verifiable manner, and a person's motor behavior can be observed, recorded, and cross-checked by different observers. However, if a person is asked to report on his or her thoughts or feelings, it is impossible to determine the authenticity of the report. Indeed, if the individual is observing his or her own thoughts, this may well change the nature of these cognitions. Further, it is possible to observe motor behavior without the individual being aware that assessment is taking place, but it is impossible for self-observation to take place under similar conditions.

It would, however, be unwise to say that directness and high authenticity should be the aims of every assessment. Although these are desirable, circumstances may dictate that nondirect assessment is necessary, as in the case of, say, child abuse, or that assessment must be low in authenticity, for example, in the assessment of private behaviors such as anger and pain. There is a temptation to prefer methods high in authenticity, and historically behavioral assessment has favored the direct, observable measurement of motor responses. Contemporary behavioral assessment is beginning to move away from this position for two reasons. First, there is growing doubt about how "pure" direct measures really are, and second, it is questionable that a singular concentration on motor behavior always gives a full assessment (Jacobson, 1985a,b). Bellack and Hersen (1988) summarize the position: "Rather than selecting assessment instruments on the basis of how well they meet preferences for motor responses and direct methods of measurement, it is better to select such assessment instruments on the basis of how well they meet the particular purposes in mind" (p. 25). The purpose in mind here is offending, but before considering the assessment of this particular behavior, it is as well to note briefly the different strategies in behavioral assessment.

Interviewing. The interview is a traditional means of gathering clinical data, and behavioral interviewing has been in use for a number of years (Hersen & Turner, 1985; Kanfer & Grimm, 1977). The behavioral interview can serve a number of functions in the process of assessment, and the interviewer should be clear in advance what these functions are. The interview may well be the first meeting, at least the first formal meeting, between interviewer and interviewee and so is the first exchange in which it is possible to agree on the agenda for what lies ahead. It is necessary to glean information from the client, and there are a number of schedules of the type shown in Table 2.2 that suggest how the incoming information might be organized as, for example, background information, behavior descriptions, and clarification of expectations (Murphy, Hudson, King, & Remenyi, 1985). It is always worth remembering the caution administered by Peterson (1968) that about three-quarters of the material exchanged in a traditional interview is redundant in terms of its eventual impact on the formulation of an intervention. This is not only wasteful of the time and effort of all concerned, but it may also represent an unethical intrusion into areas of the interviewee's life which he or she would prefer not to discuss. It is recommended therefore that the first stage in interviewing be adequate preparation to clarify exactly the goals of the interview.

Although the goals will vary from interview to interview, there are two particular functions traditionally associated with the behavioral in-

Table 2.2.   Interview Schedule (after Murphy et al., 1985)

Stage 1: Introduction, small talk, seating

Stage 2: Purpose of interview, permission on note taking, client
          perception of issue

Stage 3: Background information including family, educational,
          personal details, and medical background

Stage 4: Problem-specific information including definitions, indications
          of extent, antecedents, and consequences

Stage 5: Clarification of expectations including agreement on goals and
          responsibilities

Stage 6: Homework such as diary keeping

Stage 7: Review and scheduling next appointment

---

terview. The first is identification of the behavior in question. Many clients will use fuzzy terms such as *nervous, wound-up, fed-up,* and so on. Identification should be concerned with establishing an agreed-on definition of such terms with the client. The literature is replete with examples: Morganstern (1988) offers a typical exchange in which it is established between interviewer and interviewee that *uptight* refers to certain physiological changes (sweating, headaches), accompanying thoughts of failure, and the avoidance of certain situations.

The second primary use of the interview is the selection of targets for assessment and possible intervention. Nelson and Barlow (1981) offer four pointers related to the selection of target behaviors: (a) The behavior is dangerous to the client or to others; (b) the behavior is not producing the desired reinforcement; (c) the behavior is undesirable; (d) the target behavior should be of benefit to the client. Of course there are ethical issues to be debated: To whom is the behavior undesirable? What are the client's motivations for change? Are the targets realistic and legally and morally justifiable? Is the client in a position to give full, informed consent? (Feldman & Peay, 1982).

The interview can also serve to establish the priorities for assessment and intervention. Although life-threatening targets will probably be the most urgent, there will need to be some negotiation around the practitioner's and client's expectations and views on what is appropriate.

In total the interview can set the stage for the assessment and can form part of the assessment procedure. It is a rich source of information, but attention must be paid to the quality of this information. In the main, the client is giving a *self-report* on his or her previous behavior.

Self-report is an indirect method of assessment prone to bias and distortion through natural processes of memory functioning and deliberate withholding or falsifying of information by the client. While these constraints indicate that information from an interview must be treated with some caution, it may be possible to cross-check it against findings from other assessment methods.

Observation. For many years direct observation of motor behavior was the mainstay of behavioral assessment. It is therefore not surprising that this method of assessment has been thoroughly researched and reviewed (Foster, Bell-Dolan, & Burge, 1988). Once a motor behavior has been selected and defined, the assessor has a number of points to consider. The first concerns *sampling.* In some instances interest is centered on recording whether or not an event has occurred. This may necessitate a frequency count of, say, the number of aggressive incidents on a ward or the number of times an autistic child engages in conversation. Along with the recording of the behavior, observers can also record environmental events to inform the eventual A:B:C analysis. As well as event recording, observational data can also be gathered using interval recording. With interval recording the assessor divides the observation period into blocks of time. Observers may observe and record simultaneously, or they may spend a short period observing, followed by a short period making the recording. There are a number of advantages to interval recording, including the generation of measurement of duration of behavior as well as frequency and greater practicability for assessing a number of behaviors together (Hawkins, 1982). As anyone who has engaged in observational studies will testify, close observation of behavior demands considerable attention and concentration. The assessor should be aware of these limitations of observational data and, where possible, cross-check between observers for disagreements in recording.

Observers also require a means of recording their observations. The simplest means is a checklist and a written record. The design of such a checklist should be elegant yet sufficiently plain to allow full recording that can later be "decoded" accurately. Herbert (1987) offers examples of well-designed checklists and coding sheets. High-frequency behaviors, such as facial tics, may be most accurately recorded with a hand-held counter; stopwatches are necessary to record durations; and more recently portable computers have been used in recording behavior. Another technological advance in video recording has been utilized in observation. If a behavioral sequence is highly complex, then the ability to replay the sequence several times may yield valuable information.

Another decision the assessor must make concerns the environment in which the observation is to take place. A number of alternatives are available, but the choice is principally between naturalistic observation and observation of analog situations. Naturalistic or *in vivo* observation is perhaps the most desirable, as real behavior is observed as and when it happens in the home, workplace, or hospital. If *in vivo* observation is not possible, an alternative is a staged naturalistic interaction. Here a client is observed in a situation such as a planned waiting room encounter, unaware that the observation is taking place (e.g., Gutride, Goldstein, & Hunter, 1973). More usual, however, is an analog role-play in which the client is required to enact his or her behavior as it would occur in the natural environment. This form of role-play assessment has produced some highly sophisticated tests such as the Revised Behavioral Assertiveness Test (BAT-R; Eisler, Hersen, Miller, & Blanchard, 1975). While many experimental clinical studies have used role-play assessment, several studies have cast doubt on the assumption that role-play behavior is analogous to behavior in the natural environment (Bellack, Hersen, & Lamparski, 1979). Arkowitz (1981) provides a full discussion and concludes that although caution is needed in the use of role-play assessment, its use should not be abandoned. However, the caveat should be added that single-response role-plays are generally agreed not to be helpful.

Finally, the observer should not be neglected. Observers must be physically suited for the task, be able to record accurately and reliably, be trusted to complete the task properly, and respect confidentiality. It is undoubtedly beneficial to train observers and to keep them informed of progress during recording to counteract the phenomenon of observer drift as the individual gradually shifts his or her observational criteria (Hartmann & Wood, 1982). There should always be some check of inter-observer agreement, which may be a simple visual comparison of data or, if the data set is large and complex, involve the use of statistics (Foster & Cane, 1986).

Whereas observation by others is limited to motor behavior, *self-observation* can be used to assess private behaviors such as cognition, emotional arousal, and physiological state (Bornstein, Hamilton, & Bornstein, 1986). As with observation of motor behavior, self-observation is a direct method of assessment as it takes place at the time of occurrence of the behavior. As with public observation, self-observation has its strengths and weaknesses. There may be observer error, a reluctance to report what is experienced, and errors in recording. In practice, self-observation and rater observation might well be used concurrently.

Self-report and Rating Scales. The distinction between self-report and rating scales is somewhat arbitrary. As used here, self-report scales are those that individuals complete about their own behavior; rating scales are similar but are completed by another person.

A *self-report* is one's report of one's perception of one's own functioning. Self-report inventories have been developed for many types of behavior, for example, social skills (Hersen & Bellack, 1977), alcohol consumption (Sobell & Sobell, 1978), and depression (Levitt & Lubin, 1975). It is important to note that a discrepancy between self-report data and information from another assessment method does not necessarily mean that one of the assessments is inaccurate. A discrepancy between an individual's perception of his or her own behavior and the perception of an observer can be clinically illuminating. The principal issue in the use of self-report data surrounds the reliability and validity of the information—points which may be particularly pertinent in the case of young offenders.

Rating scales are typically devised for another person to report on the client's behavior in a systematic form. Thus there are scales designed for use by the practitioner to assist in the assessment of psychiatric symptoms, such as the Brief Psychiatric Rating Scale (Overall & Gorham, 1962). There are rating scales for children's behavior to be completed by teachers, for example, the Connors Teacher Rating Scale (Conners, 1969), and by parents, such as the Child Behavior Problem Profile (Achenbach, 1978). Other rating scales focus on certain types of behavior, such as the Social Situations Questionnaire for assessing social skills (Trower, Bryant, & Argyle, 1978). Rating scales may be completed on the basis of observation (direct measurement) or from memory (indirect measurement). In the former instance they may incorporate the biases found in any observational data; in the latter they are prone to the distortions of memory and recall. When used in conjunction with observation, it is necessary to train the observers in their use.

As a generalization, to which there are a number of exceptions, rating scales do not have the most sound psychometric properties. A number of scales have not been rigorously devised with respect to reliability and validity, and in many cases norms are not available or no subscales have been identified within the body of the scale. Although there is some debate about the exact value of good psychometric properties for methods used in behavioral assessment, current opinion holds that behavioral assessment has much to gain from psychometrically sound measures (Barrios & Hartmann, 1986).

Cognitive Assessment. The methods of cognitive assessment are no different in essence from those discussed above, with the obvious exception of observer assessment. Thus the two principal methods are self-report and self-observation of cognition and emotion, using both unstructured and structured formats for recording the data.

At an unstructured level, clients may be asked simply to "think aloud," talking their way through situations, experiences, and so forth. A more sophisticated approach attempts to measure private speech, a type of speech that is almost silent and considered to be closely allied to thinking (Roberts & Tharp, 1980). Other attempts to tap into thinking include articulated thoughts (Davison, Robins, & Johnson, 1983), thought listing (Cacioppo & Petty, 1981), and thought sampling (Klinger, 1978). Self-statements, the way in which individuals comment to themselves on their own or others' behavior, appear to play an important role in behavior. Self-statements can be assessed in a number of ways, including asking clients to report on their self-statements as they find themselves in various situations (e.g., Stefanek, Ollendick, Baldock, Francis, & Yaeger, 1987).

Not all cognition takes the form of language, and there are assessment methods for imagery such as fantasies, daydreams, and visual and auditory images (Strosahl & Ascough, 1981). The assessment may be concerned with complex cognitive processes such as attribution (Försterling, 1986), locus of control (Rotter, 1966), and problem-solving strategies (Heppner, 1982). There are tests for just about every aspect of cognitive performance the clinician could ever require (Kendall & Hollon, 1981; Parks & Hollon, 1988). The assessment of emotion has followed broadly similar lines, again using both structured and unstructured self-observation and self-report methods. Thus there are a variety of instruments such as the Anger Inventory (Novaco, 1975), the Children's Anger Inventory (Finch & Eastman, 1983), self-control rating scales (Rosenbaum, 1980), and depression scales (Beck & Beck, 1972).

The difficulties with cognitive assessment are threefold: The first is that it is impossible to know if the data reflect accurately the cognition, because what is said verbally may not be what is thought privately. The second is that some aspects of cognition may not be open to conscious inspection. The third difficulty is described by Barrios (1988): "In self-observation, the act of observing is inherently confounded with the act of responding. There is no way around this confound: thus, there is no way around questions concerning the authenticity of the procedure's measures" (p. 23). This confound extends, as Barrios suggests, beyond psychometric considerations of reliability and validity; there is the possibility that the act of self-observation may influence cognitive processes. Thus, for example, when thinking privately topics shift, on average, about every 5 to 6 s. But when asked to think out loud, people change topics much more slowly, about once every 30 s (Pope, 1978). This problem of *reactivity*—a change in behavior due to the change in contingencies following the onset of assessment—is not peculiar to cognitive assessment. Any direct assessment of which the individual is aware can cause a change in behavior with obvious implications for the accuracy of the assessment (Haynes & Horn, 1982).

Psychophysiological Assessment. Although physiological activity is an integral part of the triadic nature of behavior—the physiological response, motor behavior, private experience—its assessment has been limited for technical reasons. However, recent technological advances have introduced a range of sophisticated devices both to monitor physiological activity and to quantify the output of such assessment. A considerable body of knowledge on psychophysiological assessment is beginning to be amassed (Coles, Donchin, & Porges, 1986).

Human physiology is a complex interplay of nervous systems, skeletal musculature, hormonal systems, and so on. Thus the first task in psychophysiological assessment is to decide which aspect of physiological functioning is to be monitored. Kallman and Feuerstein (1986) describe five discrete response systems—somatic, cardiovascular, electrodermal, central nervous system, gastric—each with its own characteristic psychophysiological responses. The electrodermal system, for example, can be monitored in terms of skin resistance, skin conductance, and skin potential. In addition, Kallman and Feuerstein (1986) note three specialized psychophysiological responses: the sexual response, temperature, and respiration.

Although not as widely employed as in medical assessment, where it can be used for the detection of organic injury and dysfunction, psychophysiological assessment has been applied within a behavioral context. Monitoring of the responsivity of the musculoskeletal system using electomyography (EMG) recording has been used, for example, in the assessment and treatment of muscle contraction headaches (Blanchard et al., 1985). Similarly, electrodermal recording has been widely used in the study of anxiety (Katkin & Hastrup, 1982).

Archival Data. Any person who has passed through a formal system will have accumulated a history held in the form of case notes, psychologists' reports, psychiatric reports, and so on. Feindler and Ecton (1986) list no fewer than 40 potential sources of data that may be culled from school records, inpatient records, and outpatient records. In most cases these data must be treated as indirect recording of distal events. Although potentially valuable in giving a fuller understanding of the individual and for the sake of completeness in the eventual functional analysis, archival data must be treated with the utmost caution. The records may reflect the opinion of the writer rather than the individual's behavior; there can be recording errors; the content of later reports may be influenced by the content of earlier reports; and the data may be incomplete, erroneous, or even falsified. In all probability there is no way of checking the reliability and validity of the records, and so they should be treated as background information rather than hard data.

Baseline

As time progresses, so the assessment produces a string of data, and it is usual to plot these baseline data graphically for either visual or statistical inspection. There are several variations on the pattern or trend of baseline activity that appears in the assessment data. A *stable* baseline is one in which the behavior (in terms of frequency, intensity, etc.) remains constant over the period of assessment; an *increasing* baseline indicates that the behavior is increasing over the assessment; a *decreasing* baseline indicates exactly the opposite; and a *variable* baseline shows fluctuations as time progresses, the fluctuations may be regular or irregular in their occurrence (Barlow & Hersen, 1984). A stable baseline is perhaps ideal, although all baselines are informative. The decision to begin intervention will also be determined, in part at least, by the type of baseline. An increasing baseline may indicate a deterioration and so precipitate intervention, a decreasing baseline can have the opposite effect. When plotting baselines graphically any trend in the data may be apparent by visual inspection, however, in cases of uncertainty there are straightforward ways to analyze the data statistically (Tyron, 1982). In cases where more than one behavior is being assessed, or more than one measure of a single behavior is being used, a *multiple baseline* may be taken (Barlow & Hersen, 1984). A multiple baseline can be informative in showing relationships between behaviors, although statistical analysis becomes rather more complicated (Wolery & Billingsley, 1982).

BEHAVIORAL ASSESSMENT AND YOUNG OFFENDERS

As noted earlier, Reid (1982) details a variety of potential targets for behavioral assessment and intervention. These can broadly be dichotomized as *offending behaviors* and *current behaviors*—the former being behavioral sequences concerned with the commission of the crime and the latter being behaviors seen at present in the institution, community, or wherever. Initially at least, these two sets of behavior should be seen as distinct from each other and assessed separately.

Offending Behavior

It will certainly be the case that offending behavior took place before the beginning of the assessment; it is almost certainly the case that subsequent offending will take place outside the clinician's sphere of observation. Further, it is also doubtful—both practically and ethically—that it will be possible to recreate artificially for the purposes of assessment a situation in which offending will occur. There are a multitude of obvious dangers in attempting, for example, to recreate the setting conditions for arson, sexual attack, and violent assault. These constraints mean that in the vast majority of cases it will be impossible to observe the behavior in question. Therefore most assessments of offending behavior can instantly eliminate the possibility of direct assessment—either through direct observation of the behavior or by setting up analog situations such as role-play. Assessment must therefore rely on indirect methods.

Interview. The interview is perhaps the method of assessment most widely used with offenders. Questions can be asked about the situation leading up to the offense; details can be gleaned about the offense itself—what the offender did, what planning took place, what emotions and thoughts were experienced, and so on—and about the consequences of the offense—what happened afterward, whether there was any material or social gain, whether he or she worried about what might happen, and so forth. Undoubtedly this can provide a rich fund of material, thereby informing an A:B:C analysis about the offense. However, as noted previously, there are limitations to the strength of this self-report data: The offender may be withholding, elaborating, or falsifying information for perfectly rational reasons—shame, uncertainty as to the use the information is to be put, or a wish to present a certain image. The veracity of information offered by the offender may be dependent upon the strength of the relationship between the clinician and the offender. A strong, trusting relationship may well produce a better assessment than a superficial relationship.

On a practical note, it is as well to have issues of confidentiality well established before gathering information. If an offender, trusting in the confidentiality of the interview, admits to, say, knowledge of other crimes or institutional malpractice, the clinician may be placed in a position of conflict. I have experienced the dilemma of knowing that an assault on a particular young person in an institution was planned, but at the same time was bound by the confidentiality of the clinical interview not to reveal this to the appropriate authorities so that preventative action could take place. Colleagues have been told, in confidence, of drug possession, malpractice by other members of the staff, and even plans to escape from institutions. On one occasion in my experience a young offender confessed (to a colleague) to killing another person, an act for which he had not been apprehended. There are two stances the clinician might adopt: The first is to treat *everything* as confidential; the second is to treat only *some* things as confidential. There are advantages and disadvantages with both approaches. Taking everything as confidential may result in more honesty and more information, but the other side of this coin is that sensitive information about assessment and program planning may have to be withheld from others concerned in the work. In the event of any incident the clinician may have to defend his or her decision not to warn others about an act of which he or she had forewarning. Conversely, making it clear at the outset that only certain agreed-on topics are confidential places the balance of power even more firmly with the clinician and may well inhibit the offender; the advantage is that the clinician will not be placed in a position of conflict over client rights and public responsibilities. It is impossible to prescribe a correct approach; rather it is important that all clinicians or, better, teams of clinicians, have a clear policy understood by themselves, their clients, and their own managers and employers.

Self-report. In the field of offending there are a number of self-report studies; the sample shown in Table 2.3 is typical of the measures used. As noted above, veracity is the principal concern in this type of assessment: Does the offender always tell the truth? Are some offenses withheld and others invented or exaggerated? The most commonly used verification check in the research literature is to compare self-report with police records. Studies using this check have found high degrees of agreement between the two measures (Blackmore, 1974). Other verifica-

Table 2.3. Examples From a Typical Self-Report Scale (after Shapland, 1978)

I have stolen goods or money from slot machines, juke boxes, telephones, etc.

I have struggled or fought to get away from a police officer.

I have stolen things from small shops or private trades people.

I have used any kind of weapon in a fight.

I have stolen things out of cars.

I have broken into a shop, store, or garage.

I have entered a house or flat and stolen things.

tion measures include using peer informants to ensure matching of reports, testing respondents twice to determine the consistency of their responses, and including lie questions in the inventory as a general check on honesty (Huizinga & Elliott, 1986). Although at a general level it is possible to show guarded optimism about the overall accuracy of self-report measures of offending, this may change somewhat at an individual clinical level. It is one thing for a young offender to give details of his or her offenses in an anonymous survey, but quite another in a clinical context when another issue such as parole or release from custody may also be involved. With young offenders in a clinical context it would therefore be prudent to use as many verification checks as possible, rather than relying on the broad consensus regarding accuracy, as might be the case with self-report inventories designed for clinical populations.

Cognitive Assessment. This assessment may be of two types, formal and informal, the first being concerned with standardized cognitive measures such as the locus-of-control scale, and the second with the offender's own perceptions of his or her offending. The first might be used to give a rounded assessment or as a potential measure of therapeutic change. Thus, it is known that offenders tend toward external locus of control and that successful interventions tend to precipitate a shift to internal control; a knowledge of pretreatment locus of control may therefore be of value in assessing change. The offender's own sense of his or her offending may reveal rational reasons for apparently irrational acts; similarly, the offender's self-talk before, during, and after the crime may be clinically valuable. There are no cognitive assessment procedures specifically designed for offenders.

Psychophysiological Assessment. There are a number of theories of delinquency that incorporate physiological factors (Trasler, 1987). The most widely known is Eysenck's (1987) theory which proposes a complex relationship among genetic endowment, nervous system reactivity and liability, and conditionability. Other theories seek to account in physiological terms for certain offender groups, such as the psychopath (Blackburn, 1983). With the exception of (mainly adult) sex offenders, it is rare to find psychophysiological assessment used with offender populations. It is not difficult to see why this is the case. There is little in the way of historical precedent to spur practitioners toward this style of assessment; such assessment methods can be highly intrusive and, particularly if conducted in a closed setting, are open to public misrepresentation; the assessment requires expensive equipment and knowledge of how to use it; and the assessment data can be difficult to interpret and understand.

With offender groups it is in the assessment of sex offenders that psychophysiological assessment is most widely practiced. Monitoring of male sexual arousal can be accomplished using penile plethysmography (PPG), an assessment that measures both penile volume and circumference (Rosen & Keefe, 1978). PPG can be used to assess deviant arousal patterns in response to stimuli (presented by audiotape, videotape, or self-imagery), say, to children or to nonconsenting sex (Quinsey, Chaplin, & Upfold, 1984). While informative, psychophysiological assessment is not without difficulties: Sex offenders do show sexual arousal to deviant stimuli, but this is not invariably the case (Baxter, Barbaree, & Marshall, 1986), and similar patterns of arousal to sex offenders have been found in offenders and in nonsex offenders (Quinsey, Chaplin, & Varney, 1981). This uncertainty reflects a general picture in psychophysiological assessment: It can be anticipated that there will be a growing understanding of the meaning of such assessments as theory catches up with technology, but as Kallman and Feuerstein (1986) note, "Unfortunately, at present there is little information relating psychophysiological activity to overt behavior" (p. 346).

Archival Data. There is liable to be a wealth of archival data reaching well back into the offender's past. From the point of offense analysis, it is useful to obtain copies of witness and/or victim statements (perhaps the nearest thing to observational data), copies of police reports and the offender's statement to the police, records of court proceedings, and any photographs taken of the victims or scene of the crime. The usual limitations apply to such data, but they can be a rich source of detail about the behavior.

In total, while direct observation is impossible in the vast majority of cases, the resourceful practitioner will nevertheless be able to compile a reasonable assessment of the offense behavior.

Current Behavior

Current behavior can be taken to be all behavior other than offense behavior (see Table 2.1). According to the type of behavior, there should be no barriers to a full assessment using a combination of the standard methods. The crucial task is to determine which, if any, aspects of current behavior are functionally related to the previous offending behavior and thereby constitute legitimate criminological-clinical targets as opposed to pure clinical targets. Such a distinction gives a valid focus to intervention, although it is *not* being suggested that one type of target is more important than the other, or should assume priority. Rather, the clinician working with young offenders should be as clear as possible in his or her perception of the likely impact of the intervention on future criminal behavior. The case study at the end of this chapter illustrates these points.

Finally, the assessment should pay attention to the suitability of the offender for a treatment program. As Howells (1987) notes, a major problem in working with offenders is low motivation for change. Motivation may be low for a number of reasons: The offender may view his or her behavior as legitimate, even desirable, and see no reason for change; the offending may offer rewards not attainable in any other way; the offender may adopt a rational stance, judging, perhaps accurately, that the payoffs outweigh the disadvantages; the offender may refuse to consent to treatment. The motivation for change is important as many, if not all, clinical methods require the participation and cooperation of the client. While it would be pleasing to imagine that a clinical approach could touch the lives of all offenders, in practice this is unlikely to be the case. Perkins (1987), for example, found that even of those (sex) offenders judged suitable for treatment, a substantial number dropped out of the program. Nonetheless, by adopting a strategy for selection, it may be possible to cut down on wastage of time and effort for all concerned.

CASE STUDY

This case, involving a young offender called John (pseudonym), was one in which I was involved several years ago when working in a secure institution for male young offenders.

The Referral

As was the system, any young person in the institution who caused concern was referred to the psychology department. John's referral came as, "Totally withdrawn . . . requires social skills training."

Preliminary Assessment

The first stage in the assessment process was to gather sufficient preliminary detail to judge if a full-scale assessment was warranted. I spoke first to the staff working in John's unit. They described him as a loner: In the 2 months he had spent in the institution he had made no friends, had not joined in with activities, and had formed no relationships with staff. The unit manager told me that John did not contribute to review boards—formal meetings at which each offender's progress was discussed and new targets for work, education, and so on, agreed on—

although he would talk occasionally on a one-to-one basis. John's offenses were a string of minor drunk-and-disorderly offenses and one case of arson for which he had received this, his first, custodial sentence. I spent several short periods in John's unit and in his workplace (within the institution) ostensibly for other reasons, but with the purpose of observing John's behavior. It was exactly as the staff described: He kept to himself, very rarely acknowledging the presence of others, working hard during the day, and reading newspapers and smoking cigarettes in the evening. The staff reported no evidence of him being victimized by the other young people, who seemed to treat him with some respect although rarely approaching him, and he was not a management problem.

Having formed the initial impression that John was probably waiting out his first taste of custody in as discrete and unobtrusive a manner as possible, I asked to see him on an individual basis to begin a more formal assessment. The house manager put it to John that there was some concern about him and, if he wished, it would be possible to meet with a member of the psychology department. John readily agreed to this.

Assessment

The two principal methods of assessment employed in this case to gain as full a picture as possible and to select potential targets for intervention were archival sources and interviewing.

Archival Sources. The official notes carried details of offenses, family background, criminal record, and intellectual and educational ability. John came from a lower-middle-class family; both parents were employed, and his only sibling, an elder brother, was a member of the armed forces. There was no history of family involvement either with the police or with social services. John's criminal record showed a first conviction, for drunk-and-disorderly behavior, when he was about 17 years of age. A string of similar convictions followed, being penalized by cautions and fines, over the next year. The arson, committed when John was about 18 years old, was detailed in a police report. The fire had been started in an upstairs room in a neighbor's house close to John's own home and had caused extensive damage to the property. John had been seen leaving the house shortly before the fire was reported, and when questioned by the police he readily admitted setting the fire. After being held for a period in custody, John was tried and given his present sentence.

The reports showed John to be of average intellectual and educational ability. He had left school with a number of examination passes and had begun an apprenticeship training to be an electrician. He had, however, held this position for only a short while; his more recent employment record showed alternating periods of unemployment and casual manual work.

Interview. Space does not permit a full recording of the whole series of interviews, and only the main points are presented here. However, it is worth recording some of the information obtained from the first interview.

My expectation was that the first meeting was going to be difficult and that there would be problems with communication. But nothing could have been further from the truth. From the start, John was articulate, attentive, and helpful in all our sessions. He was open and frank, to the best of my knowledge holding nothing back at our meetings. Certainly everything he said checked with other sources such as records, staff, and his probation officer. Following the initial explanations, clarifications regarding confidentiality, and so on, it was clear that John wanted to talk about his withdrawn behavior.

The explanation for his withdrawn behavior was perfectly straightforward: If he spoke when there was a group of people present, he blushed, turning bright red. Not unnaturally, this drew attention to him, causing people to remark on his appearance; such remarks, in turn, made him color even more. If he adopted the strategy of not speaking, then his problem was neatly solved. The history unfolded over a number of interviews.

He recalled that the extreme blushing (which I was later to witness: He flushed from the neck upward, turning crimson red, sweating, and looking extremely ill at ease) had begun at home. Several years ago, aged about 16–17 years, a minor incident occurred in which he clumsily spilt a tray of coffee and a parent scolded him in front of a group of family friends. He recalled blushing with embarrassment and leaving the room feeling very self-conscious. That evening he went out with friends, including his girlfriend, and halfway through the evening someone spoke to him and he felt himself start to color. It became worse, and his friends began to tease him; this made things worse still, and he left without his girlfriend. Next day at work the same thing happened again, and then again in the company of his friends.

At this point the first A:B:C sequence can be formulated as shown in Table 2.4.

The most powerful antecedent of the blushing was the presence of other people: Beginning at home, this had rapidly generalized to other social settings. The consequences were the comments from other people and the strain on his relationship with his girlfriend: He wanted to spend more time alone with her, but she still wanted to be part of a social group.

Table 2.4. Suggested Functional Analysis of Initial Stages

(Proximal)	A:	Reprimand in front of family friends Groups of people Center of social attention
	B:	Thought of looking foolish Blushing and other indications of increased autonomic nervous system arousal Fidgets, stops talking
	C:	Verbal comments from those present Strained relationship with girlfriend

John experienced an approach-avoidance conflict: He wanted to be with friends, workmates, and so on, but did not want to experience the severe blushing and the aversive consequences it produced. Like any intelligent person faced with a problem, John looked for solutions. Thinking carefully about his blushing, he realized that if he had had a drink (usually beer), then the blushing was less pronounced. He experimented with drinking before leaving home to go out with his girlfriend and their social group. He found that five or six large cans of beer more or less prevented the blushing, and he was able to face a group of people. The drawback was that he was half-drunk before the evening started; if the evening's entertainment included drinking, then he would become very drunk; drinking made him feel aggressive, and he could not drink at work.

A second A:B:C sequence can now be formulated.

As can be seen from Table 2.5, the heavy drinking was successful in diminishing the frequency and intensity of the blushing but produced a number of other, unwanted, consequences. He became involved in

Table 2.5. Suggested Functional Analysis for Second Stage

A: Sequences as in Table 2.4

B: Heavy drinking
   Physiological changes caused by alcohol
   Increase in feelings of aggressiveness

C: Fewer comments from friends about blushing
   Resumption (later deterioration) of social activity
   Increase in fighting and arguments
   Several arrests and court convictions (drunk and disorderly)
   Loss of job
   End of relationship with girlfriend
   Family problems

brawls and street fights, although he claimed not to remember most of these as he was so drunk. A typical night out would see him drunk, fighting, and waking up the next morning in a police cell unable to recall what had happened the night before. His friends disowned him, and his girlfriend left him after several months of this behavior. He appeared in court several times, receiving fines and cautions. He was asked to leave work because of his poor attendance record and attitude toward his workmates. His family was becoming increasingly concerned, although remaining supportive and helping by giving him money until he pulled himself together. (It is possible to envisage the family in some confusion as they struggled to cope with an unfamiliar situation.)

Over the next few months he rarely ventured outdoors, taking one or two casual jobs but nothing of any consequence. He continued to drink heavily, up to a bottle of whisky a day, and reported becoming more and more depressed over his social isolation. In a little more than 18 months his world had been turned upside down. Now the outlook was bleak: no friends, a drinking problem, no job, and a deeply concerned family. (I spoke later with John's mother who confirmed John's story; she spoke of "terrible times" for her and her husband during this period.) One day, in a black mood, he decided to commit suicide: In the evening, after a day of heavy drinking, he left his own house and went to a neighbor's house where he made his way upstairs, set fire to a bed, and sat down in the room to die. After a short time he panicked and rushed out of the house, leaving the fire to burn.

Once more an A:B:C sequence can be formulated as shown in Table 2.6.

In custody he was unable to drink and was surrounded by other people. The first weeks without drinking were very difficult, but several months later, including time spent in custody awaiting trial as well as

Table 2.6.   Suggested Functional Analysis for Third Stage

A: Sequences as in Tables 2.4 and 2.5

B: Thoughts of worthlessness and hopelessness
   Low mood and emotional disturbance
   Physiological changes as in depression?
   Fire setting

C: Severe damage to property
   Potential life-endangering act
   Prosecution and custodial sentence
   Family problems intensify

at the present institution, the need to drink was gone. Unfortunately the groups of people had not gone; it was impossible to escape from them and from the blushing and ridicule that would surely follow. The strategy for solving this problem was, of course, social withdrawal, which finally leads to an A:B:C sequence for the referral problem.

Functional Analysis. The detailing of the A:B:C sequences allows an analysis to be made, in cognitive-behavioral terms, of the situation. A variety of hypotheses can be generated to account for the initial incident that produced the blushing reaction: that adolescence is a time of physiological change which may have increased the likelihood of an extreme reaction of the type experienced, or that adolescence is a time of particular social and personal sensitivity. In any event, the initial learning experience was generalized to other settings, with the presence of a group of people with whom he had to interact socially acting as a powerful discriminative stimulus. The consequences of the blushing he saw as highly aversive, and clearly they had to be avoided. The avoidance strategy was either withdrawal from social contact or, he discovered, drinking. The preferred solution, heavy drinking, can therefore be seen as being negatively reinforced, as it led to the avoidance of unwanted consequences. The drinking was associated with increased aggression and loss of inhibition, producing arguments, fights, and so forth. With time this led to a loss of the positive reinforcers—friends, work, and so on— the drinking was supposed to maintain by preventing the blushing. In addition, the drinking produced aversive consequences in the form of police arrests, convictions, and family difficulties.

All the contingencies were now producing aversive outcomes: The drinking led to problems; the alternative of social isolation was undesirable; to face the world blushing and be subjected to mockery was out of the question. The belief that there was no way out of these negative contingencies produced a "helpless" cognitive set: There was no way

Table 2.7. Suggested Functional Analysis
for Final Part of Sequence

A: Sequence as in Tables 2.4, 2.5, and 2.6

B: Thoughts of preventing blushing
   Social withdrawal

C: Little social contact (no blushing)
   Institution staff register concern
   Referral to psychology department
   Interview with Clive Hollin

out, and hopelessness and depression followed, together with thoughts of suicide. The arson followed as an attempt at the only solution perceived as possible. It failed, and more aversive consequences followed. Withdrawal from social contact within the institution was an example of a negatively reinforced coping strategy to avoid blushing.

Critique

The assessment detailed a logical sequence in which one set of events produced consequences which then become the antecedents of subsequent behavior. The assessment was concerned with cognition, mood, physiology, and motor behavior—with the emphasis on seeing the behavior as attempts at problem solving rather than as indicators of psychopathology. Throughout there was emphasis on the sense that John saw in his actions.

The assessment methods were mainly indirect in that they were removed in time from the behavior. This was inevitable for the offense behavior, and although it would have been possible to construct an analog situation to produce blushing, it was judged unnecessary to make John suffer in this way. (Later blushing during intervention justified the lack of observational verification during assessment.) As the assessment relied principally on self-report, this was a potential source of error. Some verification was possible by checking with parents, records, and so on. I was never happy with the description of the arson and the events leading up to it. Although John's recounting of it stayed the same over time and, if he had been drunk, his memory would be expected to be vague. As in most analysis of offense behavior, the limitations of self-report, indirect assessments are insurmountable. Observational monitoring over a period of 2 weeks showed a stable baseline of very low levels of social interaction, verifying this aspect of John's account of his behavior.

Observation and discussion also highlighted a number of other problems for John: He had had a slight stammer since childhood, and he was also concerned about the number of cigarettes he smoked (he had been a heavy smoker from about 14 years of age).

The intervention program is discussed at the end of the following chapter.

Three
Individual Programs

The focus in this chapter is on individual programs—individual in the sense that they focus singularly on the offender as opposed to, say, the family, and individual in the sense of *individualized*, in that they are designed for particular offenders rather than for all offenders in an institution or community project. Community and residential programs are discussed in the next chapter. The literature on individually focused interventions can be classified into three broad types: individual behavior therapy, social skills training, and cognitive-behavior modification.

INDIVIDUAL BEHAVIOR THERAPY

Individually based behavior therapy is, of course, widely practiced with a range of client populations (Bellack, Hersen, & Kazdin, 1982). Traditionally drawing on operant learning theory, as well as concepts derived from classical conditioning, behavior therapists have a range of techniques at their disposal. Drawing on the operant terms *reinforcement* and *punishment*, these clinical techniques can be dichotomized as those intended to increase (i.e., reinforce) behavior and those used to decrease (i.e., punish) behavior. Examples of the former include the token economy, shaping, chaining, and contingency contracting. Examples of the latter include time out and response cost, together with extinction (although the latter, in a strict operant sense, is not a punishment contingency as it involves removal of reinforcement rather than presentation of an aversive event); and this list can be expanded to include desensitization, biofeedback, and aversion therapy, more generally associated with classical conditioning.

A glance at any text on behavior therapy will provide a wealth of examples of the application of the above clinical techniques on an individual basis with a range of client populations and a variety of presenting behaviors (Bellack et al., 1982; Herbert, 1987; Masters, Burish, Hol-

51

lon, & Rimm, 1987). Inspection of the recent major reviews of behavioral intervention with young offenders suggests that this particular group, indeed offenders generally, are not numbered among the client populations for which individual behavior work is popular (Blakely & Davidson, 1984; Burchard & Lane, 1982; Gordon & Arbuthnot, 1987; Milan, 1987; Nietzel, 1979). Although there are case reports and individual programs recorded in the literature, they are very much in the minority compared to the much more widely used institutional and family programs. The exception to this statement is in the treatment of sex offenders, where a substantial individual case study literature has been amassed (Perkins, 1987), and to a lesser extent in probation and parole (Nietzel & Himelein, 1987). However, in both cases the intervention is primarily with adult, rather than young, offenders. To describe individual behavior therapy with young offenders, examples have been selected from what literature there is to illustrate reinforcement and punishment programs.

Reinforcement

The principle guiding reinforcement programs is that a desirable behavior is selected and rewarded until it becomes an established part of the individual's behavioral repertoire. Fo and O'Donnell (1974, 1975) devised a "buddy system" in which trained adult nonprofessional volunteers were paired with young offenders. The aim of the program was to increase the offender's socially acceptable behavior by making both social rewards (companionship and praise) and material rewards (money) contingent upon good behavior. Monitoring revealed that there was no change in academic performance, although truancy decreased in the reinforcement group but not in a control group. A follow-up revealed mixed findings (O'Donnell, Lydgate, & Fo, 1979): Two years after completion of the project the arrest rate was lower for the young offenders in the buddy system group as compared to the no-intervention controls. However, for those young people who had committed only minor offenses, the reverse was found: Their arrest rate was significantly higher than that of the control group. The researchers suggest that the group meetings that brought together the "serious" and "nonserious" young offenders may well have contributed to this effect.

Daniel (1987) reports a case study with a young arsonist that utilizes the technique of *stimulus satiation*. This technique is based on the principle that massed practice of a behavior without contingent reinforcement will lead to extinction. Following Welsh (1971), the program was devised for a young offender, held in custody, who had committed a string of fire-setting offenses and, it was observed, was fond of matches. The satiation program consisted of a series of 50-min sessions, all of which could be spent striking matches according to prearranged rules. After eight sessions the time spent striking matches per session began to decrease. After ten sessions the young offender refused to continue with the "boring" sessions—and stopped carrying matches as had always been his habit. At a 6-month follow-up there had been no further convictions for fire-setting offenses.

Punishment

As Blakely and Davidson (1984) note, "Punishment paradigms are infrequently instituted in and of themselves. However, variations on this theme do occur" (p. 259). Although intended to punish (i.e., suppress) offending, the programs to be described here are, as Blakely and Davidson note, best thought of as variations. There are two reasons for this: The first is that it has not been established that the programs are aversive; second, the programs aim to do more than simply punish offending. The punishment programs selected for discussion are based on the twin notions of *restitution* and *reparation*. The former demands that the young offender makes amends, either financially or through work efforts, for his or her offense. The latter requires the young offender to make an apology to the victim of the crime. In practice the two are often combined.

Schneider, Griffith, and Schneider (1982) studied the effect of restitution—both in terms of financial penalty and time—on juvenile crime. The influence of restitution was looked at either alone or in conjunction with another penalty such as a suspended sentence. It was found that when restitution was the *sole* intervention, young offenders were more likely to complete their obligations under its terms. In a similar fashion, these young offenders for whom restitution was the sole intervention showed lower recidivism rates than other groups.

Although not intended as behavior therapy in its reporting, the description by Blagg (1985) perhaps illustrates the aversive nature of reparation. Blagg distinguished two types of reparation: *Institutional reparation* refers to the situation in which the young offender is required to apologize to a representative of a business; in *personal reparation* the young offender makes his or her apology directly to the victim, as in the case of an assault or burglary. From Blagg's description it is clear that institutional reparation has little effect on young offenders, whereas personal reparation appears to make a significant impact. The offenders required to face their victims spoke of being "terrified," "feeling sick," and "finding it difficult to talk" while making reparation. Indeed parents of young offenders claimed that reparation was *too* punitive and humiliating a process. Once completed, again from Blagg's accounts, young offenders who made personal reparation said they had benefited enormously from the experience.

The type of program described by Blagg is awaiting long-term evaluation, but there are clear lessons for the design of intervention programs. The major problem from an evaluative viewpoint, admittedly less troublesome from a purely clinical perspective, is disentangling the components of such interventions. Undoubtedly there are aversive aspects of restitution and reparation, but there are also positive aspects such as learning about the effects of crime on victims and modification of self-image.

SOCIAL SKILLS TRAINING

The technique of social skills training (SST) is in widespread use both in clinical and nonclinical settings (e.g., schools, professional training). Comprehensive reviews of its use are available in extended (Hollin & Trower, 1986a,b) and abbreviated forms (Hollin & Trower, 1988). As the technique has a somewhat different theoretical base than cognitive-behavioral theory, it is as well to be familiar with the social skills model.

Social Skills

In drawing together a range of research findings from the social psychology of human interpersonal behavior, Argyle (1967) drew on the analogy between social skills and motor skills in suggesting that social behavior could be viewed in the same way as motor behavior. The model stemming from Argyle's proposal is shown in Figure 3.1.

The social skills model has three stages, beginning with a social *goal* (such as having more friends) that the individual wishes to achieve. The second stage begins with the *perception* of relevant cues from the social environment; this refers to the individual's sensitivity to verbal and, especially, nonverbal communication and his or her ability to identify feelings and emotions from interpersonal communication. The second stage continues with a process Argyle terms *translation*. Here the individual is required to evaluate his or her perceptions and make decisions as to which response, if any, would be appropriate in a given social context. Obviously this process takes place at a cognitive level. At the culmination of this second stage the individual finally makes a motor response; that is, he or she performs some piece of overt social behavior. This response may be verbal, nonverbal, or a combination of the two. The motor response then sets into motion the third stage of the model, emphasizing the interactive nature of social transactions. The individual's

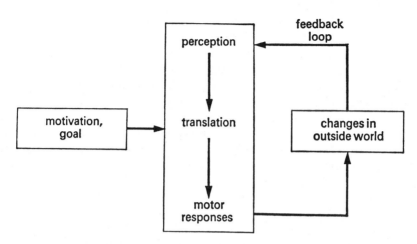

FIGURE 3.1. The social skills training model. From *The Psychology of Interpersonal Behavior*
(p. 94) by M. Argyle, 1967, Harmondsworth, Middlesex, England: Penguin Books.
Reprinted by permission of Penguin Books Ltd.

behavior operates on the social environment to produce some *environ-mental change*, primarily in the form of a reciprocal piece of social behavior from the other people involved in the exchange. These social reactions complete the *feedback* loop that closes the system and continues the flow of individual perception to translation, and so on. This latter point is often forgotten, and so it is worth emphasizing that social behavior is a dynamic process, an interaction between the individual and his or her social environment that demands a smooth integration of perceptual, translation, and response skills.

Argyle (1967) noted a variety of potential uses for the social skills model, including a clinical application: "Some psychiatric patients might be treated by training in social skills: this would cure those symptoms which consist of disturbances of social behavior, as well as others that result from it" (p. 18). This struck a chord with clinicians, and after the first applications of training social behavior, primarily with schizophrenic, depressive, and neurotic populations, the first texts began to appear (Liberman, King, DeRisi, & McCann, 1975; Trower, Bryant, & Argyle, 1978), with further texts appearing on a regular basis (Curran & Monti, 1982; L'Abate & Milan, 1985; Hollin & Trower, 1986a,b).

Social Skills Training

As with most behaviorally orientated interventions, SST has developed its own particular assessments and techniques. In the main the favored assessment methods are familiar ones such as observation, self-report, and role-play (Becker & Heimberg, 1988). However, although there has been much emphasis on such traditional behavioral measures, the response stage is only one part of the social skills model. Assessment methods for social perception have included methodologies in which the potential trainee observes and describes a videotaped social interaction (Archer & Akert, 1977). This appears to be a potentially powerful means of assessment, but it is not in widespread use, at least as indicated by the skills training literature. Assessment of cognition during the translation stage is once again sparse in the literature, although the growing sophistication in this area will surely lead to significant developments (McFall, 1982).

The major training techniques are familiar: *instruction*, usually verbally, in the required behavior; *modeling* (or *demonstration*) of the social behavior by another person; *practice* and *rehearsal* of the skills, either in role-play or real life; *feedback* on performance, either by videotape or verbally; and *contingent reinforcement* for the skill, either in the form of praise or a tangible reward. In addition, *homework* tasks may be given to be performed between training sessions. There have been a number of studies on the relative effectiveness of these training techniques. Twentyman and Zimmering (1979) suggest that rehearsal, modeling, and feedback are not consistently effective when used alone, but are more effective when used in combination. Similarly, Stravynski and Shahar (1983) conclude that instruction, modeling, rehearsal, and feedback make up the most powerful combination of techniques. Shepherd (1983) agrees, suggesting that modeling is perhaps the most powerful component for skills acquisition, whereas homework and reinforcement are important for effective transfer of training to the natural environment. As was the case with assessment, there has been some neglect of training in social perception and translation. However, recent studies have used skills training methods in attempts to increase the sensitivity of social perception (Milne & Spence, 1987) and to influence social problem solving (Kagan, 1984). It may again be anticipated that this area is ripe for innovation.

SST with Young Offenders

In the 1970s expanded use of SST began to influence the practice of those who worked with young offenders. Since that time a considerable body of experimental-clinical studies has amassed. The following synopsis of this research draws on the published reviews (Henderson & Hollin, 1983, 1986; Spence, 1979, 1982).

Although the content and style of SST programs will vary, the program for a typical SST course for young offenders is shown in Table 3.1.

Table 3.1.   Timetable for a Typical SST Program

The social skills training course consisted of ten 90-min sessions held at the rate of one per week. The basic structure of the course is given below:

Session 1: Introduction to social skills training methods, first exposure to videotape and demonstration role-plays. Trainees to agree on personal aims and objectives to be achieved from the course.

Session 2: Relaxation training, leading to posture, leading to nonverbal communication (NVC) in full: eye contact, facial expression, personal space, gestures, etc. Emphasis on the importance of NVC in impression formation.

Session 3: Verbal skills: listening and talking skills. Blend with NVC for competent social performance.

Session 4: Verbal skills continued: development of conversational skills; "ice breaking,"—use of appropriate topics to instigate conversation in a variety of social settings.

Sessions 5–9: Application of social skills as taught above to trainees' specific problems. Included were sessions on job interviews, interactions with prison and aftercare staff, confrontations with police officers, conversation with members of the opposite sex, handling aggressive encounters with peers.
A typical example was the session led jointly by a police officer from the local juvenile bureau. The officer, familiar with social skills training techniques, assisted in the enactment of various incidents the trainees had experienced with police officers. After role-play of the original incident, training in how better to manage similar incidents was given using the police officer's skill and guidance. The most common incidents were being stopped in the street for questioning and being called on at home.

Session 10: Overview of course, final points answered. Postcourse evaluation.

Note: From "The Effects of Social Skills Training on Incarcerated Delinquent Adolescents" by C. R. Hollin and M. Henderson, 1981, *International Journal of Behavioural Social Work and Abstracts, 1,* p. 148.

Micro Skills Training. A number of SST studies with young offenders have been concerned with the minutiae of social behavior such as eye contact, bodily posture, and tone of voice. Braukmann, Fixsen, Phillips, Wolf, and Maloney (1974) used SST techniques to teach appropriate interview behaviors to six delinquents. Observers' ratings of the target behaviors in a multiple-baseline design showed significant improvement on the micro skills of posture, volunteering information, personal appearance, and social behavior; the findings were inconclusive for eye contact. However, Ollendick and Hersen (1979) found improved eye contact and improved speech content following SST with nine incarcerated young offenders. These improvements were superior to those in discussion and untrained control groups, but other behaviors failed to differentiate the training group from controls.

Spence and Marzillier (1979) also reported mixed results following SST with young offenders. Training increased eye contact and reduced "fiddling" movements in the five offenders using multiple-baseline measurement. This improvement was maintained at a 2-week follow-up. However, three other interactive behaviors—question type, acknowledgments, and head movements—were not significantly changed. A second study replicated the improvements in eye contact and fiddling with 32 young offenders and also noted improved attention feedback responses and head movements (Spence & Marzillier, 1981). These improvements were maintained at a 3-months follow-up for all target behaviors except head movement. Spence and Marzillier suggest that certain skills are more difficult to train than others and that this is in turn related to the overall complexity of the skills involved. McGurk and Newell (1981), reporting a single case study, found superior post-training observer ratings on all 12 of the specific micro behaviors monitored. Long and Sherer (1984), using observer ratings from a social skills checklist, found that SST tended to produce an improvement in micro skills.

Macro Skills Training. A second method of assessing the effects of SST is through performance in complex amalgams of behavior—macro skills—rather than discrete micro behaviors. Kifer, Lewis, Green, and Phillips (1974) used SST methods with three young offenders and their parents to train complex negotiation and agreement skills. A multiple-baseline design showed significant improvement in the level of complex skill performance. Werner, Minkin, Minkin, Fixsen, Phillips, and Wolf (1975) trained three young offenders in behavioral skills previously identified as crucial in police-juvenile encounters. The training group showed significant improvement using both multiple-baseline and no-treatment control evaluation. Police officers' ratings of subjective impressions such as "politeness" and "respect" were also more favorable following training. Using SST techniques in a multiple-baseline design with six young offenders, Thelen, Fry, Dollinger, and Paul (1976) achieved behavioral change in the complex skills of expressing positive feelings and discussing problems. Significant improvement was also obtained in home adjustment ratings, but this improvement was not maintained at a 2-week follow-up.

Hazel, Schumaker, Sherman, and Sheldon-Wildgen (1981) reported both a pilot and a main study on training complex skills such as resisting peer pressure to court-adjudicated young male and female offenders. A within-group examination of the pilot study findings showed an improvement in all five trained skills, however, this improvement decreased on four skills at a 2-month follow-up. Hazel et al. made several modifications in the training program following their pilot study and reexamined its effectiveness with a large sample of young offenders from the same population. Once again an improvement in all trained skills was found. Hazel, Schumaker, Sherman, and Sheldon-Wildgen (1982) used a similar training procedure and evaluation method in a skills training program for 13 young offenders placed on formal probation by the juvenile court. The training was effective in improving all the skills attended to during the program. With the exception of the skill of "negotiations," the increase in skilled performance was found to be maintained at an 8-month follow-up. In addition, the young offenders and their parents, as well as the offenders' probation officers, expressed satisfaction with the results of the training program.

Cognitive Measures. A number of studies have investigated the effects of SST on various measures of individual difference. A measure of particular concern with delinquents is locus of control. As discussed previously, young offenders tend toward external control, and it is argued that a shift toward internal control is desirable and should accompany SST (Henderson & Hollin, 1983). Sarason and Ganzer (1973) and Ollendick and Hersen (1979) both reported movement toward internal control with young offenders following SST. Spence and Spence (1980) reported a similar finding but noted that the effect was not maintained at a 6-month follow-up. Hollin and Henderson (1981) reported a small, nonsignificant change to internal control following SST with incarcerated offenders. Ostrom, Steele, Rosenblood, and Mirels (1971) administered an abbreviated locus-of-control scale to 26 young offenders 9 months after completion of the training program. The trained offenders gave significantly fewer external responses than the controls. Although this result was predicted by Ostrom et al., the lack of baseline data, or even a pretraining level, makes interpretation of this finding difficult. Long and Sherer (1984) found SST precipitated a shift to internal control which was maintained at a 2-week posttraining follow-up.

Moving to other measures, Hollin and Henderson (1981) also found no change following SST on the personality variable of "under control" (McGurk, 1979), although there was a significant reduction in the number of self-reported problems over the training period. This change in self-reported difficulties was the only evaluation measure employed in the Hollin and Henderson study that correlated significantly with intelligence, so it may have been that the more intelligent trainees were "faking good." Spence and Marzillier (1981) noted that their SST group reported significantly fewer social problems after training, although a similar reduction was also evident for both attention and no-treatment controls. Similarly the SST group did not differ from controls on a staff questionnaire on social problems; on independent ratings of social skills, friendliness, anxiety, and employability; or on social workers' ratings of school, work, and family relations. Spence and Spence (1980) found a significant increase in self-esteem during SST, but this change was also evident in a placebo-attention control group. These changes had not been maintained at a 6-month follow-up for either group. Ollendick and Hersen (1979) reported a reduction in state anxiety following training. Long and Sherer (1984) found that SST had no influence on the level of self-concept.

Institutional Behavior. As many training programs have been conducted within institutions, several studies have examined the effects of SST on the offender's institutional performance or behavior. Spence and Marzillier (1979, 1981) found no significant differences in staff ratings of institutional behavior following SST in a community home setting. Ollendick and Hersen (1979) assessed behavior at a training center in terms of performance on a token economy and frequency of disruptive behavior. They found no significant differences in disruptive behavior between SST and control groups, however, the training group obtained significantly more points on the institutional program after training. Hollin and Henderson (1981) utilized two types of institutional offending against discipline as indexes of institutional behavior in a penal establishment. Both measures showed significant improvement following SST for the seven incarcerated young offenders compared to a no-treatment control group. This improvement was maintained at a 2-month follow-up. Hollin and Courtney (1983) used skills training techniques in an attempt to modify institutional rule-breaking behavior. Although a decrease in self-reported institutional offending was found, official rates of rule breaking were not changed. However, Cullen (1987) found "substantive improvement" in institutional offending following skills training in the management of aggressive situations for inmates of a secure penal establishment.

Recidivism. A number of studies have looked at the long-term effectiveness of SST with young offenders by examining recidivism rates. Spence and Marzillier (1981) found that 6 months after training the SST group showed the lowest level of official police convictions, although the difference between the SST group and the control groups was not statistically significant. Spence and Marzillier also measured self-reported offending and found that the SST group reported a higher incidence of offending than the controls. A 1-year follow-up by McGurk and Newell (1981) showed that the trainee in this single-case study had not reoffended, at least as recorded in official records. At a 6-year follow-up there still had been no reconviction (McGurk & Newell, 1987). Hazel et al. (1981) found that of their pilot study population, none of the 5 young offenders in the SST group had further court contact after 1 year, compared to 41% of the 22 offenders in the no-treatment control group. In the main part of their study, Hazel et al. used a self-report delinquency scale as well as the official measure of reoffending. For 14 of the young offenders in the SST group, there was a drop in self-reported offending from pre- to posttreatment. However, there was no statistical analysis, nor were these data recorded for the 22 offenders in the no-treatment control group. Therefore it is difficult to judge exactly the significance of the change in recidivism in the SST group. At a 10-month follow-up, 21% of the SST group had had court contact, compared with 37% of the no-treatment control group; again no statistical analysis was presented, so it is unclear whether the variation is significantly different than what would be expected on the basis of chance.

Ostrom et al. (1971) reported a significantly lower arrest rate for the experimental group over the 4-month period following training. However, this improvement was not maintained after 9 months for the group as a whole. Sarason and Ganzer (1973) compared the effectiveness of three treatment modes—SST, structured discussion, and no treatment—in reducing recidivism. At a 3-year follow-up both SST and discussion proved equally effective in reducing recidivism compared to no treatment. Gross, Brigham, Hopper, and Bologna (1980) found a reduction in the number of police arrests for their trained offenders at a 1-year follow-up.

In summary, six studies have employed recidivism as a measure of the long-term efficacy of SST. One study found no effect of SST on offending (Spence & Marzillier, 1981); three suggested that SST might reduce offending, but two of these can be criticized on the grounds of using only official measures of offending (McGurk & Newell) and limited design and evaluation (Hazel et al.), whereas Gross et al. (1980) used other techniques alongside SST; one found that offending was reduced, but the effect could not be distinguished from the effects of attention (Sarason & Ganzer, 1973); and one indicated that offending was reduced at short-term follow-up but that the effect was not durable at long term (Ostrom et al., 1971). It may be worth noting that the most apparently successful studies were not carried out with incarcerated young offenders.

SST Issues with Young Offenders

The outcome evidence discussed above raises issues on a number of levels, including clinical practice, criminological theory, and policy for management of young offenders. The immediate concern is with clinical practice, and the other points are discussed later in the book.

Assessment. As has been argued throughout, assessment of candidates for training should be a starting point for all training programs, yet several studies have attempted to monitor the efficacy of SST with young offenders without adequate assessment. For example, Sarason and Ganzer (1973) and Thelen et al. (1976) both failed to select their young offender trainees on the basis of social skills deficits. As Spence (1979) comments, they apparently acted on the assumption that all young offenders exhibit similar deficits and are therefore suitable candidates for training. This is a critical assumption and one that a number of empirical studies have addressed.

Freedman et al. (1978) found that male young offenders' verbal responses to a series of problem situations, assessed using the Adolescent Problem Inventory (API), were rated as less competent than those of a matched nondelinquent control group. The young offenders used a more limited range of response alternatives in solving interpersonal problems and relied more on verbal or physical aggression. Hunter and Kelley (1986) tested the hypothesis that the degree of impaired social performance, as assessed by the API, should be related to the level of offending. Thus for a sample of 60 young offenders, the API score was correlated with a range of indexes of offending such as number of arrests, most serious offense, and so on. It was found that "contrary to prediction, the API was not significantly related in the expected direction to any of the criteria" (Hunter & Kelley, p. 302). Hunter and Kelley suggest that the format adopted by the API may not be the most advantageous means of assessing social competence. *In vivo* observation in the natural environment, they further suggest, may be required for accurate assessment of social skills.

Spence (1981a) analyzed the social performance of 70 convicted young male offenders in a short, standardized interview. It was found that certain nonverbal behaviors, particularly eye contact and smiling, and verbal behaviors, such as initiating conversation, were strongly related to ratings of social skills, friendliness, and employability. Spence (1981b) used a similar experimental situation, a short interview, to compare 18 young male offenders with 18 nondelinquent controls matched for age, academic performance, and social background. The delinquents showed significantly less eye contact and speech but more fiddling and gross body movements—an aggregation of behaviors known to relate to poor ratings of social skill (Spence, 1981a). Indeed, on global ratings of social skill, social anxiety, and employability members of the delinquent groups were rated less favorably than the nondelinquents.

Gaffney and McFall (1981) developed the Problem Inventory for Adolescent Girls (PIAG), a self-report measure of social competence in dealing with awkward social situations. The PIAG was validated by comparing the performance of delinquent and nondelinquent groups of adolescent girls. Those in the delinquent group were rated as less socially competent on the basis of their descriptions of their behavior in the various situations. Further, it was found that delinquency was more closely related to skill deficits in interacting with adults in positions of authority rather than in interacting with peers. This study replicates with a female sample the findings of Freedman et al. with male delinquents. Ward and McFall (1986) reported an extended validation of the PIAG. It was found that female young offenders gave overall significantly less competent verbal responses to the problem situations. In addition, performance on the PIAG was related to self-report measures of offending: There was a significant negative correlation between self-reported offending and PIAG score. Dishion, Loeber, Stouthamer-Loeber, and Patterson (1984) found that offending was related to a number of skills, such as academic performance, but not to rated interpersonal skills. Long and Sherer (1984) found that low-frequency offenders were rated significantly higher on social skills than high-frequency offenders.

McCown, Johnson, and Austin (1986) report an experimental study on the ability of young offenders to recognize facial affect. Compared with a control group of nonoffenders, McCown et al. found that the young offenders were significantly less accurate in their social perception of emotional expressions. Within this overall finding, the young offenders were significantly less accurate at recognizing the facially expressed emotions of sadness, surprise, and disgust; there were no significant differences for happiness, anger, and fear. McCown et al. suggest that the social difficulties experienced by many young offenders "might be due, in part, to their comparative inability to understand facial expressions" (p. 493).

Although the weight of evidence indicates that delinquents are less skilled in certain tasks than nondelinquents, in total the range of studies is limited. As Freedman et al. note, external validation of their findings is necessary, since verbal reports may not be consistent with actual behavior. An identical point applies also to the findings of Gaffney and McFall. The Spence and McCown et al. studies used somewhat artificial experimental situations, which may have had a greater effect on the performance of delinquents than of nondelinquents. What is required, but is lacking in the extant literature, is a much more detailed knowledge of social cognitive-behavioral norms in the natural environment.

Training. In moving on from assessment to the process of training itself a number of points can be made. The technique of modeling is one of the principal training methods used in SST, and it seems an obvious point that similarity between the model and the trainee is important to maximize transfer of training (Meichenbaum, 1971). However, several SST studies have employed adult models in teaching adolescent delinquents (e.g., Long & Sherer, 1984; Sarason & Ganzer, 1973; Thelen et al., 1976). It is an advantage of group SST over individual training that trainees can provide their own peer models, particularly in situations where the trainer may not be able to model behavior appropriate to the age and social background of the trainees. Training sessions should also mirror real life for the trainee which, in the absence of peer models, requires knowledge by the trainer of the norms and appropriate behavior for the client population. Such norms are, however, not to be found in the extant literature. Further, as Henderson and Hollin (1983) have argued, if a highly detailed functional analysis were conducted for each potential trainee, it is possible that training needs would become so highly individualized that group training alone would be insufficient.

The rate of training sessions is generally uniform: A prearranged number of sessions (usually in the region of 7 to 10), of set length and conducted at a predetermined rate of 1 or 2 per week, is typical of many SST programs. However, as Shepherd (1980) has also noted, changes in this routine might be beneficial according to the client group. Overlearning and close spacing of sessions have been shown to be clinically advantageous (e.g., Goldsmith & McFall, 1975), and a slower rate of presentation may assist those with difficulty in information processing (e.g., Nettleback & Kirby, 1976). Hollin and Courtney (1983) found that with young offenders the standard format of weekly training sessions reduced self-reported institutional deviance significantly more than a shortened intensive training course, but that group cohesiveness occurred more quickly with the shortened course. However, practical limitations such as institutional routines and staffing levels tend to restrict the flexibility of regulating SST sessions with incarcerated young offenders. Long and Sherer (1984) used a structured SST format based principally on modeling, role-play, feedback, and homework, and an unstructured format using only a discussion of problematic social situations. Although both forms of training were associated with similar changes in rated social performance skills, an interaction between type of offender and type of training was found when cognitive change occurred. For the locus-of-control scale, high-frequency offenders showed a greater shift to internality with the structured training format; low-frequency offenders moved most toward internality with the unstructured format.

It is clear that the same criticism can be leveled at SST with young offenders as has been leveled at the practice of SST generally: namely, that practitioners have focused on the *response* phase of Argyle's model, largely neglecting the areas of social perception and social cognition (Hollin & Trower, 1988). Another group of studies with young offenders, although not within the SST domain, have focused on cognition, and these studies are discussed in the following section.

COGNITIVE-BEHAVIORAL PROGRAMS

In the discussion of cognitive functioning in young offenders it was suggested that cognitive processes such as impulsivity, role taking, and social problem solving are less well developed in young offenders. Similarly, it was suggested that young offenders may use less mature moral reasoning than nonoffenders. There are a number of programs that have addressed these issues using cognitive-behavior modification programs. Before discussing these studies, it may be appropriate to attempt to clarify the distinction, implicit in much of the literature, between cognitive-behavior modification and cognitive therapy. The distinction at a surface level is somewhat blurred: A technique, such as self-instructional training, can be found under the classification of both cognitive-behavioral intervention (e.g., Gordon & Arbuthnot, 1987) and cognitive therapy (e.g., Brewin, 1988). A difference in classification does not mean that there is any difference in what is being carried out but most probably reflects conceptual differences between practitioners. As a guide, to which there will always be exceptions, the term *cognitive-behavior modification* is preferred by practitioners whose practice is guided by behavioral (including social learning theory) principles; *cognitive therapy*, on the other hand, appears to be preferred by practitioners who are persuaded by another theoretical position from cognitive psychology, such as information processing, in which cognition is the prime focus for intervention. Brewin (1988) explains this succinctly: "Ellis (1962) and Beck (1967) have also argued that dysfunctional emotions such as anxiety and depression follow from people's perceptions and evaluations of the events in their lives rather than from the events themselves" (p. 5). The crux is in the last six words—*rather than from the events themselves*—in which primacy is given to cognition rather than to the events (which would be preferred by radical behaviorists) or to the interaction between events and cognition (as might be preferred by social learning theorists). Thus although there is some interchange in the use of techniques, the theoretical base differs significantly between advocates of cognitive-behavior modifications and of cognitive therapy.

Self-control and Self-instruction

The development of self-control in the normal child has been described by Luria (1961) as following three stages: (a) The child's behavior is controlled and directed by the verbal community; (b) the child's own overt speech regulates behavior; (c) covert or "inner" speech governs voluntary actions. In order to train or modify self-control (variously referred to as *self-management* or *self-guidance*) Kanfer (1975), following cognitive-behavioral principles, described three steps to guide practice: (a) self-observation, (b) self-evaluation, (c) self-reinforcement. In seeking to achieve increased self-control, along with regulation of covert speech, the technique of *self-instructional training* has become a popular clinical technique (Meichenbaum, 1977).

With self-instructional training the aim is to modify the individual's self-statements. The technique itself uses modeling, practice, and cognitive rehearsal to change self-statements. A typical sequence is found in Camp, Blom, Herbert, and Van Doornick's (1977) "Think Aloud" program. The trainees meet difficult situations with four basic questions: (a) "What is my problem?" (b) "What is my plan?" (c) "Am I using my plan?" (d) "How did I do?" Kanfer's principles of self-observation, self-evaluation, and self-reinforcement are implicit in this scheme. For example, if a goal is achieved, a rewarding self-statement is appropriate— "Good, I did that well!" And if there is a failure, a self-statement of the type, "Everything goes wrong now and then; all I've got to do is keep on trying" is encouraged.

Following the developmental sequence described by Luria, training moves through a sequence of the type described by Goldstein and Keller (1987). A model performs the task, say talking with an authority figure, making overt, appropriate self-statements; the trainee then practices the same behavior; the model carries out the same task, but whispers self-instructions; the trainee then follows; the model performs the task with covert self-instruction, perhaps showing nonverbal indications of thought (raising eyes, pauses, etc.); the trainee then follows. The development from overt to covert self-talk thus progresses as the program matures.

The technique of self-instructional training has been used with a range of client populations, although with some emphasis on aggressive children (Camp & Bash, 1981). However, there have been fewer studies with young offenders. Williams and Akamatsu (1978) applied cognitive self-guidance procedures (Meichenbaum & Goodman, 1971) with a group of male and female young offenders in a medium-security institution. The cognitive self-guidance consisted of modeling in appropriate self-instruction for completion of a task requiring cognitive sophistication, followed by training in overt verbalization, and then fading from overt to covert verbalization. After training there was no significant difference in test performance between the cognitive self-guidance group and an attention-control group. On a similar cognitive test used to assess generalization, members of the cognitive self-guidance group were at a significant advantage as compared to the controls. Williams and Akamatsu conclude, however, that "results suggest that generalization is limited to cognitive and not social behaviors" (p. 188).

Snyder and White (1979) used cognitive self-instruction in the treatment of aggressive adolescents with a history of criminal behavior. The focus was, first, on identifying existing verbalizations in potential problems situations. Snyder and White give the following example:

Situation	Verbalization
A cottage counselor says, "Time to get up."	"The hell with that, this feels too good."

The analysis goes on to explore the consequences that follow such a verbalization, such as losing token economy points for staying in bed. In the second phase, more adaptive verbalizations were modeled, rehearsed, and practiced both overtly and covertly.

Situation	Verbalization
A cottage counselor says, "Time to get up."	"Already? Damn. It feels good to stay in bed, but if I get up I'll get the points I need for cigarettes. OK, just open my eyes, sit up. Good I made it."

Thus the modified verbalization, including self-reinforcement, leads to a new behavior and different consequences—getting out of bed, avoiding a confrontation with the counselor, and gaining points for tangible reinforcement (although cigarettes might be less likely to be found in the enlightened eighties, rather than in 1979 when this study was reported). In the third phase of the program homework assignments were used to develop further self-observation, self-instruction, and self-reinforcement skills.

In the experimental design, a control group undertook contingency awareness training in which specific problems were raised, as in the self-instruction group, and then discussed in detail. This group did not utilize any behavioral training methods or employ self-instruction, although the group members were encouraged to use the suggestions from the discussion in their day-to-day behavior. A no-treatment control group received no training or discussion. Three measures of the effects of intervention were used: absence from class, failure to complete social and/or self-care duties, frequency of impulsive behavior. On all three measures the cognitive self-instruction group showed a performance superior to that of both control groups. This improvement was evident both after training and at an 8-week follow-up. As Snyder and White note, this provides clear evidence that cognitive self-instruction was a valuable addition to the institutional token economy in which all the young people—treatment and control groups alike—were participating during the course of the study.

Anger Control

A further application of self-control and self-management procedures has been in interventions specifically designed for anger control. Although perhaps most closely identified with the work of Novaco (1975, 1979, 1985), anger control has become a popular technique, generating a large experimental-clinical literature. A guide to adolescent anger control, utilizing cognitive-behavioral methods, has recently become available (Feindler & Ecton, 1986). In brief, anger control training does not seek to suppress the emotional arousal of anger but rather to lower the probability of unwanted behaviors by self-regulation of arousal and associated self-statements and by training in appropriate coping skills. In the original model proposed by Novaco (1975) there is a reciprocal relationship between emotional arousal and cognition, so that the angry state is maintained and influenced by the self-statements made in provocative situations.

A typical anger management program consists of three stages. First, *cognitive preparation* focuses on educating the client about the "triggers" for anger; the behavioral, cognitive, and physiological components of anger; and the consequences that can follow from behavior carried out while in a state of anger. In the second stage, *skill acquisition*, the emphasis is on coping skills for use in response to provocation. Self-instruction is one coping skill, with statements for preparing for provocation (e.g., "This is going to upset me but I know how to deal with it"), for coping with the impact of the situation (e.g., "I'm not going to let him get to me"), for coping with arousal (e.g., "Time to slow down and relax"), and for reflecting on the incident (e.g., "I'll get better with this as I get more practice" or "I got through that without getting angry"). Goldstein and Keller (1987) provide a range of self-statements suitable for anger management programs. Other coping skills include simple cognitive thought-stopping strategies such as counting backward or imagining a peaceful scene, deep breathing or muscle relaxation to counter physiological arousal, and techniques borrowed from assertion training such as the "broken record" method in which the individual continually makes the same verbalization rather than be drawn into a confrontation. The familiar skills training methods—role-play, modeling, and so on— are used to improve these self-management skills. In the third stage of intervention, *application training*, the learned skills are put to the test in a variety of imaginary, role-played, and real-life situations, at all times under careful supervision.

Anger control has been used with a wide range of offenders, including young offenders. Schlichter and Horan (1981) report a comparison of anger management techniques, simple relaxation, and no treatment across a range of measures with groups of aggressive institutionalized male delinquents. It was found that both active interventions were superior to the no-treatment control on three self-report scales, that only the anger management group improved on a role-play test, and that there was no treatment effect on institutional behavioral ratings. Feindler, Marriott, and Iwata (1984) used group anger control training with students attending a specialized program after being suspended from school because of offending. The intervention consisted of learning the self-management skills described above, together with performance skills and application training. Compared with a no-treatment control group, the anger control group showed a number of improvements both after training and at follow-up. There was evidence of less aggressive behavior in the treatment group, an increase in observer-rated self-control, an improved trainee problem-solving ability; however, the treatment had no effect on locus of control. Feindler et al. suggested that the anger control proved a useful adjunct to the program's token economy designed to decrease aggressive, disruptive behavior. McDougall, Barnett, Ashurst, and Willis (1987) report the development of an anger control course at a secure establishment for young offenders following the principles described by Novaco (1975). The effectiveness of the course, for 18 young offenders, was evaluated by comparing the level of institutional offenses committed by the treatment group and by a waiting-list control group. It was found that overall the anger control was beneficial in lowering the level of institutional offending.

Role Taking

As noted previously, a number of studies have suggested that young offenders lack the ability to take the role of the other person and to see the situation from the other person's perspective. The single intervention following this research with young offenders to be found in the literature was reported by Chandler (1973). This study used three groups: a no-treatment control, a placebo treatment control, and a perspective-taking skills training group. The last-mentioned group was engaged in both drama and film making as a means of enabling the young offenders to see themselves from the perspective of others and to develop their own role-taking ability. The results showed that role-taking abilities could be enhanced by training and, further, that at an 18-month follow-up the perspective-taking training group had committed significantly fewer offenses than the control groups. While there are some theoretical difficulties, leading Gordon and Arbuthnot (1987) to suggest that "role-taking abilities may perhaps best be viewed as necessary but not sufficient for delinquency prevention and treatment" (p. 301), it is remarkable that Chandler's study has not been replicated.

Social Problem Solving

Spivack, Platt, and Shure (1976) detail a series of interpersonal cognitive problem-solving skills necessary for successful social interaction. These cognitive skills include sensitivity to interpersonal problems, the ability to foresee the possible outcome of actions (consequential thinking), the ability to generate solutions (alternative thinking), and the ability to plan the stages for attaining specific goals (means-end thinking). The skills training techniques of modeling, role play, and discussion are blended with cognitive techniques, principally self-instructional training, to teach problem-solving skills. The specific problem-solving skills include problem recognition, problem definition, identifying feelings associated with the problem, obtaining information, generating alternative solutions, considering consequences, and deciding on the best solution.

Problem-solving programs have been used successfully with a range of client groups, including heroin addict offenders (Platt, Perry, & Metzger, 1980). Hains (1984) reported a study on the use of problem-solving skills training with four male young offenders in residential care. Following the training scheme outlined above, it was found that the young offenders were able to generate more solutions to hypothetical social dilemmas. This skill was not generalized as fully as might be hoped, and Hains noted that "any reported improvement in problem solving of personal problems was not consistently maintained" (p. 282).

Moral Reasoning Development

If, as studies have suggested, young offenders are characterized by delayed or impaired moral reasoning, it follows that attempts to facilitate moral reasoning development may be beneficial. A typical study was reported by Gibbs, Arnold, Cheesman, and Ahlborn (1984). Sixty incarcerated young offenders, 30 male and 30 female, took part in a program of eight small group discussions on sociomoral dilemmas. In the discussions a variety of opinions were aired on a particular dilemma involving a moral choice; the offenders not only gave their views but were required both to justify their opinions and to attempt to reach a group consensus on the best solution. The main outcome was that, compared to the results from a no-treatment control group, the discussion led to a significant upward shift in moral reasoning as assessed in terms of Kohlberg's moral judgment stages. Although conducted with adolescents at risk for delinquency, rather than young offenders, Arbuthnot and Gordon (1986) also reported beneficial effects from a moral reasoning development program. The intervention not only raised the level of moral reasoning but also led to improvement on several behavioral indexes including academic performance and police and/or court contact.

MULTIMODAL PROGRAMS

Rather than using just one mode of intervention, a number of programs for young offenders have integrated several clinical techniques in a multimodal approach. This section illustrates the diversity of the programs that have been devised. Gross et al. (1980) used a combination of SST, other behavior modification techniques, and self-management training in a multiple-baseline design with 10 females referred to the courts for problem behavior. They found an improvement in self-control and number of problems as rated by parents and teachers, and the improvement was maintained at a 2-month follow-up. The program also reduced school absenteeism and suspensions, and this improvement was maintained over the follow-up period. DeLange, Barton, and Lanham (1981) developed a program, dubbed the WISER way, which combined problem-solving and social skills training. The acronym WISER followed the training goals of Wait, Identify the problem, generate Solutions, Evaluate consequences, self-Reinforce. The training methods included the skills training methods of role-play, practice, and discussion. An empirical test of the model was carried out by DeLange, Lanham, and Barton (1981) by comparing standard skills training to both the WISER method and no treatment. A total of 50 incarcerated young offenders, 35 males and 15 females, took part in the study. Assessment took the form of a direct measure of behavioral change using a role-play test, a self-report measure of self-concept, a self-report measure of assertiveness, and a measure of locus of control. The role-play test showed an increase in skills for all three groups, with no significant differences among groups. There were no significant differences among the three treatment conditions on changes in the two self-report measures; all three groups shifted to a greater internal locus of control, but there were no differences among treatment groups.

Hollin, Huff, Clarkson, and Edmondson (1986) compared SST with SST combined with self-instructional training. The effects of both training methods were compared against attention-placebo and no-treatment groups. Thirty incarcerated delinquents, all male, took part in the study. Assessment consisted of a role-play behavioral test, a number of psychometric tests including the Eysenck Personality Questionnaire and a measure of locus of control, staff ratings of institutional behavior, and offenses against discipline within the institution. The two skills-training groups improved significantly on the role-play assessment, but neither of the control groups showed this change. All three trainer-contact groups showed a significant improvement in offenses against discipline, whereas the no-treatment group deteriorated markedly in the time spanned by the study. No other measures differentiated among the experimental groups, nor were any significant differences found between the effects of the two skills-training methods.

Bowman and Auerbach (1982) used a "cognitive-behavioral treatment program employing relaxation training, cognitive training in problem solving, self-statement modification, and behavior rehearsal techniques" (p. 432) with a sample of 40 male young offenders. The assessment took the form of a number of tests of cognitive ability, institutional performance, a test of social problem solving, a measure of locus of control, and staff and peer ratings of impulsive behavior. The experimental design included a no-treatment control group. The results were positive in showing that the treatment group improved on institutional performance and on the tests of cognitive reasoning ability. There was no significant effect of training on ratings of impulsive behavior, social problem solving, or locus of control. McDougall, Thomas, and Wilson (1987) successfully used a combination of role-play, perspective taking, and discussion to modify the attitudes toward violence of a group of young offenders imprisoned for violent offenses at football matches.

One of the most comprehensive multimodal programs for aggression has been developed by Glick and Goldstein (1987). Aggression replacement training (ART) utilizes a variety of methods grouped under three main classifications: *Structured learning training* includes both social skills training and social problem-solving training, *anger control training* is of the style discussed above, and *moral education* is used to advance levels of moral reasoning. Glick and Goldstein (1987) reported an evaluation of the training program as used with groups of male young offenders at two institutions. At the first institution, for less serious young offenders (stolen property, drug use), ART proved highly successful: Compared to controls, the young offenders acquired and used structured learning skills to a significant degree, displayed improved institutional behavior, and showed lower ratings of impulsiveness. Ratings from probation and parole officers showed significantly better functioning in the community after discharge from the institution. The second study was conducted with serious offenders (murder, sex offenses, violent crimes), and the findings were similar to those in the first study. The main differences were that ART had significantly less effect on some aspects of the institutional performance of the serious offenders, and that unlike the less serious offenders, the serious young offenders showed a significant improvement in moral reasoning.

The bold, perhaps unorthodox, step of mixing techniques from different treatment philosophies has been attempted in a small number of studies. Carpenter and Sugrue (1984) devised a psychoeducational program, "Getting It Together" (GIT), for tackling a range of targets from improving skills and changing cognitions, to tackling denial of feeling. The results "suggested that the delinquents had increased ego strengths, were less impulsive, and had greater knowledge of appropriate social behavior after completing the G.I.T. program" (p. 121). Carpenter and Sandberg (1985) attempted to integrate cognitive-behavioral techniques with a "psychodramatic group therapy framework." The treatment group, complete with director and "auxiliary ego and co-director," utilized a mixture of psychodrama techniques, contracting, discussion, and social and tangible rewards. The results showed a significant improvement in "the delinquents' asocial index . . . ego strength . . . and introversive tendencies" (p. 599).

CONCLUSIONS

The cognitive-behavioral interventions discussed in this chapter all have a common thread in that they focus on the individual young offender as the agent of change. While this raises a number of issues in itself, the studies have also prompted a range of questions at the clinical and experimental levels. These are important issues, but before going on to discuss them, it is important to look at another set of studies in which the focus shifts to consider environmental as well as individual change. Three distinct subgroups can be formed—institutional programs, family programs, and school programs. Each is discussed in the next chapter following the conclusion of the case study described in the previous chapter.

CASE STUDY: INTERVENTION

Following the assessment and functional analysis, the next stage with John was planning the intervention. Target selection is of crucial importance and should be informed both by the behavioral analysis and by negotiation with the client (Kanfer, 1985). In John's case two targets were selected: the severe blushing and the frequency of social interaction. These targets were selected for a number of reasons: They were of immediate concern to John; they were judged to be functionally related, so that improvement in one might be anticipated to assist in improving the other; the functional analysis suggested that they were not only clinical targets but also of criminological importance. There were other minor clinical targets—the mild stammer and the smoking—but these were seen by both of us as being of secondary importance.

Blushing

The blushing was characterized by two reactions: A fierce physiological reaction, beginning with a pounding heart quickly followed by a churning stomach and facial blushing; accompanying this were thoughts such as "Oh no, it's happening again," and "I must look a fool; I must get away." In order to modify these two targets a program was designed that incorporated elements from anxiety management, self-instructional training, and social skills training. However, before beginning the intervention three practical details were given attention. A "service contract" was drawn up with John, stating my responsibilities and his responsibilities in the intervention, along with the length of time we would continue the intervention before pausing to assess its effectiveness. This can be helpful if the client expects instant success and becomes disillusioned when this does not happen. An agreement was made initially to continue for a set period (ten 90-min sessions in this instance). Second, with John's agreement, other members of the institution's staff were informed, by both informal and formal means, of the program's goals and its progress. Finally, the resources necessary for the intervention were worked out: It was anticipated that standard anxiety management and social skills training equipment would be required, all of which were available in the psychology department.

Desensitization. The first stage in the program was anxiety management for the blushing. The principal technique was the classic method of systematic desensitization, with one or two minor modifications. As detailed by Wolpe (1983), systematic desensitization consists of three stages: training of a response incompatible with the target behavior, construction of a hierarchy of situations in which the target behavior occurs, pairing of the trained response with the hierarchy items. As the blushing involved a highly aroused autonomic nervous system, *relaxation* was selected as a response incompatible with this arousal. Relaxation training consisted of taking John step by step through a commercially available audiotape of deep relaxation. The training required him to progress through various breathing and muscle relaxation exercises. In conjunction with this John began to construct his hierarchy of feared situations: For a 2-week period he kept notes on what made him blush and recorded the situations he avoided.

While the diary recording went smoothly, there were initial problems with the relaxation training. Despite continual practice, both in and out of sessions, John reported that he could not tell whether or not he was relaxed. In order to obtain the appropriate self-monitoring of arousal and/or relaxation, *biofeedback* was used in the form of galvanic skin response (GSR) monitoring. (This had been anticipated, so equipment was at hand.) The biofeedback equipment was set at John's resting level to emit a continuous tone. As he worked his way through the relaxation tape, the tone became lower and lower in volume until eventually it was silenced. This proved a crucial step in the relaxation training, and eventually John was able to relax without the tape and then without the biofeedback. The hierarchy was completed, and examples are shown in Table 3.2. The least fearful situation is at the bottom of the hierarchy, the most fearful at the top. The ordering of the situations was, of course, made by John.

While the relaxation training and hierarchy construction were taking place, John was also practicing self-instructional training. Based on the methods noted previously, new self-statements were planned to signal the onset of the blushing (e.g., "Here it comes. I'll use the relaxation

Table 3.2.   Examples From the Hierarchy

1. Having to speak to a group of people of one's own age

2. Attending review boards (institutional procedure)

•

•

•

6. Working at serving meals on unit

7. Talking to a female community service volunteer when others might see

•

•

10. Talking to a personal officer if others might see

11. Asking for a light for a cigarette.

now"), to monitor changes (e.g., "I can feel I'm getting it under control"), and to self-reward (e.g., "That was good. I did well").

The third stage was the pairing of relaxation with scenes from the hierarchy. A slight departure from the more traditional method was made here, in that the relaxation *followed* the presentation of the scene rather than vice versa. This style is more in keeping with a coping rather than a counterconditioning use of systematic desensitization (Goldfried, 1971). The procedure was as follows: In a one-to-one setting, John was asked to imagine himself in a given situation—starting at the *bottom* of the hierarchy—and to signal when he started to feel as if he was going to blush. (At the beginning of the intervention, biofeedback was used to monitor rising arousal.) When he signaled, the instruction was given to relax, to concentrate on calming himself, and to feel the blushing (i.e., the physiological arousal) coming under control and draining away. The self-statements used in the earlier training were repeated aloud at first and then used later at a covert level.

As is apparent, this demands a great deal in the first instance: to imagine the scene, to monitor arousal, to relax, and to use self-statements. It follows that progress is generally slow at the onset of the intervention. With practice the various components begin to fit together, and in John's case progress was made in two sessions with homework practice over the 2-week period. Thus the stage was reached at which John could imagine himself in the situation lowest in the hierarchy and could bring his blushing under control. At this point the traditional approach, based on counterconditioning, moves to the next item on the hierarchy. A coping, skills acquisition approach takes one further preliminary step: *in vivo* desensitization to accompany the gains made in the comparative security of the one-to-one sessions. This introduces the skills training aspect of the program.

Skills Training. The primary aim of the skills training was to act as part of preparation for the *in vivo* desensitization. A role-play of a given situation was prepared, and John tackled events as he would in real life. The role-play was always followed by discussion, feedback (using videotape where appropriate), and instruction on points to remember. In the early stages appropriate self-statements were spoken aloud to reinforce their use. Some situations demanded the involvement of other people, and it was here that the planning with other staff paid dividends. They were aware of the program and willing to participate.

Thus the skills training was preparing John for real-life encounters, and it was also serving another important function. Whereas the desensitization was designed to reduce the blushing, the skills training aimed to prompt appropriate social behavior. This notion of constructing new behavioral repertoires rather than leaving a vacuum by suppressing a behavior is important in guiding good practice. Indeed, the constructional approach to behavioral casework is an approach in its own right (Schwartz & Goldiamond, 1975). The skills training was taken a stage further with John in preparing for failure. It is realistic to expect failure at some stage and so, in each role-played session, a period of problem solving was included to find strategies to cope with blushing. These ranged from legitimate avoidance strategies ("I must go now, I've just remembered something!") to acknowledgment of the blushing ("I know I'm blushing. I get like this sometimes"). In much the same way John was prepared for the occurrence of *extinction bursts*—the unexpected recurrence of the unwanted behavior when it seems to be coming under control.

Progress and Outcome

As in perhaps the majority of cases, progress was slow at first, but by beginning with the less difficult situations at the bottom of the hierarchy, improvement was gradually achieved. For the purpose of evaluation John kept a record of his progress, and although blushing was experienced in the early stages, it did begin to come under his control. The essential practical strategy to note was that he was not allowed to advance up the hierarchy until there was complete mastery over the lower-level situation. As John became more successful—as testified not only by John's self-report but also by staff reports and my own covert observations—so the speed of change accelerated and he moved up the hierarchy.

The concern at this stage was whether John would be able to tackle the real world outside the institution. It was arranged that he would undertake a period of community work at a nearby hospital. (It is difficult sometimes to gain permission for arsonists to work in the community while still under jurisdiction of the institutional authorities, and the involvement of management and staff in the program again paid dividends.) At this stage, perhaps 3 months after the first meeting, the sessions became less frequent as John spent more and more time away from the institution. He reported some difficulty at first, particularly in the staff room at the hospital during coffee breaks, but with some role-play and discussion he was able to manage these situations. The main anxiety of all those concerned was with the chance of arson; happily this did not occur nor, despite the opportunity, did John use his freedom to drink. Finally, it was agreed that John would stop coming to sessions altogether, although he would always be able to ask for advice if needed. This continued until his eventual discharge from the institution to return to his parents. It was unfortunate that John lived over 300 miles from the institution, and so throughout the program I had only minimal contact with both his parents and probation officer.

Just before John's discharge from custody one of the staff told me a rather pleasing story. A new member of staff had joined the institution and was finding it difficult to discuss personal matters with young people. This member of staff was stopped by an offender, and he asked about some arrangement or other. As they talked, the staff member began to color, going red around the cheeks and neck. John was nearby and saw what was happening. When the conversation was over, John approached the staff member, saying that he had seen her blushing, but not to worry because he could put her in touch with someone who could help!

Follow-up. About 4 months after his discharge I received a telephone call from John's probation officer. John had been arrested for arson. He claimed that he was not guilty, and the evidence was not conclusive. I wrote a detailed court report, submitted by the probation officer, which led to the compromise of John being returned to the institution for a 3-month period. (He would have had a much longer fresh sentence.) He maintained throughout that he had not set the fire and had not been involved in any way. He was of the opinion that once you have a record, you are simply at risk of being arrested. Whether or not John was telling the truth will, of course, never be known.

John did report, however, that the blushing was just about gone and that his main concern was finding a job and getting a girlfriend. After the second discharge from custody he kept in touch for a short while, and he was successful in finding employment. After 1 year he had not offended (as far as anyone knew), and his probation officer said all was well at the point of his leaving probation. Thus John stepped back into a life of his own—when last heard of without police, probation officers, psychologists, and custody.

Four

Institution and Community

In contrast to the individual approach discussed in the previous chapter, the emphasis here is on change not primarily through one-to-one work with the young offender (although this does take place) but via some agency such as a residential establishment or family. This approach thus follows a tradition of changing behavior by attention to the environmental contingencies as much as by modifying individual behavior while the contingencies remain stable. This means that the behavior of the agency is important and so must be considered in detail. Two very different types of institutions can be defined. In the first the emphasis is on custody with clinical intervention a secondary consideration; these institutions are generally prison establishments. In the second the aim is on treatment with security secondary; these are generally residential establishments. The use of cognitive-behavioral interventions in each type of institution will be discussed separately.

SECURE INSTITUTIONS

There have been a number of reviews on the use of behavioral techniques in secure institutions (Geller, Johnson, Hamlin, & Kennedy, 1977; Milan, 1987; Nietzel, 1979), although they include programs for adult as well as young offenders. It is clear from this literature that a *token economy program* (TEP) has been the main method of behavior modification in prisons. The present discussion will limit itself to the use of TEPs with young offenders held in security.

Token Economy

The token economy was one of the earliest of the behavior modification techniques, hence its use with young offenders stretches back further than most other behavioral methods. A TEP is based on the principle that behavior is, in large part, related to the consequences it produces; if the consequences can be managed, the behavior can be modified. In the western economy members of society are, in the main, reinforced for appropriate behavior (work and production) not by tangible rewards but by money which can be exchanged at will for preferred rewards. Thus as we work for money it is clear that the money is reinforcing our work behavior. On its own the money is worthless; "backup" reinforcers must be available to maintain the token value of the money.

This type of economic system can be imposed on any closed environment such as a prison or hospital. Identified behaviors can be reinforced or punished by presentation and withdrawal of contingent tokens (or points or some other symbol of earning). Performance of the identified behavior earns tokens which can then be exchanged at an agreed-on rate for the backup reinforcers. A fine system may be operated for unwanted behavior *(response cost)* in which tokens are taken away, so removing accessibility to the backup reinforcers. As Bootzin (1975) notes, there are a number of advantages to the use of tokens: They can be given immediately following the appropriate behavior; they provide a visible, easily monitored record of behavior; they encourage staff to reinforce appropriate behavior; they do not lose reinforcement value given a wide range of backup reinforcers; they cater to individual differences in allowing access to a range of backup reinforcers. To be effective, TEPs require a range of backup reinforcers. Bootzin (1975) lists six classes of reinforcers, as shown in Table 4.1, used in a psychiatric hospital TEP. As with

Table 4.1. Examples of Reinforcers in a TEP (after Bootzin, 1975)

Privacy
    Own room
    Personal cabinet
Leave from ward
    Grounds pass
    Trip to town
Social interaction with staff
    Time alone with staff
    Time alone with a social worker
Devotional opportunities
    Extra religious services
Recreational opportunities
    Use of radio
    Use of television
Commissary items
    Consumables such as candy and cigarettes
    Miscellaneous items such as an ashtray, newspapers, magazines, ornaments

any system there are problems: As in the real world, the availability of tokens can lead to gambling, borrowing with interest, bankruptcy through poor behavior, and the intrusion of outside forces that rock the stability of the system. Nonetheless token economies have become highly popular and have been widely used in a range of settings with a variety of client groups (Kazdin, 1982; Kazdin & Bootzin, 1972).

One of the earliest uses of a token economy was reported by Tyler and Brown (1968) who used the technique to improve academic performance with institutionalized young offenders. Similarly, Sloane and Ralph (1973) used a TEP to modify educational standards and social behavior in a group of young offenders. The points gained for meeting the defined standards of academic and social performance counted toward a parole recommendation, accessibility to various privileges and activities within the institution, and freedom of movement within the institution. A penalty system operated so that inappropriate behavior resulted in an increase in the number of points required for a parole recommendation. Evaluation of the program suggested that it led to an improvement in academic standards, an increase in discharges within a set period of time, and a lower rate of recidivism.

Milan (1987) details the development of the technique with young offenders, including the CASE project (Cohen, 1973), the Karl Holton projected operated by Jesness and DeRisi (1973), and the TEP at the Robert F. Kennedy Youth Center (Karacki & Levinson, 1970). Given Milan's excellent review it is unnecessary to repeat the details of all the programs; therefore for illustrative purposes a recent study by Cullen and Seddon (1981) has been selected for detailed discussion.

Working within a secure establishment for male young offenders, Cullen and Seddon (1981) conducted a 6-month project involving the application of a behavioral regime. A total of 12 young offenders took part in the project, which was housed in a small unit designed for offenders unable to cope with the rigors of life in the larger institutional units. The aims of the project were "(a) increasing positive, adaptive behaviors; (b) decreasing disruptive, maladaptive behaviors; (c) assisting in the learning of new behaviors" (p. 287). The token economy was based on a points system in which 1 point was equal to 1 penny of earnings, and the money to be spent as wished by the offenders. The maximum weekly earning was 100 points, divided into 50 points for work standards and 50 points for standards of behavior. These two standards were carefully specified so that, for example, standards of behavior was divided into five categories of personal cleanliness, room cleanliness, behavior at meal times, behavior toward other prisoners, and behavior toward staff. The points for each offender were awarded by staff, using agreed-on behavioral checklists, and recorded daily on a public display in the small unit.

Alongside the TEP a system of behavioral contracts was also put into operation. The use of contracting ensured attention to individual difficulties, each young offender being guided through a series of six contracts with targets as diverse as controlling temper outbursts, helping other young offenders, and reducing encopresis. Success in meeting the terms of a contract was rewarded by access to a pool of privileges and the award of a star, symbolizing success, on the publicly displayed progress chart. As stars accumulated, more privileges became available. In the case of the final contract, successful completion was rewarded with a recommendation for discharge from custody.

The intervention demanded not only program design but also training staff in the principles and running of the project. The staff training consisted principally of structured learning packages, completed over a 4-month period, covering the following: introduction to behavior modification, operant psychology, increasing and decreasing behavior, intervention, and contracting. The staff also visited other institutions to observe behavioral units in operation, viewed appropriate films, and spent time individually with one of the psychologists.

The program was evaluated using various measures of behavior. On a measure of both minor and serious offenses against institutional rules, the young offenders showed a significant improvement in behavior. With regard to the contracts, 46 were issued during the program, of which 38 were successfully completed. Earnings on the TEP improved as offenders spent more time in the program; this, of course, reflects improvements in work and behavioral standards—particularly room and personal cleanliness. A staff feedback form revealed an interesting dichotomy: "Staff were generally critical of the preparation they'd received and of their working relationships with the psychologists. They were much more favourable towards the elements of the programme and considered it a qualified success" (p. 289). An attempt at a follow-up failed to gather enough data to give any meaningful indication of behavior change following discharge from custody.

In discussing the effectiveness of the program, Cullen and Seddon are right to claim its success in achieving its original goals: Positive behaviors were increased, and maladaptive behaviors decreased. However, as Cullen and Seddon note, much can be learned at an organizational level. Clearly staff training is of fundamental importance, which should be recognized by higher management to ensure that trained staff are suitably rewarded. That the staff were asked to change their own behavior required greater attention and reinforcement. As they note, there is for staff a fundamental difference between the goal of a quiet life in a well-disciplined setting and the goal of rewarding inmates for social interaction with staff. There were also differences in opinion among psychiatrists: Any attempt to reduce drug dosages as part of the contracts "was apparently seen as an infringement into the province of the psychiatrist" (p. 291). Psychiatrists were also involved in transferring young offenders out of the institution, regardless of contracts, points, or progress in the program. However, Cullen and Seddon's main concern was with the relationship between themselves as psychologists and the staff running the program. They were criticized for being specialists, hence being of limited effectiveness and perspective and unlike the staff who saw things as they "really were." With refreshing candor, Cullen and Seddon concede that they were too prescriptive rather than collaborative with staff and that they concentrated on the effect of the program on the offenders rather than on the staff. Although of little use or comfort to Cullen and Seddon, the comment made by Burchard and Lane (1982) strikes home: "With respect to . . . resistance to change . . . behavior-modification advocates who do not recognize that much of their time will be spent trying to change the behavior of staff and policy of administrators are in for a rude awakening" (p. 616). It is to their credit that Cullen and Seddon realized they had been shaken awake and were bold enough to say so in print. By way of a postscript, I worked in the same institution several years after the completion of Cullen and Seddon's project. The staff who had worked on the project remembered it fondly. I recall being told of how things were really happening then, how psychologists used to get involved, and how much worse things had become since the project was concluded. Life, it seems, was always better yesterday.

In summary, a number of points can be made about token economies. The first is that, in the main, they are a successful means of changing behavior. There have typically been three targets with young offenders: self-maintenance and discipline within the institution (e.g., Cullen & Seddon, 1981) and self-improvement such as in higher educational and academic standards (e.g., Bippes, McLaughlin, & Williams, 1986). Whether such improvements are generalized beyond the institution remains a matter of debate: There are very few follow-up studies, with generally pessimistic outcomes, particularly with regard to recidivism. Indeed, Ross and McKay (1976) indicated a higher rate of recidivism in female young offenders who had passed through a TEP. Further issues raised by these conclusions are considered in the next chapter, following a discussion of programs in other settings in the remainder of this chapter.

RESIDENTIAL ESTABLISHMENTS

There are many criticisms of closed, secure institutions: that they reinforce criminal behavior; that they label people; and that they are, by their very nature, unsuitable for interventions aimed at rehabilitation to the community. At the same time, there are arguments in favor of some type of closed community: to protect the public and to give some structure to an attempt at rehabilitation. The alternative to traditional institutions, in ethos as much as physical structure, is a residential setting in which the emphasis is transferred from security to treatment. There have been many such residential facilities for young offenders offering a range of styles of intervention from transactional analysis to behavior modification (Sinclair & Clarke, 1982). Of the residential establishments that offer behavioral intervention, there can be little doubt that Achievement Place has generated the most interest and influence.

Achievement Place

The residential establishment, Achievement Place, has generated a large number of publications and evaluative studies for which reviews are available, the most recent being by Braukmann and Wolf (1987). In the treatment program that operates at Achievement Place, first established in Kansas, a specially trained married couple live in a family-style home with a small group, on average six, of young offenders. The married couple has the role of teaching parents: That is, they bear responsibility for both specific interventions, such as skills training, and the less structured care and attention associated with parenting. As Braukmann and Wolf (1987) note, the task of the training parents is highly demanding, and the average stay of such couples in this type of work is about 2 years.

The system of intervention employed at Achievement Place is based on social learning theory principles and seeks to modify existing behavior using a variety of cognitive-behavioral techniques. When the young offenders arrive at Achievement Place, they enter a token economy system in which points are earned or lost according to their performance on defined appropriate and inappropriate behavioral targets. The points are exchangeable for a range of backup reinforcers such as extra television privileges and more free time. Initially the points are exchanged on a daily basis in order to shape the young person's behavior in the appropriate fashion. When this has been achieved, the process of fading begins so that points are exchanged for privileges on a weekly rather than a daily basis. This is followed by progression to a merit system which dispenses with points so that privileges do not have to be earned but are contingent upon appropriate behavior as in the natural environment. Evaluative studies indicated that the scheme of token and merit systems was beneficial with regard to behavior within the residential setting (e.g., Phillips, Phillips, Fixsen, & Wolf, 1971) and also affected behavior positively outside the group home both at school and with natural families (e.g., Bailey, Wolf, & Phillips, 1970).

Although behavior can be modified by contingency management, this approach is somewhat artificial in that contingency management of the type exemplified by a token economy does not operate in the real world. Intervention must also aim at developing one's powers of self-government in relation to both one's own behavior and that of one's peers. Achievement Place pioneered two forms of self-government: a peer manager system which gives offenders the responsibility of supervising and running sections of the day-to-day program, and a family conference in which the young offenders contribute to a daily meeting dealing with the business of program design, administration, and rule violation. The self-government systems proved to be a significant part of the running of the establishment (Fixsen, Phillips, & Wolf, 1973), and more recent research has illustrated the potential of self-government procedures for managing aggressive behavior in a residential setting for young offenders (McNeil & Hart, 1986).

Although the token and self-government procedures contribute to the structure of the organization and assist in achieving broad behavior change targets, individual work in teaching social, educational, and self-management skills also takes place. Using the full range of skills-training techniques, the teaching parents directed the young offenders toward an array of new behaviors. Burchard and Lane (1982) offer a summary:

> Some of the specific behaviors that have been modified in teaching-family programs include classroom behaviors (Bailey, Wolf, & Phillips, 1970; Kirigin, Phillips, Timbers, Fixsen, & Wolf, 1975); interview skills (Braukmann, Maloney, Fixsen, Phillips, & Wolf, 1974); negotiation skills (Kifer, Lewis, Green, & Phillips, 1974); communication skills (Bailey, Timbers, Phillips, & Wolf, 1971; Maloney, Harper, Braukmann, Fixsen, Phillips, & Wolf, 1976); vocational skills (Ayala, Minkin, Phillips, Fixsen, & Wolf, 1973); and more effective skills to employ with encounters with police (Werner, Minkin, Minkin, Fixsen, Phillips, & Wolf, 1975 (pp. 622–623).

This range of intervention depends on staff competence, and so a comprehensive staff training program was constructed. Newly trained parents spent a year in training, which involved skills workshops, feedback from established teaching parents on day-to-day work, and periodic evaluation by other professionals and by the young offenders themselves. In short, the new staff were trained using the cognitive-behavioral methods they were eventually to practice. A comprehensive training manual was produced (Phillips, Phillips, Fixsen, & Wolf, 1974) together with a number of favorable outcome studies on the effectiveness of the staff training procedures (Braukmann, Kirigin Ramp, Braukmann, Willner, & Wolf, 1983).

In total, Achievement Place offers a complex, integrated model for residential treatment. Indeed, Rutter and Giller (1983) comment that Achievement Place "is a highly imaginative, well thought out programme which includes a range of measures appropriately designed to maintain behavioral change after the youth leaves the institution" (p. 278). As a model for residential care, Achievement Place has been of immense influence: It has been estimated that, in the United States alone, there are more than 200 teaching-family homes (James, Beier, Maloney, Thompson, Collins, & Collins, 1983). The majority of these homes are for adolescents in trouble with the authorities (e.g., Liberman, Ferris, Salgado, & Salgado, 1975; Weber & Burke, 1986), with perhaps the Boys Town program being the most widely publicized (Phillips, 1978); although there are others for different client groups such as autistic children (McClannahan, Krantz, McGee, & MacDuff, 1984). In Great Britain the influence of the model has also been felt although, as the next section illustrates, not on the same scale.

British Developments

In their summary of behavioral intervention with young offenders outside North America, Yule and Brown (1987) note a number of small-scale projects such as Gilbey House in Birmingham (Brown, 1977) and Unit 1 at Orchard Lodge in London (Brown, 1975). Other larger-scale projects include Aycliffe School in Durham (Hoghughi, 1979), the Shape project in Birmingham (Reid, Feldman, & Ostapiuk, 1980), and Glenthorne Youth Treatment Centre (YTC) in Birmingham (Reid, 1982). The latter is a large-scale government-funded establishment and merits further discussion.

Glenthorne YTC. The two youth treatment centers, of which Glenthorne is one, were designed to offer a treatment facility for the most disturbed children and adolescents in the child care system (Barlow, 1979). Not all the young people at Glenthorne YTC are offenders: About half the population, in total about 40 young people, have been convicted of serious offenses, although a substantial proportion of the remainder may have committed serious acts, such as violence toward staff, that would be legally punishable. As detailed by Reid (1982), the decision was made at Glenthorne YTC to operate an approach based on social learning theory, similar to that at Achievement Place. Thus attention was devoted to three aspects of the institution's functioning: the staff, the management and administration, and the treatment program.

The care staff are drawn from a range of professions—including nursing, teaching, social work, and psychology—all with the generic title of "group worker" and all performing the same tasks. The center is managed by a director and a deputy director with the support of an administrator, psychology and social work departments, and unit leaders who manage teams of group workers in the center's four units. Specialist staff training is organized jointly with a local university (see chapter 6).

On arrival at Glenthorne YTC the young person initially spends a period of time in a secure assessment unit before progressing to another secure unit for treatment. The final move is to an open unit with the goal of returning to the community. Originally a token economy was operated as at Achievement Place, but this has been replaced with a levels system. This system operates by allowing the young person a structured, graded access to increasingly higher levels of privileges contingent upon meeting appropriate behaviors (Ostapiuk & Westwood, 1986). As detailed earlier (see Table 2.1), Reid has defined seven classes of behavior ranging from offense behaviors, clinical targets, and institutional problem behaviors. The individual programs are designed, following the initial assessment, to modify each of these targets. The intervention techniques include offense counseling, anger control training, anxiety reduction, and skills training. The Center has developed behaviorally based strategies for the management of institutional violence (Gentry & Ostapiuk, 1988). Each young person progresses at his or her own rate from security to an open setting, culminating in time spent away from the Center on work experience programs, family visits, and other activities in preparation for a permanent return to the community. As yet there are no outcome data from Glenthorne YTC, although Ostapiuk and Westwood (1986) note that a major study is in progress. There are, however, a substantial number of outcome studies on residential programs in the United States.

Outcome Studies

Following a number of small-scale evaluations (e.g., Kirigin, Wolf, Braukmann, Fixsen, & Phillips, 1979), the first major outcome study on Achievement Place was reported by Kirigin, Braukmann, Atwater, and Wolf (1982). Kirigin et al. (1982) compared 13 Achievement Place homes with 9 comparison group homes that had not used a teaching-parent approach. The treatment group consisted of 102 male and 38 female young offenders and the control of 22 and 30 males and females, respectively. The groups were compared on a number of measures 1 year before treatment, during treatment, and 1 year after treatment. The pretreatment to during-treatment results were encouraging: "Teaching-Family programs for boys and for girls were superior to non-Teaching-Family programs on during treatment measures of percentage of youths involved in alleged offences, rates of alleged criminal offences, and youth and teacher ratings of the quality of treatment" (Kirigin et al., pp. 10–11). The posttreatment results were altogether less encouraging: "The post-treatment differences seen in the percentage of youths involved in offences were not statistically significant nor were there significant differences in the rates of criminal offences or in the percentage of youth institutionalized" (Kirigin et al., p. 11). In other words, the residential program is highly successful while in operation, but this success does not transfer from the group home to the community. Similarly Braukmann et al. (1985) found superior effects of teaching-family homes compared to no-treatment controls on measures of drug and alcohol use. But in the year following treatment no outcome measure significantly distinguished the two groups.

A national study on the teaching-family model was reported by Weinrott, Jones, and Howard (1982). This study involved 51 programs across 10 states, providing outcome data on 354 young offenders who had experienced teaching-family care in 26 different programs and a comparison group of 363 young offenders from 25 traditional group homes. The study spanned a 5-year period. Weinrott et al. concluded that although the teaching-family homes were superior on measures of educational progress, there were no significant differences on offending or social adjustment. Weinrott et al. also commented on the large number of program failures: They estimated that only 45% of those in both samples completed all the stages of the program.

The most recent outcome data were reported in 1985 by Braukmann, Wolf, and Kirigin Ramp (cited in Braukmann & Wolf, 1987). This study involved 168 young offenders (125 males and 43 females) from teaching-family homes and 205 young offenders (149 males and 56 females) from comparison homes. The two groups were compared before treatment, during treatment, and after treatment on eight *self-report* delinquency measures. The use of self-report makes a significant move away from relying on official measures of offending. The analysis revealed exactly the same pattern as in the earlier evaluation by Kirigin et al. (1982). There were no differences between the groups before treatment, there were significant differences favoring the teaching-family samples during treatment, but there were no significant differences 1 year after treatment. Exactly the same pattern was found for males and females. An identical analysis with official measures, including police and court data, yielded exactly the same result as with the self-report data. This same study examined a range of program variables and found higher ratings of improvement in skills and behavior for the teaching-family group.

Braukmann and Wolf (1987) provide a succinct summary of the position to date: "The data again appear to support a conclusion of an immediate and considerable impact on the behavior of the participating youths. Again, however, differences favouring the Teaching-Family approach do not seem to survive the treatment period" (p. 152). As is abundantly clear from outcome studies involving other therapeutic approaches (Sinclair & Clarke, 1982), this problem is not unique to the teaching-family model or to behavioral regimes in general or, indeed, to interventions with young offenders. The lack of transfer of treatment gains is an issue that plagues most of the clinical literature. There are a number of explanations for this failure of generalization, including the view that despite a treatment ethos, residential care is simply too far removed from the natural environment for effective treatment to take place. Such a view formed the basis of programs designed to operate in the community in which the young offender lives.

COMMUNITY PROGRAMS

School-Based Intervention

In the field of research on the etiology of juvenile crime, school performance has been long held as an important correlate of offending. This relationship can be viewed in two ways. The first emphasizes *academic* difficulties, including learning difficulties, which are seen as a characteristic of the young offender population. These academic limitations are associated with poor social adaptation, which in turn increases the probability of offending (Loeber & Dishion, 1983). At a second level, *social* behavior within school is seen as related to later offending (Elliot & Voss, 1974). Although it would be inappropriate to state that school difficulties, either academic or social, *cause* offending—indeed, it is likely that this is *not* the case (Rutter & Giller, 1983)—this does not mean that school-based interventions are not required. Even though it is not the cause of the criminal behavior, if school performance increases or maintains the probability of offending, then intervention at this level may nevertheless prove beneficial. Thus, for example, if dropping out of school increases the probability of offending (Thornberry, Moore, &

Christenson, 1985), then programs for maintaining school attendance may well be advantageous in reducing the probability of criminal behavior.

The typical reaction of the educational authorities to offending is summarized by Lane and Murakami (1987): "Traditionally, the school's response to the behaviorally disordered or delinquent youth has been exclusion" (p. 309). This exclusion can take a number of forms such as reduced school time or removal from mainstream classrooms to special schools or residential establishments. More recently there has been a growing emphasis, across a range of populations, on community-based interventions and a concomitant move toward deinstitutionalization. This shift in emphasis has provided the impetus for schools to develop their own programs rather than depending on facilities outside the mainstream educational system (Kauffman & Nelson, 1977).

In order to give a realistic flavor to a description of this work it is necessary, for this section only, to modify the earlier definition of a young offender. Much school-based intervention has been with lesser (i.e., noncriminal) behaviors such as absenteeism, school suspension, and breaking school rules, although the interventions do include as referral criteria law breaking and police contact.

PREP Programs. One of the programs most widely cited in the literature is the Preparation Through Responsive Education Program (PREP) described in a number of publications between the late 1970s (e.g., Filipczak & Friedman, 1978; Friedman, Filipczak, & Fiordaliso, 1977) and the early 1980s (e.g., Filipczak & Wodarski, 1982; Wodarski & Filipczak, 1982). PREP, based in the United States (Maryland), was intended for pupils of all ages recommended for the program because of academic and social problems, including (but not exclusively) offending and police contact. The program was composed of two related components: academic tutoring, social and interpersonal skills training, and family skills training for the pupils, alongside which a staff training program was conducted to facilitate the work with students. Academic learning took place mainly through self-instruction, with the use of contracts, teacher ratings, and a positive reinforcement program that rewarded progress. Skills training, using traditional methods, was conducted in both small and large groups.

The outcome studies, with data from over 600 pupils, are presented in a series of research reports by Filipczak and his colleagues; a succinct review of the findings is given by Burchard and Lane (1982). The results can be summarized according to short-term and long-term outcome. Short-term outcome was gauged in terms of standardized test scores, grades for academic work, and school behavior and attendance. It was found that overall the PREP pupils performed better than controls on tests of academic achievement and received better grades for academic work. The program also increased school attendance. However, PREP had no significant effect on school behavior—suspensions, teacher ratings, discipline—relative to a control group.

The long-term outcome findings resulted from 1- and 4-year follow-ups of the PREP pupils and matched controls. At the first follow-up the advantage clearly lay with those who had experienced PREP: These pupils showed fewer suspensions and discipline problems, with greater school attendance and higher grades for academic work. At the longer-term, 4-year, follow-up the position had changed: The PREP pupils, mean age almost 18 years, were not distinguishable from the controls. The academic improvements had faded, there was no difference in school dropout rates, and, as measured by self-report, parent report, and official records, there was no significant effect of PREP on offending. As Burchard and Lane (1982) comment, "Overall, the PREP program was impressive . . . unfortunately, however, the results do not tend to support the efficacy of the program" (p. 638).

Contingency Contracting. A series of studies have investigated the use of a contingency management program within a school setting to modify both academic and social behavior. In a typical study, Heaton, Safer, Allen, Spinnato, and Prumo (1976) employed individualized academic tuition and a points system for academic and social target behaviors; the targets were agreed on in weekly negotiated contingency contracts between teachers and pupils. The points could be exchanged for a variety of both social and tangible backup reinforcers. A form of response cost also operated in that pupils who seriously misbehaved were sent home and required to participate in a parent conference before returning to school. The efficacy of the program was assessed by comparison with a control group, although the validity of the control is somewhat uncertain as these pupils were drawn from a different school.

The program ran for 5 years, with annual outcome and follow-up data available (Safer, Heaton, & Parker, 1981). These annual reports showed that the intervention group was better behaved within school and achieved better grades for academic work. A 4-year follow-up showed that those in the intervention group were less likely to drop out of school but no more likely to be academically successful. The data on offending suggested some initial effect on offending but that the overall effect on offending was not significant as compared to the controls (Safer et al., 1981).

In summary, it is possible to note a number of consistent findings from school-based behavioral interventions. In the short-term the programs are, in the main, successful at improving academic performance and in ameliorating school disciplinary problems, and they have an additional beneficial effect on family problems. However, it is doubtful that these changes will be maintained over the long term. There is very little, if any, evidence that school-based behavioral programs reduce the probability of future conviction for criminal behavior. Indeed, this latter point appears to hold for school-based prevention generally (Hawkins & Lishner, 1987).

Family-Based Intervention

The role of the family in the etiology and maintenance of juvenile crime is documented in legions of publications from criminology, psychology, and sociology. The role of the family ranges from genetic transmission; disrupted family life, as with a broken home; the social status of the family as gauged by housing, employment, and so on; family management practices as reflected by style of parenting; and family interaction as reflected in approved behaviors within the family (Snyder & Patterson, 1987). As was the case with academic and school-based behavior, it is uncertain whether family processes are a cause or a correlate of juvenile offending. What is more certain is that there are liable to be complex relationships, perhaps shifting from family to family, among parental functioning, family interaction, and other social influences on the young offender. This complexity is reflected in the performance models being constructed by theorists such as Patterson (1986). However, although there is some debate as to the exact role of the family, there is little dispute that the family does, either wittingly or unwittingly, play a part in the development of young offenders. A range of family interventions have attempted to counter the family processes thought to lead to juvenile offending. Not all family therapy for "delinquent" families is based on behavioral theory (Wells & Dezen, 1978), although there is a considerable literature on behavioral family intervention (Morton & Ewald, 1987). Although it is difficult to force classifications, for convenience a broad distinction is made between interventions aimed at training parents and interventions designed to modify patterns of family functioning.

Parent Management Training. Parent management training (PMT) aims to modify, through training, the way in which parents interact with their children. Originally developed for use with parents of younger children, PMT became increasingly popular and has been used with parents of older children, including young offenders. Specifically, empirical research has suggested that the level of parent skills, such as monitoring

the child's whereabouts, using effective discipline strategies for antisocial behavior, applying effective problem-solving strategies, and reinforcing appropriate behavior, may play a role in the etiology of offending behaviors (Patterson & Stouthamer-Loeber, 1984). These parenting
behaviors therefore are the focus of PMT. In broad terms, parents are
taught to praise more, to be less critical, and to be more vigilant and
consistent in their parenting style.

The training follows the behavioral principles of defining the target
behavior, setting targets, and reinforcing appropriate behavior while
punishing inappropriate behavior. As described by Bank, Patterson,
and Reid (1987), the starting point is training parents to observe their
child's behavior, beginning with simple behaviors, so as to be able to
track (i.e., monitor and record) its frequency. When this skill has been
mastered by the parent(s), a reinforcement system is devised. Most typically this is in the form of a token or points system in which the child
earns tokens which can later be exchanged for agreed-on rewards. As a
discipline procedure, time out is favored with younger children, and a
response cost, such as loss of privileges, with older children. Training
in problem-solving skills may be added to the program. Clearly PMT
requires a great deal of parental commitment and, as many practitioners
have experienced, parental resistance can be very strong (Chamberlain,
Patterson, Reid, Kavanagh, & Forgatch, 1984). Thus it is important to
build into the program a reinforcement system for the parents, particularly in view of the likely antagonism between offender and parents
which is not going to predispose the latter toward reinforcement
schemes. It must also be recognized that the social support system for
the parents is important: Parents who have few positive social contacts
outside the home with relatives and friends are less likely to respond to
PMT (Dumas & Wahler, 1983).

There is a large literature on PMT with children and a substantial
number of studies dealing specifically with young offenders (Bank et
al., 1987; Morton & Ewald, 1987). A recent study by Serna, Schumaker,
Hazel, and Sheldon (1986) illustrates the general procedures. Serna et
al. used skills training with parents and young offenders referred via
the probation services. Following initial assessment, skills training programs were conducted for the offenders, for the parents, and then for
parent-offender interaction. The training took place in rooms assigned
to county juvenile court services. Using standard skills training techniques, the program focused on various problematical situations such
as giving feedback on the behavior of others and giving instructions (see
Table 4.2).

The outcome data showed that the skills training was effective for
both offenders and parents in that it increased their skills level. Further,

Table 4.2. Reciprocal Parent-Youth Social Skills: Giving Instructions and
Following Instructions

Parent Skill: Giving Instructions	Youth Skill: Following Instructions
1. Face the person.	1. Face the person.
2. Maintain eye contact.	2. Maintain eye contact.
3. Keep a neutral facial expression.	3. Keep a neutral facial expression.
4. Keep a straight posture.	4. Keep a straight posture.
5. Get the youth's attention (e.g., call his or her name).	5. Give attention feedback (head nods) to the person.
6. State the instruction in the form of a request—be specific about the required behavior.	6. Listen carefully to the instruction.
7. Give a rationale for the request.	7. Make a statement of acknowledgement of the instruction.
8. Ask the youth if he or she understands.	8. Ask for clarification (if necessary).
9. If the youth does not understand the instruction, explain again.	9. Say you will follow the instruction.
10. If the youth understands the instruction, ask if he or she will perform the instruction.	10. Follow the instruction.
11. If the youth agrees to follow the instruction, state a positive consequence for following the instruction. If the youth does not agree to follow the instruction, give another rationale for the request. Repeat Steps 8–11.	

Note: From "Teaching Reciprocal Social Skills to Delinquents and Their Parents" by L. A. Serna, J. B. Schumaker, J. S. Hazel, and J. B. Sheldon, 1986, *Journal of Clinical Child Psychology, 15,* p. 67.

the training benefited the level of communication between parents and offenders, producing better family relationships. However, as Serna et al. note, "What is unknown is the extent of the generalization of the trained skills to the home environment" (p. 77). It is also unknown whether the training had any influence on offending. However, an un-published study by Marlowe, Reid, Patterson, and Weinrott (cited in Gordon & Arbuthnot, 1987) did show some effect of PMT on recidivism. A total of 55 young offenders took part in a program in which the intervention was either PMT (plus contracting) or conventional community treatment. The results showed that during the treatment year the intervention group offenders committed fewer offenses than the community group. At a 1-year follow-up the intervention group had spent significantly fewer days in institutions, resulting in considerable financial savings; but the difference in rate of offending was similar for the two groups at the end of the follow-up period. It is interesting that this study combined PMT with another technique, contracting, to produce at least promising outcome evidence. Contracting has formed the basis of another style of behavioral family intervention in which the emphasis is placed on family functioning.

Functional Family Therapy. Functional family therapy (FFT) is based on the premise that behavior within family systems, including antisocial behavior, serves a functional purpose in meeting some interpersonal need such as intimacy or discipline. While there are similarities between FFT and PMT, in FFT the emphasis is more explicitly focused on the interactions between members of the family. A number of studies have suggested that particular patterns of family interaction are characteristically associated with offending in young people. These can be summarized as follows: (a) greater frequency of parental disagreements than in "nondelinquent" families, (b) less decision making by the parents and a concomitant greater influence of the child, (c) less expression of positive and greater emphasis on negative affect, (d) a greater level of misperceived interpersonal communication within the family, (e) a greater reluctance to negotiate toward a compromise in times of dispute (Jacob, 1975). These maladaptive family processes are the focus of FFT: "The main goals of treatment are to increase reciprocity and positive reinforcement among family members, to establish clear communication, to help specify behaviors that family members desire from each other, to negotiate constructively, and to help identify interpersonal problems" (Kazdin, 1987, p. 192).

One of the techniques most widely used in pursuit of these therapeutic aims is *contingency contracting.* A contract is a written, negotiated statement that specifies behavior and outcomes based on the assumption of a need for reciprocity in family communication together with an emphasis on positive reinforcement. As Stuart (1971) notes, good behavioral contracts contain a number of elements. The first is a detailing of privileges to be obtained for meeting defined responsibilities; with young offenders this may be free time, spending money, and so on. The contract should also specify the responsibilities, such as school attendance and keeping parents informed of their whereabouts, related to securing privileges. The contract should also include a system of sanctions, such as loss of privileges for a specified time, to be implemented in case of failure. On the other hand, good performance merits reward, and so a "bonus clause" may be written into the contract. Finally, the contract should include a system for monitoring progress. Stuart (1971) gives an example of a contract used with a female young offender; see the case study at the end of this chapter for an extended discussion.

There have been a number of studies on the use of contingency contracting with delinquent families. Stumphauzer (1976) used a combination of self-control techniques, including self-instructional training, and family contracting in the treatment of stealing in a 12-year-old female. The contract was designed to shift parental (and school) attention away from negative sanctions for stealing and toward positive rewards for not stealing. The program was successful in eliminating the stealing, remained so at an 18-month follow-up, and improved family relationships significantly. Welch (1985) also reported a single-case study, in this instance with a 16-year-old male who, at the outset of the intervention, was awaiting institutional placement for assault and refusal to attend school. The consequences of a successful program would be that the offender would return home; an unsuccessful intervention would mean that the court would carry out the order for institutional placement. The intervention was based on specific family contracts involving temper control, curfew regulations, and household responsibilities. While the path to a satisfactory conclusion was far from smooth, the intervention successfully reduced both physical and verbal aggression and increased appropriate behavior. In summary Welch notes that "the court ordered Ralph to be returned to the custody of his mother and stepfather and set aside the order committing him to institutional placement. At the seven-month telephone follow-up, the subject and his parents each stated that there were no major adjustment problems" (p. 258).

Examination of successful contracting with the families of young offenders suggests that the therapist's skills of negotiation and facilitating communication are important, as is supplementing of the contract with other techniques as in Stumphauzer's (1976) study. An example of a multimodal program, involving family contracting, is given by Henderson (1981). Henderson's approach to eliminating stealing is based on changing "both the internal and the external environments of each individual client" (p. 232). Control of the internal environment is achieved through relaxation training, biofeedback, and self-instructional training, and control of the external environment through a system of family- and school-administered contingent reinforcement for not stealing. The contingent reinforcement, detailed and agreed on before intervention, involves the awarding of points for not stealing which can be exchanged for individualized rewards. Henderson reports follow-up data for 10 young offenders indicating that the intervention program was successful in 8 cases.

Following an early study on family functioning in families of young offenders (Alexander, 1973), a series of interventions by Alexander and his colleagues involved FFT. Their approach was developed to include skills training, contingency contracting, and problem-solving training, all aimed at improving patterns of family communication and exchange of reinforcement. The therapist plays an active and supportive role in facilitating the process of family interaction and change while directing the focus of the intervention toward specific behavioral targets (Alexander & Parsons, 1982). In the first studies contingency contracting was used in conjunction with skills training to improve family communication and negotiation (Alexander & Parsons, 1973; Parsons & Alexander, 1973). In an experimental program comparing treatment approaches, over 100 first-time offenders were randomly assigned to behavioral systems family therapy (i.e., FFT), client-centered family therapy, psychodynamic-eclectic family therapy, or a probation-only control group. The outcome evidence indicated FFT was superior to client-centered and probation-only treatment in improving family interaction and conflict resolution. With regard to recidivism, at a variable 6- to 18-month follow-up (Klein, Alexander, & Parsons, 1977), the FFT group had the lowest rate of reoffending, almost half that for the group with the next most effective intervention (client-centered family therapy). A longer follow-up, at 2.5 to 3.5 years, was also reported by Klein, et al. (1977). This investigated the hypothesis that the previously successful intervention in modifying family functioning would have a beneficial effect on the younger siblings of the offenders. The results showed sibling recidivism rates of 40% for the probation-only group, 59% for the client-centered group, 63% for the psychodynamic-eclectic group, and 20% for the FFT group. Statistical analysis supported the hypothesis that the intervention had also acted to reduce sibling offending. (It is unfortunate that offender recidivism rates were not also reported at the longer-term follow-up, especially in view of findings suggesting that treatment gains tend to fade after a year.) In an interesting subanalysis, Alexander, Barton, Schiavo, and Parsons (1976) found that the personal qualities of the therapist contributed significantly to a good outcome. They identified two therapist variables of particular importance: "relationship" skills, such as warmth and humor, and "structuring" skills, including directness and self-confidence.

In summary, it appears that family-based interventions can be successful on a number of levels: Intervention can modify parent skills, family interactions, and family functioning; there are indications of reduced recidivism within the family for both the targeted individual and for his or her siblings. It may also be the case, and certainly it is with the more recent studies (e.g., Serna et al., 1986), that the distinction between PMT and FFT becomes blurred, at least in practical if not theoretical terms. Overall, Patterson (1985) has defined three essential ingredients for producing change in families: a technology of child management, a high level of clinical skills for countering parental resistance to change, and a therapist support system for when the going gets tough. One cannot help but feel that this family-oriented style of community intervention has more to recommend it than the movement toward home incarceration with electronic monitoring (Ball & Lilly, 1988). Is a therapist preferable to an electronic jailer as a form of social control?

Probation and Diversion

Probation. As documented by Prins (1982), the role of the probation officer is wide and varied, ranging from court work and supervision of offenders to carrying out treatment programs. Probation officers make use of a range of treatment techniques, from psychotherapy (Romero & Williams, 1983) to methods based on social learning theory (Nietzel, 1979). In Britain, as Hudson (1986) notes, behavioral casework is being reported with increasing frequency by probation officers, with social skills training proving particularly popular. In a recent review of behavior modification in probation work, Remington and Remington (1987) suggest that many of the problems faced by offenders, such as anxiety, depression, and alcohol and drug abuse, are precisely those in which behavioral intervention has proved efficacious. However, for behavioral casework to be acceptable, Remington and Remington suggest that three criteria must be met: (1) It must be shown that training can successfully equip probation officers with the skills needed to conduct behavioral casework, (2) that there is room for trained probation officers to incorporate these skills into their work schedule, and (3) that behavioral methods lead to positive changes in client behavior.

While assessment of the effects of professional training is notoriously difficult, there is evidence that probation officers can be trained to be competent and knowledgeable behavioral practitioners (e.g., Novaco, 1980; Wood, Green, & Bry, 1982). However, the evidence from post-training studies suggests that there is a failure of generalization: Jesness, Allison, McCormick, Wedge, and Young (1975) found that probation officers trained in behavioral skills were slow to put their learning into practice. There may be a variety of reasons for this, but one should be aware of an increasingly outspoken view held by probation workers that the individual treatment model (behavioral or otherwise) is not an appropriate one for probation given the dual responsibilities of help and control inherent in probation work (Willis, 1986). Enthusiastic probation officers may thus find themselves attempting to practice behavioral intervention in an environment hostile not only to behavioral methods but also to a treatment philosophy.

With regard to Remington and Remington's final point, there is empirical evidence that probation officers can be effective behavior therapists with both young and adult offenders (e.g., Nietzel, 1979). There is no reason why more cognitive techniques should not be used by probation officers with equal effectiveness. Remington and Remington conclude: "We have little doubt as to the promise of behavior modification in probation service contexts. However, as our review of the literature shows, the promise has yet to be adequately fulfilled" (p. 170).

Diversionary Projects. During the 1960s there was mounting concern about the number of young people held in custody. The concerns were twofold: the potentially damaging effects of custody on young people and the financial costs of a growing prison population. On both sides of the Atlantic steps were taken to provide alternatives to custody for young offenders. The most radical changes occurred in Massachusetts where a program of decarceration was begun which involved closing down all training schools and institutions for offenders under 17 years of age (Miller, Ohlin, & Coates, 1977). Despite opposition, the program was successful and continues today (Rutherford, 1986). One of the results of this policy was a growth in successful community programs. Elsewhere competition between institutions and community programs remains, forcing community practitioners into the unenviable position of having to convince judges and magistrates of the superiority of community treatment to custodial measures. Clearly this extends treatment issues into the realm of politics and social policy, about which more will be said later.

Of the various diversionary measures, *intermediate treatment* (IT) has attracted a great deal of attention (Thorpe, 1978). The term IT refers to an ideal rather than a specific technique, its goal being to prevent both custody of and offending by young people. The manner in which this goal is pursued varies from IT program to IT program. In a review, Preston (1982) comments: "IT schemes vary greatly, from playgroups for the under fives, through evening groups for young people who go to school, to day-care facilities for school truants and/or young offenders" (p. 171). One of the difficulties with such diversity is that it makes it hard to quantify and assess the effectiveness of the intervention. However, Preston (1982) describes an IT scheme that utilized behavioral principles and yielded some indications of effectiveness.

The Birmingham Action for Youth (BAY) scheme, based in a renovated school building, was structured to commence with an assessment period, gathering details of each young person's (not all were offenders) general education level, work skills, and social and self-management skills. At the end of the assessment phase, a contract was negotiated detailing short- and long-term goals, and the negotiation included parents or guardians whenever possible. The intervention had two components, a general program running for the center as a whole and individualized programs. The general program incorporated a points system for rewarding targets such as keeping to a work routine. This general approach was supplemented by an individual program for reinforcing work and social skills. A work experience scheme, organized in conjunction with local employers, ran alongside the other components of the project. At a 6-month follow-up, there was a disappointing drop in the high levels of employment achieved on leaving the program. The offending figures were more encouraging, with indications of some reduction in official measures of offending.

There have been a number of not dissimilar projects in the United States: A recent study by Davidson, Redner, Blakely, Mitchell, and Emshoff (1987) illustrates the approach. Following a previous study that had demonstrated the efficacy of behavioral and advocacy interventions (Davidson et al., 1977), over 200 young offenders were assigned to one of four intervention conditions or to one of two control groups (attention-placebo and treatment as usual). The four intervention groups were as follows: an *action condition,* using mainly advocacy and individual contracts with offenders and significant others; an *action condition family focus,* in which advocacy was combined with behavioral contracting used exclusively with family members—either parents or siblings of the offender; an *action condition court setting,* which was essentially the same as the action condition, with the work taking place in a court setting and being carried out by a juvenile court member rather than a psychologist; and a *relationship condition,* which focused on the development of the offender's empathy, communication skills, and genuineness in interpersonal relationships, all factors thought to play a role as determinants of antisocial behavior. The study used a range of measures to assess treatment integrity, the dimensions of change fostered by the intervention (e.g., job seeking, peer involvement), and police records, court records, and self-report measures of offending. The results showed a high degree of treatment integrity; that is, the style of intervention was followed in a thorough and proper manner. Although the different conditions produced different processes of change, the findings for recidivism are of particular interest. For court recidivism the action condition, action condition family focus, and relationship condition were superior to the control. The intervention that was court-based had no significant impact on court recidivism. It appears that the style of intervention mattered little: "Just removing juveniles from the court and pairing them with a volunteer may have more positive effects" (Davidson et al., p. 74). However, the self-report scale failed to show any effect of intervention on offending, suggesting that the intervention had modified the system's response rather than the offender's behavior. Although should this be the case, it is not clear why the attention-placebo control group involved in an intervention did not show a lower rate of court recidivism than the treatment groups. Davidson et al. have demonstrated, in total, that diversion can be successfully achieved but that diversion from the court system does not significantly change rates of offending.

In this chapter and the previous one a reasonably detailed overview of the literature has been presented. The evidence raises a number of issues: Does treatment work? Why does it work (or not work, as the case may be)? How can the probability of successful results be increased? What theoretical lessons are to be learned from the outcome studies? These important points are addressed in full in the next two chapters.

CASE STUDY

Background

Billy and Tommy are brothers, aged 12 and 11 years, respectively, when I first met them. Billy and Tommy had spent several years in care, including 4 years in long-term fostering. The foster placement had broken down with the suggestion that the older boy's stealing was the cause. However, as the foster parents separated shortly after the breakdown, this disharmony was seen as the real reason for the breakdown of the foster placement. Shortly afterward work began on looking for adoptive parents for the brothers. The search was successful, and after introductions the brothers were placed with a couple who had no other children. The adoption order was made almost a year after the initial placement. The social work notes suggest that although there were the inevitable problems involved in placing 9- and 8-year-olds in a new environment, the adoptive parents coped well and did not require a great deal of support. When the adoption became legal, contact with the adoption agency ceased.

Over 2 years later the adoptive parents took the unusual step of recontacting the adoption agency. They had discovered that Billy, the elder brother, had been stealing, and their attempts to stop him had failed. While they thought that he was stealing only small amounts of money, the frequency of the thefts appeared to be increasing. A social worker from the adoption agency, who knew the family, visited several times and began to gather some baseline information. As is often the case, monitoring appeared to stop the stealing. Several months later it started again, a family discussion "cleared the air," and once again the stealing stopped. After a second interval of several months the adoptive parents discovered that *both* brothers were stealing from local shops and from home. The adoption agency approached the clinical unit at the university for assistance, and I agreed to become involved in the case.

Assessment

The background details, as noted above, were based on information from discussions with the social worker and from the written records. The first step toward a functional analysis was to talk with the family.

At the first meeting all members of the family were present. After the preliminary introductions it quickly became apparent that the family wished to talk about the stealing. At first it was the adoptive parents who talked, mainly confirming details already seen in the social work case notes and adding other points. It transpired that when the older brother had been caught, the younger brother had joined in with the chorus of general condemnation. It must have been galling for Billy to have Tommy held up as a model of good behavior, knowing that his brother was stealing more than he was. It says a lot for his loyalty to his brother that he did not say anything, although what happened in private might best be left to the imagination.

Both parents were employed full-time, although it was only recently that the mother had returned to full-time work. While this was being discussed during the initial meeting, Billy made his first spontaneous contribution, saying how difficult this had made life for him and Tommy, forcing them to change various school and social routines. The parents acknowledged this as a source of difficulty, although the brothers had been involved in discussions about their mother's return to work and it was said that they all would have to make readjustments. The stealing however, had been taking place before the change in employment.

The boys then described their stealing, which was a highly skilled activity. In the small town in which they lived there were two or three local shops from which they stole regularly. The sequence was that they would walk past a shop, usually after school, look in the window, decide what to steal, go in, make sure they were not being watched, slip the selected item into a pocket or up a sleeve, perhaps buy something, and then walk out. Sometimes they stole together, other times alone; they took items such as drinks, sweets, pens and pencils, small toys, and batteries. The stolen items were put to a variety of uses: Confectionary was eaten or shared with friends (they would not say if the friends stole as well), and other items were played with, given to friends, or hoarded. The younger boy was a particular hoarder: It was discovered that he had accumulated quite a collection of toys. They both received a weekly allowance which they spent on items similar to those stolen, although they said they would steal whether or not they had any pocket money in their possession. Both boys said they stole when they "felt like it" rather than planning the theft well in advance. It also transpired that both boys had been stealing from home, taking money from around the house and from their mother's purse. While stealing both boys said they remained calm and unflustered, becoming neither excited nor anxious.

The stealing had become a serious issue when Billy was caught in one of the local shops and reported both to his school and his parents by a shopkeeper who was threatening to take legal action. This naturally raised the parents' concern and led to their questioning of Billy and then to discovery of the intensity of the problem and later Tommy's involvement. The parents had used a number of strategies to try to stop the stealing: The boys were not allowed any free time to themselves, they were "grounded" (not allowed out in the evenings) for long periods, pocket money was stopped, and smackings were administered. None of these proved to have any effect and eventually, feeling that matters were out of control, they recontacted the adoption agency.

The initial session ended with a request, to build on the existing self-report data, that both the parents and the boys keep a daily diary, recording as much information as possible. Realizing that the boys might well be unwilling to record stealing, it was agreed that their diaries would be read only by me and would be treated as strictly confidential. In recording stealing the boys were asked to answer a number of questions: (a) What tempted you to steal? (b) If you resisted the temptation, how did you do it? (c) Where were you when you stole and what time of day was it? (d) What did you do with the stolen item? (e) Why do you think you stole that item? The parents kept a running log of daily events, their reactions to any discovery of stealing, and so on.

In later sessions I talked with the parents separately. They showed marked differences in reacting to the stealing. The father was pragmatic: Boys steal, his had been caught, and something needed to be done. He was concerned on two fronts: The boys could well do without prosecution and criminal records that would follow them through life. His wife had reacted strongly to the stealing. In talking with the mother it quickly became evident that she was experiencing a deep sense of moral outrage: "How could they do it?" she repeated. "Stealing; people should not steal. It's wrong." She was clearly very upset, blaming herself and her husband for doing something wrong, labeling the boys as "bad" and "wrong." She and her husband had had words, and she wondered whether the boys were suited to living with them after all.

Over a 3-week period the diary recording began to reveal some useful information, as illustrated by the following extracts taken verbatim from the diaries.

Tommy: Tuesday
   On the way back from Grandad as I got to the corner by the green I saw the shop I decided to go in just seeing the shop made me go in.

   No it was not anythink school or at home. I was happy befor I went into the shop. Nothing made me steal.

   I had already decided to steal. I just wanted anything. I stole a purse, yes I was going to keep it and wear it as it look's good, as it fastens to my wrist. I keep it.

Billy: Monday
   I resisted stealing because I knew I would get found out or caught by my mum or dad.

   Wednesday

   I resisted because I did not want to be ground for a year or more.

Eventually an A:B:C sequence was formulated; this was essentially the same for both boys.

Distal A: Disrupted family life
            Breakdown of foster home placement
            Undetected episodes of stealing
            Adjustment to adoptive parents following placement

Proximal A: Sight of shop
              Goods in window
              No parents or adults present to supervise

Behavior: Decide to steal
            Select item
            Enter shop and take item

Proximal Consequences: Play with (or eat) stolen item
                         Add to hoard of items
                         Use stolen money to buy things
                         Share stolen items with friends
                         Save spending pocket money

Distal Consequences: Parents' wrath if discovered
Parents' individual reactions to the behavior
Loss of free time
Grounding
Involvement of social worker and psychologist
Prosecution and criminal record
Family breakdown

The distal antecedents undoubtedly occurred, although their exact role in the development of stealing remains uncertain. Certainly a case can be made for less than optimum socialization in early childhood, but it is too simple to use this as an explanation for stealing. It will be recalled that self-report studies reveal that stealing is very common in late childhood and/or early adolescence (Belson, 1975). It is also known that developmentally, minor offending begins to increase at about the boys' age (Farrington, 1983). These developmental and behavioral norms may in fact be a more likely explanation than poor socialization: Petty stealing is found in a wide range of young people regardless of the quality of early experience. This, however, remains a point of conjecture and is of limited clinical value.

The proximal antecedents suggest that the stealing had an impulsive quality: The sight of a shop and an item that caught the eye appeared to be all that was required. No pattern relating to home or school events was evident. The stealing had been occurring without detection for a long period of time, seemingly on an episodic basis, at a frequency of about once a week. Thus there was a long schedule of reinforcement, broken only recently by discovery, although there was the foster care breakdown in which the stealing was implicated.

The consequences were immediate: The use of the stolen items, the hoarding, and the sharing with friends were all positive outcomes which occurred on a continual basis. The negative outcome, family disharmony, seldom took place, and the boys had learned that they could survive a family breakdown having already experienced it twice in their short lives. For children who have experienced life in care, social workers and psychologists are part of the everyday routine—a nuisance to be tolerated. The distal consequences all had a question mark over them: They might happen, but some time in the distant future if at all.

Functional Analysis. Given this assessment it is possible to arrive at an understanding of the function of the behavior. The stealing was positively reinforced by the positive outcomes, both material and social, it produced; these positive outcomes, with a long history of being successfully obtained, outweighed the negative outcomes and sanctions imposed by the parents. For reasons of immaturity, poor socialization, or normal development, internal control of behavior had not developed. The potential long-term consequences were probably too distant and unreal to matter greatly to the boys. Their parents' concern may have been seen by the brothers as justified as retribution for the recent upheaval due to the changes in employment—this, however, is speculation.

This assessment left a great deal open to speculation for two reasons: The first was that it was difficult to obtain information from the boys. They did not like talking about the stealing or about family life, although they did keep good diaries. This reluctance to talk—questions were often met with shrugs, monosyllabic replies, or "Don't know"—limited the depth of information that could be obtained. The second reason was an ethical decision: Given that the stealing had been taking place over a long period of time (as the boys confirmed), its etiology clearly did not lie in the present family functioning. As the goal of the intervention was to stop the stealing, the finer points of the family relationships were none of my concern. This position therefore draws boundaries on what those involved can rightly be asked to reveal, but of course, is open to revision should future developments (i.e., a lack of successful intervention) cause the initial analysis to be called into doubt.

A further restriction, unavoidable in the circumstances, was due to the assessment methods used. All the information was gathered through self-report and parents' monitoring; there was no direct observation of the behavior, a point that applies to most criminal behaviors.

Intervention

The primary target of the intervention was the stealing. There was agreement by all concerned, Tommy and Billy included, that the time had come for the stealing to stop. A secondary target, perhaps necessary to reach the main target, was the parents' (particularly the mother's) views of the stealing. In order to modify their views on the abnormality of the behavior we talked at great length about moral development, noting that it might not be expected that the children would have clearly defined concepts of right and wrong in the same way as adults. Further, it was mentioned that stealing was statistically a far from deviant activity in late childhood and was not an indication in itself of some underlying psychopathology. This information seemed to be of use to the parents: Once assured that the position was not being advocated that stealing was not wrong, their perception of the issue changed from "maladjusted children" to "problem behavior."

The main target, however, was the stealing, and it was approached in two ways: rewards for not stealing and punishment for stealing. Although the parents, as is usually the case, had focused their efforts on the latter strategy, the notion of rewarding good behavior needed discussion. Often parents hold the opinion that good behavior is what children should do and does not merit any attention or reward. In this case the parents accepted this philosophy of rewarding good behavior following an explanation of the basic principles of behavior change. (I have had cases that have failed because of the parents' refusal to accept this principle.) The intervention was therefore designed to reward not stealing and to punish stealing. As a point of principle I am extremely unhappy about the use of physical pain as a means of inflicting punishment, although recognizing the parents' claims to use such sanctions. (For the benefit of cynics: Yes, I do have children, two in fact; both remain unsmacked but have sailed close to the wind!) It was agreed that removal of privileges would be the means of punishment in the first instance. The system of reward and punishment was clarified in the form of a contingency contract. This was a four-page document, as detailed in the tables below. The opening page (Table 4.3) defined the behavior and set out the terms and conditions of the contract. It should be noted that there are always problems with contracts, and it is advisable to name an arbitrator of disputes at the outset.

The rewards were programmed to be available, contingent upon not stealing, in the short term (daily), medium term (weekly), and long term (monthly)—see Table 4.4. I was less than happy with clause 4, but the parents were unwilling to commit themselves to long-term rewards. The clause in the contract is an uneasy compromise.

The costs were more difficult to formulate, as it was necessary to take

Table 4.3. Terms of Contract

Contract: Mum and Dad, Billy and Tommy

This contract is concerned with stealing, the word *stealing* is used for any of the following:

Taking items from a shop without paying.

Taking items from school that are not your own.

Taking anything from home that is not yours, including more than two items from the cupboard.

Taking anything from someone else's house that is not yours.

The contract sets out the rewards for not stealing and the costs of stealing for Billy and Tommy. In signing the contract Mum and Dad agree to give the rewards and administer the costs; Billy and Tommy agree to accept the rewards for not stealing and pay the costs for stealing. It is also agreed that Dr. Hollin will act as judge in any disputes. This agreement will begin on _____ and will finish on _____ . It will be reviewed after one week and minor changes may be made.

Signed _____ (Mum) _____ (Dad)

Signed _____ (Billy) _____ (Tommy)

Witnessed _____ (Clive Hollin)

Table 4.4. Rewards in Contract

---

1. At the end of each day if nothing has been stolen, Billy will go to bed 15 min later than usual (i.e., 9:00 P.M. rather than 8:45 P.M.); Tommy will receive three mask stickers.
2. If there are seven consecutive days without stealing, then Billy and/or Tommy can choose either a trip to the leisure center or a visit to the cinema, paid for by Mum and Dad.
   If there are seven consecutive days without stealing, then Billy and/or Tommy will be allowed to do extra jobs around the house to earn more pocket money.
4. If four consecutive weeks pass without stealing, then Billy and/or Tommy can choose a sporting activity at the leisure center which will be paid for by Mum and Dad.
5. If there is stealing, then any future trips, such as to Grandmas's or with the scouts may be canceled. The possibility of more freedom to go shopping alone and have part-time jobs will be explored.

---

into account the fact that the stealing could go undetected and that there were qualitative differences in the way it might be discovered. These variations are reflected in the costs section—see Table 4.5. The inclusion of social rewards was a deliberate strategy on my part to engineer situations in which the family enjoyed themselves together, rewarding each other for their progress with social activity. In situations where family relationships have become strained, this is to be encouraged for obvious reasons. The linking together of the costs for the two boys (clause 4) was to encourage each to become responsible for the other's behavior. It was also possible to buy back lost rewards by prolonged good behavior. The final page of the contract (not shown) was a record sheet on which each day's progress was recorded.

I was also concerned to undertake some self-instructional training with the boys to counter their apparent impulse to steal. I felt it was

Table 4.5. Costs in Contract

---

1. If stealing happens and the boys tell Mum and Dad: loss of rewards for that day, loss of rewards for that week, loss of reward at the end of the month, visit to caravan will have to be discussed further; also 30 min off bedtime for 1 day, loss of 1 day's pocket money, grounded for 1 day.
2. If caught stealing but admit it: loss of rewards for that day, loss of rewards for that week, loss of reward at end of the month, visit to caravan will have to be discussed further; also 1 hr off bedtime for 2 days, loss of 2 days' pocket money, grounded for 2 days.
3. If found out to be stealing but have not told or have lied: loss of rewards for that day, loss of rewards for that week, loss of reward at end of the month, visit to caravan will have to be discussed further; also 1 hr off bedtime for 4 days, loss of 4 days' pocket money, grounded for 4 days.
4. If Billy or Tommy steal, the one who has *not* stolen will lose his reward for that day.

Note: If stealing happens as in 1 and 2 above (steal and tell or admit it), then it is possible to earn back the monthly reward by an extra 14 consecutive days without stealing after the period of the contract.

---

important to look at changing self-statements at the time of deciding to steal and at subsequent statements depending on behavior. However, the boys were resistant to this suggestion, saying that they would stop. We agreed not to do the individual work, but that this decision would be reviewed in light of their progress.

Progress. The contract was extremely smooth-running; there were no major disputes, and all concerned took matters seriously. There was a minor dispute when the parents attempted to make another behavior part of the contract and the boys said it was not fair and should not be allowed. They were, of course, quite right: It wasn't, it shouldn't, and their objection was sustained. The parents had the grace to accept this decision—an important acceptance that maintained the integrity of the contract.

During the first month of the contract Tommy stole once, and Billy not at all. Tommy stole and did not tell, so clause 3 (Table 4.4) was used. The loss of rewards was hard in itself and his brother's displeasure an unpleasant experience, but seeing his brother rewarded was perhaps the most unpleasant of all. (It should be noted that clause 3 says that rewards are still available on a daily and weekly basis after the loss of one week's rewards—thus *all* is not lost, which would be counterproductive.) During the following month Billy stole once but owned up (clause 2, Table 4.4). After a third month with no reported stealing the parents and boys were eager to stop the intervention. Although I would have preferred another month with the contract, they were resistant to this and had I not agreed I think they might well have ended things themselves. We compromised with an initial weekly telephone call, soon to be a monthly call. There was more stealing, by Billy, but the parents said they had managed it properly as the contract had shown them. Indeed, my conversations with the parents suggested that they had modified their style of parenting to concentrate more on behavioral strategies rather than on trying to instill verbally and physically a moral sense of right and wrong in the boys.

At the time of writing, I had corresponded with the family only 8 weeks ago, about a year after the intervention. They said all was well and that the boys were no longer stealing. In terms of a follow-up this is not all it might be. There was no contact with the boys, for example, and even had there been it is uncertain whether they would be reliable. (I think they would, but thinking is not knowing.) Although the indications are of a successful intervention, the nature of the behavior dictates that the possibility must be admitted that the boys have devised extremely successful strategies to avoid detection. One's clinical judgment is for the former outcome, although the latter cannot be denied.

Five
Outcome and Evaluation

In the previous two chapters note was made of the success or other outcome of individual studies. In this chapter the focus shifts to give a more expansive view of the field in considering the broad conclusions that can be drawn from research on cognitive-behavioral interventions with young offenders. However, before moving to this discussion, a quotation from Roberts (1987) serves to put matters in perspective: "In view of the millions of dollars expended each year to protect society, care for, and rehabilitate juvenile offenders, it is astonishing that so few systematic research and follow-up studies have been conducted by juvenile justice agencies" (p. 44). Similar sentiments have been expressed elsewhere; for example, in their review of behavioral approaches to delinquency, Blakely and Davidson (1984) comment that "after twenty years of research, it is unfortunate that delinquent behavior is assessed directly in less than half of the available research" (p. 261). The immediate point to be drawn from comments such as these is that the research is but a sample, probably very small and highly biased, of the rehabilitative work taking place every day of the week, week in and week out. The true success of rehabilitative work with young offenders will never be known. The reasons why so little research takes place and the biases that exist will be discussed presently. The starting point is the design and analysis of the research.

EVALUATION STRATEGIES
Experimental Design

In testing the effectiveness of any intervention, the experimental clinician must first select a research design. In behavioral and cognitive-behavioral studies two styles of design have proved popular: the control group design and the single-case study.

Group Designs. With this type of experimental design the researcher selects a group of varying size as an experimental group of young offenders who are to be involved in the intervention. The researcher then selects another group of young offenders to act as a control group. The control group may be involved in another type or style of treatment, as in a *comparison control;* there may be a delay before the delivery of treatment, as in a *waiting list control;* the intervention may be nebulous and unfocused, consisting only of contact with the experimenter without any attempt at intervention, as in a *placebo control;* or intervention may not be offered at all, as in a *no-treatment control.* The assembling of control groups presents a number of problems. In order to compare experimental and control groups meaningfully, it is necessary to form groups that are as homogeneous as possible. In the case of young offenders this may mean matching across a range of variables such as age, sex, race, socioeconomic standing, criminal history, offense type, family background, and other psychological and demographic variables. In practical terms, the more variables to be matched, the larger the population required to form the groups. Indeed, if the point is taken to its logical conclusion, it begins to look doubtful whether even two individuals might be described as homogeneous (Kiesler, 1966)—a point that is hardly startling to those who adopt a cognitive-behavioral perspective stressing the uniqueness of each individual's learning history. It is certainly my experience that referrals do not arrive in matched samples; nor is it always easy to pluck groups ready for treatment even from a large population. It is possible to counter between-group differences, to some extent at least, by more sophisticated statistical analysis which, of course, requires more elaborate skills on the part of the researcher.

A second difficulty lies in the statistical management of the data from group comparison designs. The statistical methods traditionally used with such designs—*t* tests, analysis of variance, multiple regression, and so forth—rely on averaging the data and then comparing across groups. From a clinical perspective the principal difficulty with this type of data management lies in the obscuring of individual differences in the clinical outcome *within* groups in order to compare across groups. Thus within a treatment group some individuals may show marked improvement, others may show little change, and some may deteriorate; when averaged this can give only a weak clinical effect, which may or may not be significantly greater than the averaged changes in the control group. The outcome is that sensitive clinical information concerning within-subject variability is lost. When the issue is turned around, it can also be seen that there are problems in generalizing the findings from a carefully selected homogeneous group to other individuals from the same broad population. Barlow and Hersen (1984) offer a succinct statement on treatment versus no-treatment control group studies:

> This arrangement, which has characterized much clinical and educational research, suffers for two reasons: (1) To the extent that the "available" clients are not a random sample, one cannot generalize to the population; and (2) to the extent that the group is heterogeneous on any of a number of characteristics, one cannot make statements about the individual. The only statement that can be made concerns the average response of a group with a particular makeup which, unfortunately, is unlikely to be duplicated again (p. 55).

Finally, and perhaps most importantly, there are ethical considerations involved in the use of control groups. The immediate reaction to withholding treatment is rightly one of concern, but matters are not so simple. Concern about withholding treatment is based on the unfounded, and even illogical, assumption that intervention is going to achieve something significant. It may well do nothing of the sort, and the control group will have benefited by *not* being involved (e.g., McCord, 1978). Nonetheless, there are few clinicians who feel comfortable about withholding treatment, even for a limited period as in the case of a waiting list control. The combination of clinical, experimental, and ethical difficulties has over the past decade led to a significant rise in the use of single-case studies.

Single-case Designs. The case study methodology has a traditional place in psychotherapeutic literature, being the main vehicle of expression of many of the most celebrated therapists from Freud onward. In one of those parallels that give occasion for thought, the need for a methodology based on a single subject was voiced by the emerging experimental behavior analysis. B. F. Skinner was, of course, foremost in this development: As early as 1938, Skinner and his colleagues were developing a single-case study methodology based on repeated measurements with the same individual. With the advent of behavior therapy in the 1960s, the methods of the (mainly animal) experimental behavior analysts were borrowed and modified to inform *applied behavior analysis.* The advent of applied behavior analysis sowed the seeds for a method of treatment evaluation, based on a single-case design, which has now reached a point of considerable sophistication (Barlow & Hersen, 1984).

The general strategy in single-case design begins with an initial period of assessment involving repeated measurement of an individual's behavior. This initial period is the *baseline,* generally referred to as the A phase of the design; as noted previously, the behavior can assume a variety of curves during the baseline period (see chapter 3). Although several variables may be monitored during the baseline period (multiple baseline), the intervention focuses on one behavior at a time. The intervention phase is the B phase, creating an A-B design; in multiple-baseline designs each variable is treated in turn during the B phase. It is also assumed that the method of intervention remains constant during the treatment phase. The final stage is withdrawal of the intervention, so returning to a no-treatment condition, resulting in an A-B-A design. The second A phase allows the clinician to determine whether the gains made during treatment have been maintained over time. Should this not be the case, then a second treatment phase may be initiated, producing an A-B-A-B design. There are many variations on this basic model, including the introduction of two (or more) different types of treatment strategies (i.e., A-B-C-A) or a gradual withdrawal of treatment (e.g., A-B'-B''-B'''-A) by, say, changing schedules of reinforcement in a token economy. A range of statistical techniques are available for use with single-case designs, from familiar t tests to complex time-series analyses. A number of simplified time-series analyses have been formulated that are of particular value to clinicians (Tyron, 1982).

While single-case design is ideally suited for clinical purposes, like group designs it is not without its limitations. If there is a problem in generalizing from the group to the individual, then the converse is also the case. Thus in order to advance both theory and practice it is necessary to aim for clinical replication of results. This can be achieved by accumulating a series of single-case studies in which exact, direct replication might be the goal or in which systematic alterations are planned to study variations in, say, intervention, setting, or client behavior.

The literature on cognitive-behavioral intervention with young offenders is dominated by group designs involving substantial numbers of young people in treatment and control groups of different types. In light of the points made above, how confident can we be about the generalizability of the outcome literature? Although conducted with young offenders, how homogeneous is that population? My opinion is that, as in any other group, there is marked heterogeneity across the young offender population, both in terms of demographic and psychological variables. Although this does not negate the impact of the studies reviewed in chapters 3 and 4, it makes it necessary to consider very carefully what might and might not have worked with young offenders. There are some individual case studies involving young offenders, but to my knowledge there is no series of replication studies. In a seminal paper, Emery and Marholin (1977) lament the low frequency of individualized interventions with delinquents which, they suggest, "is contrary to the basic tenet of a behavioral analysis approach: Treat an individual by first conducting a thorough functional analysis" (p. 866).

Experimental Measures

Clinical Variables. As is evident from the research discussed in chapters 3 and 4, outcome studies have utilized a wide range of measures: cognitive variables such as locus of control and problem-solving ability, academic performance as measured by school attendance and examination performance, institutional behavior, social skills, token economy points, and so on. In terms of clinical outcome such measures make sense as dependent variables to gauge the success or other results of the intervention. However, the studies are being carried out with *young offenders.* What relevance do these measures have with offending as the focus of concern? Emery and Marholin (1977) suggested that the literature is dominated by a strategy based on "targeting behaviors that are believed to be incompatible with delinquency" (p. 867). This strategy contains two related assumptions: that the target behavior is functionally related to the offending and that changing the target behavior will in turn change the offending.

Establishing a functional relationship between the target behavior and the offending is an empirical concern. Although young offenders may be shown to be different on average from nonoffenders on, say, measures of academic attainment, it is an inferential leap to suppose that poor academic performance *causes* offending. There is, for example, limited empirical evidence to suggest that young offenders are less socially skilled than nonoffenders, but there is no such evidence to support or refute the assumption that poor social skills are functionally related to criminal behavior. As Gaffney and McFall (1981) observe, "Although the data show a relationship between a lack of competence in social situations and delinquent behavior, the research does not provide evidence that delinquency is caused by a lack of social skills" (p. 967). The relationship between the referral problem (i.e., offending) and the target behavior in the intervention does not appear to concern most researchers. Emery and Marholin (1977) suggest that less than one-third of the studies they reviewed established a case for relating referral and target behaviors. On the other hand, it is difficult to see how a functional relationship between a clinical behavior and a criminal behavior can be shown on a grand scale. The range of variables in real life is too large to allow such functional relationships to be expressed with confidence. Although it might be apparent in some individual cases that there is a functional relationship between offending behavior and clinical behavior, this is far removed from a theory of criminal behavior in which the clinical target is given the status of a universal cause of the criminal behavior and thereby becomes an automatic focus for intervention. To continue with the social skills example, social skills deficits and youth crime *may* be associated, and the link may be a direct one such that the social skills deficits cause the offending. It is also possible (and more likely as a generalization) that both skills deficits and offending are products of a myriad of other factors such as social class, parenting, and education.

The position could be taken that clinical efficacy provides a solution: If offending is functionally related to, say, social skills deficits, then the modification of skills levels will be reflected in a change in offending. It is difficult to progress further with this argument for two reasons: The majority of studies, across a range of target behaviors, are concerned only with clinical efficacy, and their success or failure is based upon a change in clinical measures. It is simply not known in the majority of cases whether the intervention curtails offending. (It strikes me that the cognitive-behavioral literature on young offenders is particularly vulnerable to this criticism.) In addition, as the major reviews indicate with monotonous regularity, there is little evidence that behavioral intervention has any systematic impact on offending (e.g., Blakely & Davidson, 1984; Burchard & Lane, 1982). Although the issue will be returned to in due course, it is important to note the use here of the term *systematic*. I am *not* advocating a "nothing works" position, which is clearly not the case (e.g., Gendreau & Ross, 1979). The conclusion to be reached is that at present the weight of clinical evidence is too light to inform criminology and so elevate clinical behavior to a causal status in criminological theory.

If none of the above is revolutionary in its content, why are programs continually designed to modify clinical targets in young offender populations? Blakely and Davidson (1984) make a salient point: "A great deal of importance was attached to targeting academic, prosocial, and within-treatment program behaviors. The hope was that by targeting such behaviors directly, the future incidence of unlawful behavior would be reduced. In other words temporal, setting, and behavioral generalization were hypothesized in suggesting that behavioral procedures would affect delinquency rates" (p. 261). The notion of criminal behavior as a measure of generalization of clinical targets is an important one and not without problems.

The tactic of employing criminal behavior as a measure of generalization of cognitive-behavioral (or, indeed, any other) intervention has been discussed in detail by Hollin and Henderson (1984). Like Blakely and Davidson, they suggest that the concept of generalization is a key to understanding the problems associated with using criminological variables as a measure of clinical efficacy. Following Craighead, Kazdin, and Mahoney (1976), a distinction can be made between stimulus and response generalization. *Stimulus generalization* is defined as the transfer of a trained response to situations other than those in which training has taken place. *Response generalization*, on the other hand, is said to occur when changing one response influences other responses in the individual's repertoire of behaviors. Thus, for example, if a young offender is trained to improve his or her conversational skills and this improvement is observed outside of training, say in talking with peers or parents, then stimulus generalization has occurred. However, to then measure criminal behavior following conversational skills training is to assume implicitly that response generalization will occur, that modifying one class of response, conversational skills, will influence another class of responding, criminal behavior. Perhaps a case might be made for such an association between conversation skills and offending, but this would have to be empirically justified. The point has been made that this is seldom attempted and so, in Blakely and Davidson's words, clinicians are left "hoping" for success with young offenders.

Criminological Variables. Problems of generalization aside, the use of criminological measures poses a particular set of issues for the clinician. Criminological data can be gathered in a variety of ways: self-report, official police cautions, reconviction, time until reconviction, and type of offense. There are difficulties with both official and self-report measures of offending (see chapter 1). Braukmann and Fixsen (1975) have strong views on the use of official measures: "Recidivism does not provide a sensitive measure of new law-violating behavior. To the contrary, it is a better measure of the court's behavior than of the youth's: it is an all-or-nothing measure that provides no differential qualitative feedback on youthful behavior after treatment" (p. 193).

The point is illustrated by two previously discussed studies. Spence and Marzillier (1981) used both official and self-report measures of offending following social skills training with young offenders. They found that "the most noticeable finding was the large discrepancy between the number of police convictions . . . and the number of offenses reported by the boys" (p. 362). The young offenders who had participated in social skills training had the lowest frequency of official convictions but the largest number of self-reported offenses. Davidson et al. (1987) similarly found that a diversion program produced lower rates of recidivism as measured by official indexes such as police offenses and court petitions, however, "self-report delinquency data failed to show any effects. Lack of evidence of treatment effects on self-reported delinquency was consistent with previous findings" (p. 73).

We are left with a dilemma: These (as have other) interventions satisfactorily achieved clinical targets, they reduced police and court contact, but they had no effect at all on the rate of offending. Success or failure?

Thus far criminological measures have been discussed within the context of response generalization as behaviors to be influenced by modifying individual skills, academic performance, and so on. However, there are studies that were concerned directly with offense behavior and so in which the measures of offending could justifiably be claimed as measures of stimulus generalization. This is a step in the right direction, but it raises a new set of assumptions. The use of cognitive-behavior interventions with young offenders carries with it the assumption that modifying the individual's behavior will reduce the offending, that is, that offending is to be accounted for in terms of individual factors. Such a position is at odds with a great deal of contemporary criminological theory in which stress is laid on social, economic, and political forces. From a behavioral perspective this point makes sense: The individual is seen as interacting with his or her environment, each influencing the other in a reciprocal fashion. To modify the individual is therefore to modify only part—how large a part might be debated—of the system. Realistic attempts to modify criminal behavior must strive to change the environment as well as the individual.

Follow-up. The most crucial test of the value of any intervention lies in its ability to produce long-term change. A return to baseline conditions within a week of terminating the intervention is not in anyone's best interests. If an intervention produces change, then the change must be durable. However, it is difficult to say what might be expected at follow-up: the complete elimination of offending? More modestly, a delay before committing the next offense? Perhaps even a change in the type of offense? Is it realistic to expect interventions to have an effect after 5 years? With respect to ethical issues, is it justifiable to continue to follow up young offenders for years after treatment? Alternatively, can clinical researchers afford not to collect long-term follow-up data to determine what intervention strategies are successful—what factors facilitate generalization of treatment gains?

As the reviews note time and time again, the literature is not well-served in terms of follow-up data after cognitive-behavioral and behavioral interventions with young offenders. Emery and Marholin (1977) have little doubt why this is so:

> Perhaps the reason that the literature fails to report adequate, long-term, follow-up data may be found by analyzing the contingencies on the experimental clinician. Because most researchers produce frequent permanent products (articles, chapters, books) in order to receive reinforcement in the form of raises, tenure, social acknowledgement by peers, editorships, and job offers, they are likely to avoid any delay in terminating a particular research effort, especially if the delay is as long as the 1 or 2 years often required to collect adequate follow-up data (p. 869).

Without wishing to deny the force of this statement, it is also true that most experimental clinicians experience other contingencies. A personal example illustrates the point. In 1981 my colleague Monika Henderson and I reported a study on social skills training with delinquents (Hollin & Henderson, 1981). We planned a follow-up which did not come to fruition, and we recalled why in a later paper (Hollin & Henderson, 1984):

> When contemplating a follow-up to our original study . . . we found our study population was scattered over the whole of the British Isles. The financial expense involved in visiting each individual to gather data would have been enormous; and the cost in time would also have been expensive; permission to leave other duties would have had to be obtained, further clinical work set aside (p. 338).

In other words we were defeated by time and lack of money. We did, of course, have one means of follow-up at our disposal, which was official recording of recidivism. However, as argued above, we had little reason to collect these data: We had not conducted the intervention to stop offending, but rather to increase the social skills of a group of young offenders with skills deficits. We took the view, elaborated in our 1984 publication, that criminological variables as a measure of clinical efficacy are unwarranted both theoretically and politically—theoretically because there is no ground for assuming that increasing social skills reduces offending, and politically because the very use of such criminological measures raises expectations that the intervention can reduce criminal behavior. Research that then fails to realize these false expectations fuels the "failure of treatment" argument. Indeed, it became the policy of the last department where I worked to make a disclaimer for criminological effectiveness of clinical intervention in instances where we felt no good case could be made:

> We have no long-term data available and will make no effort to collect any. While there are excellent theoretical grounds for gathering such information, the practical and financial constraints are prohibitive. Reconviction rates will be readily available, but are of doubtful worth as an assessment of behavioral training (Hollin et al., 1986, p. 298).

In summary, the picture is at best mixed: A great deal of treatment is simply not evaluated, and there are fundamental problems with the literature. Blakely and Davidson (1984) conclude:

> Less than half the studies reviewed used a sample of reasonable size, unbiased data collection, multiple outcome measures, a systematic variation of treatment, or appropriate control groups or reversal procedures. While the pattern of results reported remains positive the credibility of the methodology upon which the positive results are based remains surely lacking on major dimensions (p. 266).

This picture is blurred even further if treatment integrity is considered. The concept of *treatment integrity* refers to the extent to which the treatment is delivered as planned. As any clinician will testify, when treatment delivery takes place through a third party—a staff member, a coworker, a parent—there may be discrepancies between the intended treatment and the treatment that actually takes place. In the majority of published studies treatment integrity is assumed, although there is little justification for this. Monitoring of treatment integrity is possible as shown by, for example, Davidson et al. (1987). Allied with treatment integrity is the notion of *strength* of treatment. Even when treatment integrity is assumed, treatments can vary in intensity, duration, focus, and quality of delivery. Again this is not well considered in the experimental literature, although it has been shown to be a straightforward experimental task (e.g., Hollin & Courtney, 1983).

With the limitations of research, treatment integrity, and treatment strength in mind, we can move to a discussion of the philosophy that when it comes to the treatment of offenders, nothing works.

NOTHING WORKS

A number of reviews on the effects of treatment (of all types) have suggested that clinical intervention does not always lead to reduced recidivism (Bailey, 1966; Brody, 1976; Rutter & Giller, 1983). The ambiguity in the clinical outcome studies has been used in some quarters, both in the United Kingdom and in the United States, to fuel the doctrine maintaining that "nothing works"; that is, any attempt at rehabilitation is doomed to failure. In a highly influential paper, Martinson (1974) argued that only a small proportion of outcome studies indicated any efficacy of clinical intervention, and of those that did, sampling and methodological errors could explain the successes. This research is often quoted by those in favor of therapeutic nihilism, and so a recent reexamination of Martinson's data by Thornton (1987) is of particular interest. From the same source that Martinson used, a review of 231 studies by Lipton, Martinson, and Wilks (1975), Thornton extracted studies based on three criteria: (a) the use of recidivism as an outcome variable, (b) a research design involving either random allocation to conditions or matching across conditions, (c) a level of methodological sophistication acceptable by criteria defined by Lipton et al. Thornton found that of the 231 studies, only 38 satisfied all three criteria. The majority (34) involved a comparison between psychological therapies, such as counseling and psychotherapy, and an untreated control group. As Thornton notes, the small number of acceptable studies immediately limits the data base from which any conclusions can be drawn, and the subject matter of the studies allows no conclusions to be made about other forms of treatment based, for example, on vocational training, behavior modification, or cognitive development therapies. In examining the outcome of these 34 studies, Thornton found that 16 studies showed a significant advantage following treatment, 17 studies showed no significant difference between treated offenders and controls, and 1 study showed a significant disadvantage following treatment. Concluding his discussion of this reanalysis, Thornton states:

> Either the catalogue of studies on which Martinson based his assertions may properly be read as indicating that psychological therapy can have positive effects on recidivism, or it can be read as indicating that no conclusion can safely be drawn. The one interpretation that is not acceptable is that it has been shown that "Nothing Works" (p. 188).

The spirit of Thornton's work is to be found in other reviews (e.g., Gendreau & Ross, 1979), leading to the position that clinical intervention works with some offenders some of the time. The major difficulty, from a clinical perspective, is to distill the effective ingredients of treatment programs to devise interventions with a consistently high success rate. To a certain extent this was a technical problem, as it required reviewers to extract the significant ingredients of interventions "by hand," so to speak. However, recent advances in statistics have led to development of the technique of *meta-analysis*. There are two meta-analyses of relevance in the present context, and each will be discussed in turn following a brief discussion of the technique of meta-analysis.

Although previous attempts to integrate the literature on a given topic used strategies such as "vote taking" and combined probabilities, meta-analysis seeks to bring specificity, standardization, and replication to literature reviews. The technique, as proposed by Hunter, Schmidt, and Jackson (1982) and Glass, McGaw, and Smith (1981), is based on the principle of converting results from different studies to a common metric. Garrett (1985) explains:

> The effect size *(ES)* is the "statistic" that is used in meta-analysis to estimate the amount that a treatment group differs from a control group following treatment. In its most basic form the *ES* is the mean of the treatment group minus the mean of the control group divided by the standard deviation of the control group [$(X_E - X_C)/S.D._C$]. *ES*s can also be estimated from a number of other data elements, including t statistics, F statistics, chi square, correlation coefficients, and percent improved (p. 289).

Thus it is possible to code the various characteristics of a large number of studies and calculate their *ES* for various outcome measures, producing an overall picture of treatment efficacy. The two meta-analyses of direct relevance here were performed on studies involving residential treatment of young offenders (Garrett, 1985) and community-based interventions with young offenders (Gottschalk, Davidson, Gensheimer, & Mayer, 1987).

Residential Treatment

In her meta-analysis of the effects of residential treatment of adjudicated young offenders, Garrett (1985) incorporated over 100 studies. These studies were selected according to four criteria: (a) The study was completed between 1960 and 1983; (b) the treatment took place in an institution or residential setting; (c) the subjects were adjudicated young offenders aged 21 years or younger; (d) the study incorporated a control procedure in its design. A grand total of 111 studies satisfied these criteria. Garrett subdivided them into two groups of "rigorous" and "less rigorous" design, with 52% of the studies in the former category and 48% in the latter. A total of 13,055 young offenders were involved, of average age 15.8 years, with most studies (85) reporting results for males only. With regard to the type of intervention, contingency management techniques were the most common (21.5% of studies), then group techniques (16.5%), and then cognitive-behavioral intervention (14.0%). Most studies utilized a range of outcome measures: Psychological adjustment was the most frequently used (31% of studies), followed by institutional adjustment (21.2% of studies), with 17.6% of studies including recidivism as a measure of effectiveness.

The first step in the analysis was to calculate an overall effect size, as Garrett explains: "The overall average *ES* for all studies was + .37. This means that, across treatments, settings, offender types, and outcome measures, the treated group performed, on the average, at a level of + .37 standard deviations above the level of the untreated group, the group that received only the regular institutional program" (p. 293). What is of interest, of course, is how the *ES* varies according to variables such as type of treatment, outcome measure, and so on. The first comparison is telling: The 58 studies of more rigorous design gave an average *ES* of .24, while the 53 less rigorous studies yielded an average *ES* of .65. In other words, the better designed studies give less magnitude of effect of treatment. As Garrett points out, this does not mean that the results from the less rigorous studies should be dismissed, rather that the overall results must be treated with caution.

The treatment programs were divided into four types: psychodynamic; behavioral, including contingency management, cognitive-behavioral, guided group interaction and/or positive peer culture, and milieu; life skills, including academic and vocational training; and "other," such as music therapy and megavitamin treatment. Although the present concern is with the findings within the behavioral category, it is of interest to note that in comparing across categories the behavioral studies effected the greatest change (ES = .63), followed by life skills (ES = .31) and psychodynamic (ES = .17). The picture changes when experimental rigor is considered: Within the behavioral category the less rigorous studies showed an ES of .86 compared to .30 for the more rigorous studies. As Quay (1987) has also commented, some of the categorization seems unfortunate, especially the grouping of guided group interaction and/or positive peer culture and milieu with behavioral techniques. If the figures are extracted for the more traditional behavioral interventions, contingency management produces an ES of .86 (.23 for the more rigorous studies, 1.00 for the less rigorous). The ES of .86 for contingency management is the highest across all specific intervention procedures; with an ES of .58 for the cognitive-behavioral interventions. For the more rigorous studies only, family intervention produced the highest ES (.86), but this comparison involved only two studies.

The effectiveness of the interventions varied, as might be expected, according to the outcome measure; overall, intervention had the greatest influence on academic improvement (ES = .78). Across all studies there was a positive effect with regard to reducing recidivism (ES = .13). Looking at only the more rigorous studies, the effect on recidivism falls slightly (ES = .10) (for these studies the greatest effect was on community adjustment, ES = .72). For the behavioral interventions the effect on recidivism was larger than the average of .13, with an ES of .18. However, if the behavioral studies are separated according to experimental rigor, then for recidivism with the more rigorous studies the ES is −.08 compared to .36 for the less rigorous studies. In other words, the more rigorously designed studies on behavioral intervention (n = 6) fail to show any effect on recidivism. Having mentioned this, the reservations expressed above about the selection of studies for inclusion in the behavioral category should be restated. In regard to specific techniques, contingency management studies showed an ES of .25 on recidivism, and cognitive-behavioral intervention an ES of .24. Guided group interaction, included in the behavioral category, showed an ES of −.07 for recidivism.

On other outcome measures the behavioral interventions showed strong effects on all measures except vocational adjustment, although this was based on only one study. This general picture was maintained for the more rigorous studies. A summary of the treatment effects for contingency management and cognitive-behavioral interventions is shown in Table 5.1.

In discussing the general points arising from her analysis, Garrett suggests that "perhaps the most interesting finding with respect to specific treatments was that a cognitive-behavioral approach, a relatively

Table 5.1. Average Effect Sizes for Contingency Management and Cognitive Behavioral Studies (after Garrett, 1985)

Outcome Measure	Contingency Management	CBM
Recidivism	.25	.24
	(22/10)	(7/2)
Institutional adjustment	1.19	.55
	(6/6)	(16/12)
Psychological adjustment	1.14	.62
	(9/8)	(24/14)
Community adjustment	.63	—
	(1/1)	
Academic improvement	1.25	1.77
	(20/12)	(3/3)
Vocational adjustment	—	-.23
		(1/1)

Note: The first number in parentheses is the number of effect sizes upon which the average is based; the second is the number of studies.

recent development, seems to be more successful than any other, even in the more rigorous studies" (p. 304).

Community-Based Treatment

Gottschalk et al. (1987) performed an analysis similar to Garrett's, focusing on studies based in the community. A total of 163 studies were included in the meta-analysis, coded across a range of dimensions such as intervention components and methodology. The studies had been performed between 1967 and 1983, mostly with adjudicated young offenders (74% of studies) who were mostly males (85%) averaging 14.6 years of age. The meta-analysis included over 11,000 young offenders. Behavioral interventions were the most common (28% of studies), using a range of techniques such as positive reinforcement (27%), modeling and/or role-playing (22%), contracting (19%), and a token economy (16%). Cognitive therapy accounted for only 2% of studies, whereas 52% of the interventions concerned some type of diversion from the court system.

To produce an interesting comparison with the meta-analysis, Gottschalk et al. first generated data using the traditional method of rating the effectiveness of a study based on the inspection of each individual set of findings. This exercise revealed that both their own ratings and those of the studies' authors suggested that most interventions have either a positive effect or a null effect, negative effects are rare. This pattern of ratings holds across a range of outcome measures including recidivism but not self-reported delinquency.

The meta-analysis itself was reported in a style different from Garrett's. The studies were subdivided according to experimental design: One group consisted of studies using a pre-post design with the same sample of young offenders, and the second an experimental-versus-control group design. The studies were compared in the meta-analysis for overall effectiveness, recidivism, behavioral outcome, and attitudinal outcome. The ES values, weighted for sample size, are shown in Table 5.2.

It is noticeable that for three of the measures, the ES is greater with a pre-post design. Gottschalk et al. believe that this may reflect the offenders' maturation over the time taken to complete the research rather than treatment effects, suggesting that the experimental-control design may give a more realistic estimate. It might also be noted that recidivism showed a very small ES, similar to that found by Garrett. Although not presenting data for ES according to type of intervention, Gottschalk et al. did find that characteristics of the young offender were related to the ES. Nonadjudicated young offenders were more likely to be successful than adjudicated offenders; the more male offenders in the sample, the greater the chances of a higher ES. However, overall the results of the meta-analysis were not as positive as the initial ratings might have led one to expect.

It is evident that meta-analysis studies furnish a great deal of information in a systematic manner. However, a number of points should be made. Garrett comments that meta-analysis does not answer questions of statistical significance but shows whether there is positive change—"whether that amount of change merits the energy, expense, and time involved in a decision that must be based on social and policy considerations rather than statistical significance" (p. 304). On the other hand, Gottschalk et al. reported further statistical calculations leading them to suggest that their meta-analysis broadly failed to allow the rejection of a null hypothesis of no treatment effect. However, as they caution, prudence is required in partitioning statistical significance, effect size, and clinical change.

Table 5.2. Effect Sizes in Community-Based Interventions (after Gottschalk et al., 1987)

	Pre-Post Design	Experimental/Control Design
Overall effectiveness	.279[a]	.232
Recidivism	− .081	.218
Behavioral outcomes	.697	.111
Attitudinal outcomes	.495	.588

[a]Weighted mean effect size.

Meta-analysis does not take treatment integrity into account—it simply deals with treatment outcome. The *ES* may be produced by treatments of high or low integrity or by treatments of high or low power in terms of intensity and length; the outcome figures are treated in the same manner regardless of the process. Indeed, as both studies showed, correcting for even simple factors such as strength or type of design and number of subjects produced marked differences in the *ES*. What would happen if the *ES* were weighted for treatment power and integrity? Having said this, the *ES* for recidivism was modest in most cases but was positive. This seems to support those who oppose the nothing works position. It was also notable that few negative effects were reported, reflecting either the universal benefits of intervention or some filtering in the selection of studies for publication. In conclusion, meta-analyses are encouraging rather than negative; to place this in perspective a note of caution follows.

Potential Negative Outcomes

The American Cambridge-Somerville Youth Study (Powers & Witmar, 1951) provides a focus for a discussion of potential negative effects of treatment. Young males living in a high-delinquency area were recommended to a community program by welfare agencies, churches, and the police. When a recommendation was accepted, the young person was randomly assigned to either a treatment or a no-treatment group. Starting in 1939, counselors were assigned to the family to which each young male belonged, visiting the home on average twice a month. In addition, families were able to call for assistance when they thought it necessary. For the treatment group, the intervention included academic teaching, medical and psychiatric care, counseling, and availability of various community programs. The treatment lasted for between 2 and 8 years. The control group simply provided information about themselves. The most recent follow-up traced over 500 men who had participated in the study (McCord, 1978). Although those in the treatment group expressed fond memories of the project and remembered their counselors with affection, McCord's follow-up found no difference in the rate of offending, either as juveniles or adults, in the treatment and the control groups. Indeed, McCord notes that "unexpectedly, however, a higher proportion of criminals from the treatment group than of criminals from the control group committed more than one crime" (p. 286). Yet further, McCord lists a string of seven *adverse* effects of treatment, including more signs of mental illness, more evidence of alcoholism, and even a tendency to die at a younger age. McCord suggests that because the counselors' social values differed from those of the family with which they became involved, internal conflicts may have developed in those treated and so produced the later disorders; or alternatively, the intervention may have fostered a dependency on outside assistance that caused problems when assistance was discontinued. McCord concludes with the stark statement: "Intervention programs risk damaging the individuals they are designed to assist" (p. 289).

More recently a similar study has been reported by Palamara, Cullen, and Gersten (1986). Palamara et al. were concerned with assessing the effect of both police and mental health intervention on juvenile deviance. They conducted a longitudinal study on the impact of formal intervention on young people, using measures of both offending and psychological and psychophysiological functioning. From an original sample of 1,034 youths a follow-up sample of 732 was contacted 5 years later. Interview data were gathered at both initial and follow-up points on referral to mental health services (school counselors, psychologists, social workers, and psychiatrists), and a search of police records established those in the sample who had experienced police intervention. A sophisticated analysis revealed that "both police and mental health intervention increase subsequent levels of delinquent behavior . . . police-mental health intervention has an interaction effect, with those youths subjected to both modes of reaction having the highest levels of subsequent delinquency" (p. 99). Palamara et al. suggest that these results can best be understood in terms of labeling theory: Intervention negatively affects an individual, reinforcing the label "bad" or "mad" and compounding the very problem it is supposed to be solving. However, Palamara et al. do not dismiss the potential of intervention: Although the overall impact of intervention may be adverse, they suggest that a more refined analysis may reveal that certain types of offenders do profit from particular types of intervention. A similar observation might also be made about McCord's findings. Finally, Palamara et al. place their findings in a broad social context, stating forcefully that their study warns of "the potential danger of the current wave of punitive policies being instituted across the nation" (p. 102). In concluding this overview of outcome, it is important to adopt a sense of perspective, and so we move toward a philosophical position against which to set the outcome studies.

TOWARD A PHILOSOPHY OF TREATMENT

Although part of the debate hinges around the empirical data—behavioral versus cognitive-behavioral, psychodynamic versus behavioral, institution-based versus community-based intervention—at another level the struggle is for a dominant model of crime. A treatment philosophy is often associated with liberal political values, stemming from the belief that individuals can be assisted to overcome and cope with difficulties and ultimately contribute positively to society. This liberal ideal has taken a terrible pounding over the past decade: The ambiguity of the treatment outcome studies has not assisted greatly, but other forces have been at work. The political tone, in both the United Kingdom and the United States, has become more conservative: Bayer (1981) has written of the shattering of the optimism of postwar liberalism and the emergence of the new pessimism of the conservative perspective. Proponents of neoclassical views of crime (based on assumptions of free will and the offender's rational choice in opting to commit crime) offer a quite different perspective on managing crime, a view that removes the need to consider the finer points of individuality by reducing human motivation and behavior to economic terms. Van Den Haag (1982) argues against the notion of rehabilitation in just this way:

> I do not see any relevant difference between dentistry and prostitution or car theft, except that the latter activities do not require a license. . . . The frequency of rape, or of mugging, is essentially determined by the expected comparative net advantage, just as is the rate of dentistry and burglary. The comparative net advantage consists in the satisfaction (produced by the money or by the violative act itself) expected from the crime, less the expected cost of achieving it, compared to the net satisfaction expected from other activities in which the offender has the opportunity to engage. Cost in the main, equals the expected penalty divided by the risk of suffering it (pp. 1026–1027).

Such a position clearly pays little heed to any sophisticated psychological or sociological analysis of crime: Offending is seen principally in the economic terms of costs and benefits. It is not difficult to see where this leads. According to Van Den Haag:

> Our only hope for reducing the burgeoning crime rate lies in decreasing the expected net advantage of committing crimes (compared to lawful activities) by increasing the cost through increasing the expected severity of punishment and the probability of suffering them (p. 1035).

These views, encapsulated in a so-called justice model (Hudson, 1987) have obvious implications for the management of offenders. They dictate a response to crime not in terms of treatment or rehabilitation, but rather in terms of tougher, harsher punishments (*not* in the operant sense). Thus we witness the return of harsh custodial regimes for young offenders, repeated calls for the return of corporal and capital punishment, and the abandonment of rehabilitation in institutions for offenders. Despite the warnings of studies, such as that of Palamara et al. (1986), that *any* intervention needs to be considered carefully and the findings of empirical studies showing that harsh custodial regimes do not influence recidivism (Thornton, Curran, Grayson, & Holloway, 1984), the proponents of the justice model hold sway at present. I find this a bleak scenario, bleak in a humanitarian sense as well as in terms of a successful social response to criminal behavior. However, although fighting a rearguard action, the treatment ideal is not defeated and with the right tactics could yet emerge with honor. In the final chapter an attempt will be made to formulate these tactics, for cognitive-behavioral intervention in particular, on the basis of all the evidence discussed thus far.

Six
Success and Failure

We are now in a position to ask, Is cognitive-behavioral intervention with young offenders a success or a failure? Schrest and Rosenblatt (1987) have succinctly summarized three ways of looking at the issue: "(1) There really is no good way to rehabilitate juvenile offenders; (2) there may be good ways to rehabilitate juvenile offenders, they have just not been found; (3) owing to methodological problems in earlier research, we really don't know much of anything about which approaches to rehabilitation work or don't work" (p. 417). I tend to agree with Schrest and Rosenblatt that the third statement is perhaps the most accurate, although I believe that it is possible to begin to distill the elements of success and failure in cognitive-behavioral intervention from our existing knowledge base. This distillation will, in turn, begin to suggest strategies that can be used to increase the chances of success and decrease the probability of failure.

SUCCESS

Assessment

It is impossible to overstate the importance of assessment as a contributing factor in the success of cognitive-behavioral interventions with young offenders. Assessment should have three broad aims: to identify those young offenders suitable for cognitive-behavioral intervention; to elucidate clinical and criminological targets and any functional relationship between the two; and to facilitate the planning of the intervention. It should be acknowledged at the outset that not all young offenders will be suitable for a treatment-based intervention. To include all young offenders in a program with no selection criteria is surely to inflate the failure rate in terms of both dropout and lack of progress. The difficulty lies in deciding upon the criteria for selection. Perkins (1987) has made

129

some suggestions for treatment decisions with a sex offender population which might inform the present discussion. Perkins suggests two criteria as indicators of suitability for intervention: the offender being able to specify problems and goals to be achieved, and an expressed willingness to participate in the methods used in the particular intervention. The criteria that may indicate that intervention is not the best option, Perkins suggests, are threefold: denial of the offense; attribution of blame for the offense to others, thereby denying that there is anything about one's own behavior that is problematic; and an insistence that there will be no further offending. Clearly some of these points are relevant principally to sex offenders, particularly regarding denial of the offense, but others apply to the majority of offenders. The point regarding willingness to participate is particularly important. The ethics of coercion into treatment must be considered—the clinician must ask if it is right to deliver an intervention if the offender is reluctant or unwilling to participate. Although there is no right or wrong answer to this dilemma, it is incumbent upon the clinician to make clear the contingencies associated with a decision to participate in or to refuse treatment. Indeed, a discussion of these issues might well be a profitable preintervention strategy with all offenders. It is my opinion that when fully informed of the facts, and with ample opportunity for discussion, the offender's right to refuse treatment must be respected. If a view of criminal behavior is taken in which offenders are seen as making a rational choice in deciding to commit a crime (Cornish & Clarke, 1986b), then the same rational choice should be allowed to the offender in making decisions about treatment options. It follows that such a decision should not reap aversive consequences for the offender: A young offender negatively reinforced for participating in treatment is not desirable.

The point has been made throughout that clinical and criminological targets should be clarified at the point of assessment. As discussed in chapter 2, Reid (1982) has provided a listing of the various behavioral excesses and deficits commonly found in young offenders. The assessment should aim to establish the exact parameters of such behaviors, which will differ from young offender to young offender, and then crucially to determine the functional relationship, if any, between clinical and criminological (i.e., offense) behaviors. The assessment techniques should be as many and as varied as possible, administered over as long a period as is practically and ethically feasible, to gain as full an assessment as possible. One of the central tenets of cognitive-behavioral theory is the uniqueness of the individual, and therefore assessment should be conducted on an individual basis. Even given similar behaviors, functional analysis invariably illuminates individual differences.

Program Design and Delivery

> In comparing effective and ineffective programs we noted that all success-
> ful programs were multifaceted. They did not rely on any one intervention
> technique to achieve their effects. Rather, they included a number of dif-
> ferent modalities each of which might be expected to influence some as-
> pects of the offender. Effective programs were complex; not unlike the
> offenders they treated (Ross & Fabiano, 1985, p. 7).

This is perhaps the single most important point to make: The successful
programs are, indeed, complex, multimodal programs. They utilize a
range of techniques and often include members of the young offender's
family.

In terms of techniques, Garrett's (1985) meta-analysis has suggested,
for institutions at least, what the most effective components of a treatment program may be. It is evident that some form of contingency management is beneficial in producing change. As discussed in chapters 3
and 4, both a token economy and contracting are widely used methods
of contingency management for both clinical and criminological target
behaviors. Garrett also suggested that cognitive-behavioral techniques
were to be found in successful programs. A number of techniques were
identified, including interpersonal problem solving, self-control and
self-management training, self-instructional training, anger management, role taking, and moral reasoning development. It was perhaps a
necessary part of the development of these techniques that they were
researched individually, but the need for multimodal training is now
widely recognized. There are two particular examples of such programs
that might serve as models for future developments. Glick and
Goldstein's (1987) *Aggression Replacement Training* is a multimodal program, designed for aggressive and violent young offenders, that utilizes
techniques from skills training and cognitive behavior therapy (see
chapter 3). Ross and Fabiano (1985) have developed a comprehensive
reasoning and rehabilitation (R & R) program. This program is composed of eight discrete elements, each with its own particular training
methods and priorities. The eight elements are social skills, interpersonal problem solving, cognitive style, social perspective taking, critical
reasoning, values, meta-cognition, and self-control. An example of the
detailed techniques associated with an element (there are different techniques for different elements) is shown in Table 6.1. Ross and Fabiano
also present a comprehensive assessment program.

An empirical test of the R & R program (with adult offenders) was
reported by Ross, Fabiano, and Ewles (1988). Ross et al. trained probation officers to deliver the R & R program to 22 offenders. They note
that the program delivery demanded 80 hours of intensive training con-

Table 6.1. Example From a R & R Program
(after Ross & Fabiano, 1985)

Interpersonal Problem Solving
Interpersonal cognitive problem solving skills
Creative thinking
Think labs
Modeling and role playing
Interpreting nonverbal behavior
The promise
The choice
Thinking about thinking
The gentle art of saying no
Problem solving: using your head creatively

ducted with groups of 4 to 6 offenders on probation. In the experimental program, three treatment groups were used, with random assignment to experimental group; the groups were regular probation, regular probation plus life skills training, and regular probation plus cognitive training (i.e., the R & R program). At a 9-month follow-up the recidivism rate was 69.5% in the regular probation group; 47.5% in the life skills group, and 18.1% in the R & R group. One hopes that similar figures could be obtained with young offenders. As Ross et al. conclude, "*Some* programs—when they are applied by well trained staff—can be remarkably effective in offender rehabilitation" (p. 34).

The point made above regarding well-trained staff is an important one. Ross et al. note that the competence of the probation officers in conducting the intervention varied greatly: Some "became rather good trainers," but others were "not suited" for the demands of group cognitive-behavioral training. It is to their credit that Ross et al. were sensitive to this issue and, presumably, took steps to rectify the situation regarding poor trainers. Quay (1987) has commented on the issue of treatment integrity, noting that in one published study "the majority of those responsible for carrying out the treatment were not convinced that it would affect recidivism (the major dependent variable of the study), and the group leaders (not professional counselors) were poorly trained. The treatment was not well implemented (see Quay, 1977)" (p. 246). As Quay (1987) continues, the treatment was not successful and is cited as a "failure of treatment," although one must ask whether it ever really had any chance of success. It is vital to have some knowledge of the strength and integrity of training in order to gauge the value and standing of the intervention. Researchers would do well to follow the example of those few studies (e.g., Davidson et al., 1987) that include a measure of treatment integrity as part of their design.

A final point concerns planning and flexibility of treatment delivery. Effective programs are not designed overnight; they require considerable planning for both content and resources, including trained personnel if necessary. Further, once designed, the program and the trainers require the flexibility to cope with the varying demands and problems different individuals present. The maxim should be that the program fits the client, not that the client fits the program.

FAILURE

An intervention can fail for a number of reasons including poor treatment delivery, poor assessment, and poor design. However, with young offenders the failure may often lie not so much in the quality of treatment delivery as in resistance to treatment. This resistance, as discussed below, can come from a number of sources.

Institutional Resistance

Practitioners working within institutions can face resistance in a number of guises. Many institutions attempt to achieve what, on the face of it, are contradicting goals—custody and punishment versus rehabilitating and caring. There may be staff divisions as to the value of, utility of, and even right to treatment; staff role conflict inherent in the twin roles of jailer and therapist; conflict between different professions as to who should deliver treatment; conflict both between and within professions as to the preferred type of treatment; or a lack of commitment by management to supply the support and resources necessary to run effective treatment programs (Milan, 1987; Repucci & Saunders, 1974). Given these constraints, perhaps most typical of penal institutions, it seems doubtful that effective intervention could ever take place. Yet perhaps it says something about the strength of behavioral techniques that even given these constraints, as Cullen and Seddon (1981) have documented, it is still possible to engineer positive change in incarcerated young offenders.

Alongside the particular problems noted by Cullen and Seddon in achieving the necessary consistency for the successful operation of a token economy, even more fundamental problems can arise. At the most basic level there can be a great deal of confusion over what constitutes a behavioral program. It some cases behavioral techniques are used in the name of treatment as a means of administering punishment (in a nonoperant sense) and to force compliance with institutional rules and thereby to run a trouble-free institution. Further, opposition to behavioral intervention can be detrimental to treatment programs when there is a clash of therapeutic goals. Laws (1974) has described the problems of attempting to run a token economy in an institution with psychodynamically oriented administrators who refused to accept behavioral change as an index of improvement, requiring instead assessment and treatment of intrapsychic processes. Similarly, Schlichter and Horan (1981) concluded their study on the effects of stress inoculation on the anger and aggression of young offenders with a wry comment: "Other staff workers served to undermine the efficacy of the stress inoculation treatment: some modeled aggressive behavior in response to anger provocations. Others operating from a different theoretical perspective encouraged the subjects to experience and express their 'pent-up' anger" (p. 364).

Client Resistance

Resistance to change is well documented in the clinical literature, with all manner of theoretical explanations to account for the phenomenon. The focus of these explanations is typically either on some attribute of the client or on the opportunity for change offered by the therapist. Thus it is commonly held that those most likely to gain from treatment are clients who expect the intervention to be helpful to them, who take some responsibility for changing their own behavior, and who participate actively in the treatment program. The successful therapist is characterized, perhaps in an anecdotal manner, as possessing the facilitative skills of accurate empathy, nonpossessive warmth, and genuineness to allow the client space to grasp the opportunity for change (Truax, 1966). However, recent research suggests a more complex picture. With a sample of parents participating in a program for teaching effective child management procedures, Chamberlain et al. (1984) monitored client resistance according to the client's level of cooperation in treatment. Resistance was assessed by the degree to which he or she avoided topics, showed an unwillingness to follow suggestions, and challenged the therapist's ability. It was found that client resistance varied over time, with maximum resistance occurring at mid-treatment. As might be predicted, more high-resistance than low-resistance families dropped out of treatment, although a higher level of resistance was found in agency-referred rather than self-referred families. It follows that a higher drop-out rate was found among agency-referred families. A moderate and positive correlation was reported between client resistance and therapists' ratings of a successful outcome of the intervention.

Moving to intervention with the young offender, there are a number of points to note from the above discussion. Young offenders may, as a generalization, be characterized as a high-resistance group: Typically they may see little need to modify their behavior, hence are unwilling to take any responsibility for change or even to see intervention as necessary. Even if motivated toward intervention, a view of the world as controlling their actions may lead to low expectations of treatment. According to another of Chamberlain et al.'s findings, by far the majority of young offenders came to the clinician via an agency (usually legal) referral, a good predictor of high resistance. It is not difficult to understand why young offenders may be resistant to treatment. Most clinical intervention is based on the premise of taking away something the client wants removed: a phobia, depression, problems with a difficult child, hallucinations, disturbed eating, and so on. Certainly the taking away may be achieved by constructing new behaviors and replacing the maladaptive behavior with adaptive alternatives, but the aim is in part at least to remove a problem. For many young offenders there is no problem: Their offending, even when accompanied by violence, is something they are good at; it is a skilled behavior that brings tangible and social rewards—not a problem to be removed. It follows that the therapist must have a strong set of arguments as to why the young offender should engage in a process of change. Points for debate may include the likely outcome of further offending, the effect of offending on friends and family, and the effect on victims. It can be a useful exercise to ask the young offender to list the potential positive and negative outcomes of future offending.

IMPROVING SUCCESS: MINIMIZING FAILURE

Institutional Structure

At any time within an institution a number of needs can be identified. Ostapiuk and Westwood (1986) represent these needs as shown in Figure 6.1

The vertical axis has the institution at one pole and the real world at the other pole. For many reasons including legal requirements, protection of the individual, protection of the public, safety of staff and other residents, and the establishment of a safe working environment, the institutional pole of this axis is characterized by security and predictability of routines, in turn producing a highly artificial environment. The opposite end of the axis, the real world, is quite the opposite: It lacks structure, fails to define boundaries, and is unpredictable in many of its events. The horizontal axis separates management needs and client needs. Management needs, reflected in the characteristics of institu-

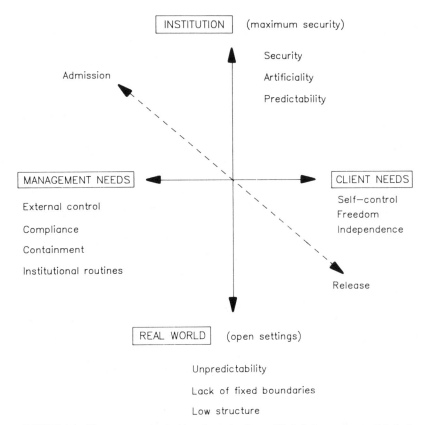

FIGURE 6.1. Client versus institutional needs. From *Clinical Approaches to Criminal Behaviour* (p. 54) edited by C. Hollin and K. Howells, 1986, Leicester, England: British Psychological Society. Reprinted by permission of The British Psychological Society.

tions, must have effective means of control to ensure compliance, containment, and adherence to institutional routines. Client needs, given the ultimate goal of a return to the real world, are characterized by a need for freedom and independence, together with the self-control to manage real-world contingencies.

Ostapiuk and Westwood make the point that at all times the treatment offered must be relevant to both the institution and the individual. Under the pressure of institutional life, the focus can become fixed on the upper left quadrant—institutional and/or management needs—to the neglect of the lower right quadrant—real-world and/or client needs. Moving across the time span from admission to release, Ostapiuk and Westwood suggest that the goal should be that the individual client progresses along the path marked from one quadrant to the next. Thus during the early stages of an individual's institutional placement, some type of system is required to establish control to satisfy management and institutional requirements. A token economy and variations such as points and levels systems have been found to be highly successful as a means of establishing this control. However, to establish external control and then discharge the young offender back into the real world is to throw an unprepared person back into an environment he or she is no more equipped to manage successfully than at admission. Instead, as time passes the strategy should be to gradually shift away from external control and an imposed structure, to greater flexibility and a relaxation of institutional restraints together with encouraging greater freedom and independence. As this progression occurs, individually tailored programs for both clinical and criminological targets should be planned; in seeking to foster self-control and increase adaptive skills and behavior, cognitive-behavioral interventions should be introduced. As release approaches, token economies should be phased out and the individual reinforced for assuming greater and greater responsibility for his or her own behavior. It is important to note that the system should be sufficiently flexible to accommodate individual differences in speed of progress along the path from admission to release.

To enable realistic transition from institution to the community to take place, it is beneficial to establish formal contact between the two environments. This might include work experience programs, social events, and family gatherings—all planned and managed in as structured and systematic a manner as possible to maximize the chances of a reinforcing outcome for the young offender. Burchard and Harrington (1986) developed the system called Transitional Program Analysis (TPA) to facilitate movement from an institution back to the community. TPA was designed for use with a range of client types including young offenders. Adopting the same philosophy as Ostapiuk and Westwood, Burchard and Harrington suggest that progression through the institution should be guided by attempts to reach three types of targets: "declaration targets" such as offense behaviors or institutional violence, "acceleration targets" such as social and self-management skills, and "acquisition targets" such as the employment skills necessary for community adjustment. Systematic monitoring of progress on all three targets informs decision making regarding the young offender's current functioning and so assists in the timing of the individual's release back into the community.

In discussing the implementation of TPA, Burchard and Harrington suggest that target identification will, in turn, lead to developments in the range of options within the institution. The principle, they suggest, should always be the same: "What can we (staff) do to improve the clients' chances of adapting to the new environment?" (p. 31). This acknowledges the most crucial variable in the equation—staff behavior. While, for convenience, staff issues are discussed here under an institutional heading, the points made apply equally to any setting in which treatment delivery is made through another agent.

Staff

When discussing the reasons for program failure, the point was made repeatedly that staff at all levels can do a great deal to counter the effects of any therapeutic endeavor. Although a variety of reasons can be advanced to account for this state of affairs, apportion of blame is not helpful. Burchard and Harrington's philosophy is more constructive. To paraphrase, what can we (clinicians) do to improve the chances of staff adapting to a treatment environment? I propose two broad avenues of approach: One is staff training, and the other is political maneuvering.

Staff Training. Antipathy or hostility among staff to a treatment approach to criminal behavior can arise for reasons such as the lack of any real understanding of why treatment goals are being pursued and why they, as staff, are being asked to follow certain treatment-related routines. In writing about the development of Glenthorne Youth Treatment Centre, Reid (1982) suggests that training was an essential part of staff development, and hence played a major role in service delivery to the center's clients. Reid noted that, at the time of his writing, a course was planned to meet the demands of staff training. This planning bore fruition with the advent of a university-based diploma in social learning theory and practice. This course, to which I was appointed course tutor at its inception in 1982, has subsequently developed in a number of ways—developing me and several others in the process! We have learned a number of lessons that may well be of interest to those contemplating setting up similar staff training programs or courses.

The selection of trainees for the course was guided by two aims: to train across disciplines and to recruit from the outside as well as within Glenthorne Youth Treatment Centre. This strategy was intended to give a broad perspective within each intake, so that the content did not become too inward looking and solely concerned with institutional work. These aims have been achieved in that teachers, nurses, social workers, psychiatrists, volunteers, and psychologists have all successfully completed the diploma program. They have come from a range of settings, from community to security, with a range of client groups, from child conduct disorders to the elderly psychotic. All, however, have a common commitment to working in a behavioral style, using behavioral analysis and behavior therapy in their professional practice. Although this mixing of professional groups has advantages, such as instilling appreciation of the the difficulties and challenges faced by other disciplines involved with other client groups, it did pose one issue that concerned us greatly. In order for the diploma to be recognized as professional training, it was necessary to negotiate with a number of professional bodies, such as The British Psychological Society on behalf of psychologists. This has led us to develop political, negotiating, and diplomatic skills previously undreamed of. It is also true to say that this has led to a number of significant developments, for the better, in the management and content of the course.

The diploma program is a part-time course, meeting one day per week and running for a full calendar year. Trainees are required to secure in advance agreement from their employers that they will be allowed to practice behavioral intervention at their places of work in order to complete the course. Trainees are required to produce five pieces of work, all of which must be passed for the diploma to be awarded. This work consists of two short essays and one long essay, a case assessment demonstrating the ability to perform a functional analysis, and a research project, generally a single-case study, designed to show the ability to implement and monitor a piece of clinical work. The latter two pieces of work are both managed by an on-site supervisor who takes responsibility for assessment of the trainee's practical work.

An outline of the core topics covered by the course is shown in Table 6.2. It should be noted that this is not an exclusive list: Other topics are included to reflect the interests and demands of any particular group of trainees in any given year. The progression over the three (extended) academic terms consists of, first, the theory and practice of behavioral assessment, followed by research and therapeutic skills and techniques, and finally the application of assessment and practice techniques to specific client groups and types of problems. (Full details about the diploma program will happily be supplied to anyone who writes.)

In a follow-up survey of those who completed the diploma program, we found that over half those trained changed employment within a year of completion. Some moved to a new post, usually with a promotion; others changed to specialist roles within their own institutions. We are confident therefore that as well as refining the practitioner's skills to the benefit of the client, the training also marks a significant step in career development for the individual concerned.

Politics. It is unusual to have, as at Glenthorne Youth Treatment Centre, the whole staff working with the same model and all committed to a therapeutic approach. In other instances it is necessary to develop politi-

Table 6.2. Core Topics From a CBM Training Course

Theories of learning: Classical conditioning, operant conditioning, social learning, the nature of reinforcement and punishment, schedules of reinforcement, secondary reinforcement, modeling, extinction, discriminative stimuli, generalization, internal and external control of reinforcement.

Behavioral techniques: Anxiety management, assertion training, aversion therapy, behavior rehearsal (convert and overt), biofeedback, chaining, coaching, cognitive behavior modification (self-instructional training, anger management, self-control, problem solving, etc.), constructional approach, contingency management, contracting, extinction programs, feedback, flooding, relaxation therapy, response cost, shaping, social skills training, stimulus control, systematic desensitization, time out, token economy.

Practical skills: Assessing contingencies, establishing baselines, evaluation skills, functional analysis, hierarchy construction, identifying and defining behaviors, identifying and defining reinforcers, interviewing skills, measuring, monitoring and recording behavior, phasing out treatment, writing contracts, single-case design and analysis.

Biological basis of behavior: The brain and behavior, genetic factors, the nervous system and behavior.

Ethical issues: The use of negative reinforcements and punishment, issues of confidentiality, clients' rights, reinforcement control, the client-therapist relationship, decision making in behavioral intervention, treatment versus management issues.

Special applications of CBM techniques: Aggression and violence, conduct disorder, delinquent and criminal behavior, disruptive behavior, enuresis and encopresis, family therapy, neuroses, self-mutilation, sexual deviations and dysfunction, psychoses, affective disorders.

CBM techniques in a wider social context: The use of behavioral techniques in various social settings: in the classroom, in family therapy, in residential institutions such as hospitals, young offender institutions, and community homes, and in field social work practice.

cal strategies to minimize disharmony and maximize the chances of an effective intervention. These strategies include involving other members of staff in the planning and implementation of training programs, thereby maintaining a sensitivity to the organizational issues (cf. Cullen & Seddon, 1981). It is helpful therefore to write regular, brief, jargon-free reports on each individual's progress through treatment, and with due regard to confidentiality these reports should be made available to others concerned about the client's future. Further, when challenged one should not apologize, and one should be prepared to respond positively to those who are antagonistic to intervention with young offenders. In this light, Perkins (1987) formulated the useful tactic of costing, in economic terms, the relative cheapness of clinical intervention in preventing future offenses. High recidivism rates can be used to argue that intervention is worth a shot to save the suffering of future victims. Similarly, one must be prepared to defend behavioral intervention—challenging false beliefs and stereotypes about behavioral methods and inviting critics to view work in operation and to talk to present clients.

One must be prepared to argue for the client's right to clinical intervention, even if it is not connected to offense behavior. The development and use of such strategies can pay dividends both in establishing that one has a cogent defendable viewpoint and may even convince skeptics to participate in intervention programs. In addition, make efforts to publish studies in professional journals. Milan (1987) suggests that there is a paucity of recent research in some important areas, particularly from closed institutions for young offenders. In the final analysis, however, not everyone will be convinced, and sabotage, either intentional or unintentional, will always be a possibility. This fact should be reflected in the content of treatment programs, along the lines of training clients in "coping with awkward situations" when overt attempts at sabotage are made. This final point brings us to the program itself and ways to minimize failure and maximize success in its design.

Program Design

In discussing program design a number of important points have been made: the need to select motivated clients, to ensure proper treatment intensity and integrity, to distinguish between clinical and criminological targets, to assess as rigorously as possible, and to evaluate the effects of the intervention as thoroughly as possible. Given all this, and a skilled practitioner, there remains one element of vital importance: the need to maximize the probability of generalization of treatment gains. The behavioral literature is replete with studies that show immediate positive gains in the treatment setting but then find that the gains are no longer seen once the client returns to his or her natural environment. Kazdin (1982) comments: "As a general rule, it is still prudent to assume that behavioral gains are likely to be lost in varying degrees once the client leaves the project" (p. 437). Given this knowledge, it is advisable that cognitive-behavioral programs make every effort to strive for generalization; there are a number of strategies that can be employed toward this aim.

The transfer of a newly acquired behavior from the treatment setting to the real world is properly termed *stimulus generalization*. The critical factor in determining the extent to which stimulus generalization occurs is the degree of similarity between the treatment environment and the natural environment. The greater the difference between the two, either in terms of setting conditions (i.e., discriminative stimuli) or reinforcement contingencies, the greater the probability that the client will discriminate between the two environments. This discrimination, in turn, will be associated with different behavior in the two environments, and generalization of behavior from one setting to another will become less likely. Thus attempts to program for generalization have two broad strategies: to match treatment *and* natural environments for both setting conditions and contingencies of reinforcement.

In thoughtful discussions Brown (1982) and Huff (1987) have made a number of practical suggestions about how to aid the process of stimulus generalization. To work toward increased similarity of treatment and natural environments it is recommended that the treatment setting strive to simulate the real world. This may refer to, in institutions particularly, the availability of work, educational, and leisure opportunities; it requires the real world to be drawn into treatment programs in the form of families, friends, and a peer group. In addition, assessment and treatment should take place in the real world. Huff (1987) makes the point:

> Graded or special release for a period before discharge (e.g., one month) or a similar period in a pre-release hostel, could be arranged during which time offenders could, even if only temporarily, re-enter certain settings in the community (e.g., pubs, sports clubs, discos, possible workplaces, etc.) which would permit at least a degree of direct observation of target behavior by treatment staff (p. 233).

The trainer can become a powerful discriminative stimulus so that the trainee can "perform" only while the therapist is present. This possibility can be countered by having more than one trainer and by training parents, relatives, or others to continue the program outside the treatment setting. Again, this blurs the boundaries between treatment and natural settings, incidentally modifying the real world (e.g., family behavior) as well as the treatment environment. Experimental studies have demonstrated that such strategies can produce improved generalization with young offender populations (Emshoff, Redd, & Davidson, 1976).

The delivery of reinforcement can be arranged to match real-world contingencies. Social praise and condemnation are the most frequent natural reinforcers and punishers, and they should both be used in treatment. If the young offender fails to respond to social payoffs—there is no law dictating that praise has to be reinforcing—then pair acknowledgment, approval, and other social rewards with tangible rewards such as points or tokens. When the association is established, gradually fade out the points or tokens so that the naturally occurring contingencies remain. In treatment there is a tendency to deliver reinforcement immediately upon observing the desired behavior; although this may be necessary in the early stages of a program in order to precipitate behavior change, continual reinforcement is seldom found in the real world.

Thus, once the behavior change is established, use delayed reinforcement and intermittent schedules of reinforcement, which are more representative of the natural environment.

Finally, turning to the behavior itself, the prime rule is to select as target behaviors those that are relevant to the real world and so will continue to be reinforced outside the treatment setting. Repeated practice and overtraining increase the strength of newly acquired behavior. This point applies equally to cognition and observable behavior. For example, self-instruction should not be situation-specific so that when a new situation arises the young offender is unable to self-talk. Rather, self-instructions should be part of a more general problem-solving strategy so that, when a new situation arises, the response is, "What can I aim for here?" Such "executive" self-instructions should be included as part of the program design. Self-statements, in addition, should include both reward, censure, and coping components. With a young offender population, given the general tendency toward external control, it is wise to engage the offender in the selection of treatment goals. Gains are therefore less likely to be written off as being entirely due to the therapist, and therefore liable to disappear when he or she does, but to be seen as due in some part to the young person's own efforts. This may assist in a move toward internal control. Finally, intervention should be gradually withdrawn rather than abruptly terminated; "booster sessions" should be planned for rather than left to chance.

The guiding principle in cognitive-behavioral theory is the uniqueness of the individual. It follows that a functional analysis of a young offender's present cognitive and behavioral repertoires, both in terms of their relationship to each other and the environmental contingencies, is a necessary prerequisite to treatment. My own opinion is that this philosophy extends into treatment: Group intervention on its own is not enough; there must be some level of individual assessment, goal setting, and monitoring of progress. Although group interventions can be a potent means of changing behavior, the individual should not be "lost," and the pitfalls of relying on group change as an index of therapeutic success have already been discussed.

In the main this book has been about the individual, focusing on cognitive-behavioral methods of changing the young offender's behavior to achieve either clinical or criminological behavior change goals. In the first chapter it was noted that whereas this approach could be justified, criminal behavior is properly seen as an interaction between the individual and the environment. In the next, penultimate, section I wish briefly to acknowledge the environment part of the equation and broaden the discussion to include questions of social policy and its modification.

SOCIAL POLICY AND THE
BEHAVIOR ANALYST

Burchard (1987a) draws the distinction between therapeutic contingencies and social and/or political contingencies. Therapeutic contingencies are those typically designed by behavior therapists to assist individuals in adapting to their environments. Almost all of this book thus far has been about therapeutic contingencies. On the other hand, social and/or political contingencies, generally referred to as rules, regulations, policies, or laws, are established by administrators or legislators. Burchard argues that social and/or political contingencies are of crucial importance for the behavior analyst concerned with young offenders for five reasons: (a) social and/or political contingencies can determine the total environment, and they are therefore relevant to any behavioral approach to working with young offenders; (b) they influence the young offender's behavior; (c) they influence the behavior of the therapist; (d) they can be beneficial or detrimental to the work of the therapist; (e) they are rarely the concern, in terms of either formulation or influence, of those trained in behavior analysis. As Burchard (1987b) points out, advocates of therapeutic contingencies and of social and/or political contingencies come from two very different worlds. The therapist is concerned with individual change, and the cognitive-behavioral therapist with applying certain theoretical principles to modify the behavior of the young offender. Almost by definition, the social and/or political policy maker is concerned with affairs on a large scale:—with laws that affect the disposal of young offenders, with budgetary control over financing of projects, with personnel (including therapists), and with the making of laws dictating who becomes a young offender. This points to a critical distinction, as Burchard (1987b) notes: "Although therapeutic and social/political contingencies are both designed to prevent or eliminate unlawful behavior, they differ significantly in terms of power and influence. The power differential is obvious. Behavior therapists are not able to change the total environment contingent upon a particular behavior" (p. 580). This power differential is expanded still further if the relative influence of the two is considered: Burchard (1987b) estimates that in the United States in 1982 there were 1,630,226 arrests involving juveniles, while the courts disposed of 1,296,000 young offenders. Compared to this level of influence of social and/or political contingencies, less than one in a hundred of the offenders experienced a therapeutic contingency. Given this state of affairs, together with the poor showing of the outcome evidence (for reasons explained previously), the prevailing political climate, and the ascendency (wrongly, I've argued) of the "nothing works" argument, the future appears at face value to be bleak.

However, I feel stirrings of optimism for two reasons: a new realism in clinical intervention with offenders and the gathering momentum of alternative approaches to preventing crime.

The new realism in clinical intervention is characterized by a growing awareness that criminal behavior is not simply another form of psychopathology or behavior disorder to be treated like a panic attack or a bout of depression. A great deal of offending is better seen as a form of social behavior (granted that the same point can be made for a number of clinical disorders) and, particularly in the case of many young offenders, it becomes increasingly difficult to call this form of social behavior "deviant" (e.g., Farrington, 1983). The steady revision of theories and models of the etiology of offending is causing many clinicians to pause to assess the force of a therapeutic contingency in the light of criminological data. As outlined in the following section, it can be anticipated that clinical research with young offenders will be influenced significantly by, for example, research on developmental approaches, research on sex differences in offending, the renewed interest in typologies of young offenders, and rational choice perspectives on offenders.

The development of new approaches to crime prevention has grown from increasing dissatisfaction with the notion of tertiary prevention as exemplified by a great deal of clinical work with young offenders. Morris (1987) distinguishes three types of prevention as applied to criminal behavior: *Primary prevention* programs seek to prevent the whole population from engaging in criminal behavior and so aim to promote law-abiding behavior; *secondary prevention* programs seek to prevent those individuals identified as being at risk from engaging in criminal behavior; and *tertiary prevention* programs seek to prevent future offending by those who have already committed a crime. Nietzel and Himelein (1986) have outlined five areas that appear promising for the design of prevention programs.

The first is diversion from the justice system of young offenders judged to be at risk of the corrupting influences the legal and penal system is argued to have on development. The second is reduction of family violence that research links with later antisocial and violent behavior in adults who experienced such violence in childhood. The third is parent training as a means of improving the behavior of children who experience impulsivity problems. The fourth is development of those personal competencies—cognitive, behavioral, academic, and occupational—that appear to be crucial to effective socialization and coping with the stresses of childhood and adolescence. And the fifth is modification of situations and victim vulnerabilities linked to higher rates of criminal behavior.

With the exception of diversion, which is tertiary prevention, the other four areas can be seen as either primary or secondary prevention depending on whether they are designed for selected at-risk groups or the population as a whole. Before briefly discussing each of the above, it is worth noting that any prevention program is only as good as the research that informs it. Identification of at-risk groups, knowledge of the effects of family violence on later functioning, and details of the supposed harmful effects of the justice system can only be as accurate as the empirical base from which they draw strength. In making claims of such magnitude for the data so as to be confident in the design of prevention programs, social scientists are forced to make value statements about the knowledge base that informs their expertise. Nietzel and Himelein are refreshingly candid: "We believe there is enough knowledge about etiologic factors in crime to justify aiming our interventions at some prevention targets" (p. 197). (I must confess that, perhaps jaundiced by problems at the level of tertiary prevention, my faith is not so strong that extant knowledge can be translated into practice with a high probability of success. Nonetheless, the targets and programs outlined by Nietzel and Himelein have, for me, an intuitive appeal.)

Diversion has been discussed previously (chapter 4) and need not be duplicated. It is sufficient to say that diversion programs are targeted at known offenders with the aim of achieving nonjudicial and certainly noncustodial alternatives to those found within the formal justice system. In its favor, diversion is cheap economically, less restrictive in the limitations it places on offenders in achieving its goals, and generally more humanitarian in being community-based and constructive in orientation. The great drawback is that there is little empirical evidence indicating its effect in terms of lowering recidivism, although, as Davidson et al. (1987) found, this whole argument very much depends on the measure of recidivism employed. The foundation of programs aimed at reducing family violence lies in research supporting the "abused-abusing" cycle of family violence. The aim of such intervention steps beyond the amelioration of family violence to prevention of the consequences of violence—more violence by abused children as adults. With the relatively recent growth in professional concern, at both research and clinical levels, about child abuse, it should be possible to test empirically the claims for the preventive powers of intervention in reducing levels of family violence.

The conceptual basis for competency enhancement follows research that has attempted to identify the predictors of later offending. Much of this research has been outlined in chapters 1 and 2 as it informs the basis for cognitive-behavioral interventions with young offenders. What is being advocated in prevention (other than tertiary prevention) is that programs to remedy poor educational achievement, low impulse control, and so on, are targeted not at young offenders but at those at risk of offending. The techniques used are identical to those covered in chapters 3 and 4. Again, the same position applies to programs designed to modify family discipline procedures. The conceptual basis, research base, and techniques are the same as those that inform work with young offenders, as discussed in this book, but the target group moves back a stage to the at-risk or predelinquent population. In both cases, competency enhancement and modification of family discipline procedures, there is, as with young offenders, some success but not as yet on a systematic or consistent basis.

The fifth approach noted by Nietzel and Himelein, situational crime prevention, marks a contemporary approach to crime prevention that moves away from the notion of intervening at the level of the individual offender and toward reducing the opportunity for crime through modification of the environment. While a full discussion is beyond the scope of the present text, situational crime prevention is a strategy clinicians should be aware of. A situational approach to crime prevention seeks to change the environment in two ways—by reducing opportunity and increasing the risk of detection (Clarke, 1983; Heal & Laycock, 1986). Opportunities to commit crime can be reduced in a number of ways. *Target hardening,* for example, relies on the use of stronger materials or locks and bars to obstruct the would-be offender. The introduction of steering column locks on cars has been shown in both British and German studies to reduce the number of car thefts. Another strategy lies in *target removal:* Theft from telephone coin boxes can be eliminated by the introduction of a system that uses credit cards rather than money. On the other side of the coin, increasing the risk of detection can be achieved in a number of ways. The most obvious strategy is to increase levels of formal surveillance. The police are the most visible manifestation of authority, but other authority figures can have a similar effect: Apartment buildings with doormen are less likely to be burglarized, public transportation with visible personnel is less likely to be vandalized, and parking lots with attendants have a lower rate of damage to cars. While the visible appearance of people, especially employees with authority, appears to be advantageous in reducing offending, the formality of surveillance can also be increased by the use of closed-circuit television (CCTV). Indeed, CCTV has become a feature in many shops, banks, and public transportation systems. In addition, there are other environmental strategies such as organizing citizen groups to prevent crime, educating the public about victimization, changing public attitudes toward crime (especially crimes against women), and architectural design of the home, the factory, and the city.

There are a number of objections to situational strategies for crime prevention such as ignoring the "person" side of the person and envi-

ronment interaction. In reality most commentators agree that it is unwise to omit either side of the person-environment equation. In a critique of situational crime prevention, Trasler (1986) articulates just such
a position: "Policies of crime reduction really demand two strategies:
deterring the occasional or low-rate offenders from committing crimes
. . . and identifying and incapacitating high-rate, persistent offenders.
Situational crime control offers effective measures for the first, but is
likely to have little impact on the second group" (p. 24).

A further objection lies in the domain of civil liberties: recordings on
videotape, photographs on credit cards, and carrying identity cards.
This is clearly an area in which moral and political decisions have to be
made regarding the relative advantages and disadvantages in trading off
cherished liberties and conveniences in order to reduce crime. A similar
argument applies to the aesthetics of, at worst, an environment bristling
with guard dogs, barbed wire, armed guards, and security cameras. As
in all things, a little moderation makes good sense—but who is to act as
moderator?

A final objection considers the notion of "displacement"—the argument that the criminal, frustrated by situational measures, will modify
one or all of the following: time, place, method, or form of the crime
(Reppetto, 1976). The empirical data indicate that, for some crimes at
least, displacement does occur. Again we are faced with moral and political decisions. If the gains in crime prevention, in both human and economic terms, outweigh any effects of displacement, then situational
measures may well be worthwhile. Overall, the main problem lies in
measuring precisely the exact impact and effect of situational interventions, so that in the final analysis their implementation becomes something of a social gamble.

New Directions: New Skills

There can be little doubt that primary and secondary prevention programs, perhaps situational strategies especially, have had a significant
effect on criminological psychology at both the theoretical and practical
levels. The relative merits of intervening with at-risk and predelinquent
groups, set against the findings of McCord (1978) and Palamara et al.
(1986), which suggest that there may be detrimental effects of early intervention, do, however, await full exploration. The thesis developed in
the text, in keeping with the meta-analysis studies (see chapter 5), is
that cognitive-behavioral intervention with young offenders can claim a
degree of success. However, as Burchard (1987a) observes, "If the issue
is the prevention of delinquency, or even a reduction in the incidence of
delinquent behavior, behavior analysts must broaden their focus. Social/

political contingencies should be brought into the realm of behavior analysis and behavior therapy" (p. 88). I agree unreservedly with this but admit to being less sure how to go about achieving this goal. History tells us that it is unlikely that social administrators and politicians are going to rush to psychologists generally and behavior analysts in particular for advice on the formulation of social policy. It follows therefore that strategies are needed to engage the attention of policy makers in order to impact on policy making and to reinforce appropriate policies. It is less than probable that this will be done on an individual basis; a concerted, coordinated strategy by professional bodies seems more likely to have an effect. The American Psychological Association and The British Psychological Society are obvious examples, but it would be interesting to see representations from multidisciplinary groups—psychologists, psychiatrists, social workers, probation officers—with a common commitment to young offenders. Lobbying of administrators can take place at a number of levels as exemplified by the work of the Division of Criminological and Legal Psychology (DCLP) of the BPS.

The DCLP seeks to represent the interests of psychologists who work in the general areas of law and crime, and to this end it can be an influential voice in shaping social and political contingencies. To exercise this influence a variety of skills are needed by active DCLP members. The most crucial is to make known, both within the BPS and at a national level, exactly what expertise is available in order to respond quickly to requests for information. This type of work also requires the skill and technical knowledge to read government papers and to make comments, from a psychological perspective, on a range of issues. In my time with the DCLP we have made comments, for consumption at a high political level, about a range of topics including sentencing for young offenders, procedures for questioning eyewitnesses, capital punishment, and community options for young offenders. It is gratifying to see the views of psychologists reflected in the final publication of government papers and policies. The process can be taken a stage further by involvement in the BPS Parliamentary Group, which actively seeks to make politicians concerned about matters rather than waiting to be approached. Again this requires discrete verbal and writing skills: The level of debate and written evidence politicians are familiar with, and hence influenced by, is not the same as that used by most psychologists in everyday communication with other psychologists. There are other areas of activity, such as lobbying for research funds, in which the DCLP might engage, but the general point has been made: Although effective prevention programs require clinical and research skills, they also demand that psychologists become involved in social and political decision making. It can be predicted that this will become a greater part of the concern of psychologists working in the forensic field, and it is to be hoped that training courses will begin to take note and attend to the necessary skills in the future.

FOR THE FUTURE

Theory and Practice

The theoretical debate both between behavioral and other theories and within the behavioral framework is set to last for the foreseeable future. Concentrating upon cognitive-behavioral theories there are continued lines of development: The radical behaviorists are expanding Skinner's position, as Skinner (1974) has maintained is essential, to encompass the role of language and cognition in human behavior and consciousness (e.g., Lowe, 1983). Some theorists seek to move away from a radical behaviorist position, seeking to incorporate other psychological theories into the cognitive-behavioral framework. Kendall and Bacon (1988) suggest, for example, that as classical and operant learning form the basis for much of traditional behavior therapy, cognitive-behavioral theorizing might well be informed by developments in social learning theory and information processing approaches. Kendall and Bacon suggest that looking to mainstream experimental cognitive psychology, as typified by information processing approaches, has a number of beneficial payoffs. The first is that if the experimental approaches have developed new measures of cognition, then these may be able to be exploited in clinical practice. The second is that mainstream theoretical research may contribute empirical findings of direct concern to clinicians and students of psychopathology. Third, the integration of mainstream cognitive research into clinical assessment and theory may well prompt developments in clinical practice. It is true that there are fundamental differences, perhaps irreconcilable, between the various theoretical positions; it is also true that there have been spirited exchanges between schools of thought within the broad behavioral church (e.g., Ledwidge, 1978, 1979; Locke, 1979). However, one begins to perceive that the exchanges are becoming less entrenched and more open to scientific debate: Lowe (1983) suggests that "a behavioural analysis of what takes place in cognitive behavior modification should provide not only a coherent conceptual basis for these techniques but also the means of enhancing their effectiveness. The cornerstone of such an analysis must surely be the recognition of the role of verbal behavior and private events in determining human behavior" (p. 87). Kendall and Bacon (1988) advance the view that although like all behavior therapists they share a committment to empirical evaluation, they "differ in the faith we hold in different theories of psychopathological process. Cognitive-behavioral therapists are betting that our faith in cognitively mediated processes will prove useful" (p. 163). Although the authors of these two quotations differ in their theoretical orientation, the impression is one of scholarly debate, with opinions open to revision, rather than maintaining a fixed theoretical stance. This recognition of the need for progress is exemplified by the recent collection of papers debating the force of the variations within a behavioral paradigm (Fishman, Rotgers, & Franks, 1988). It is to be hoped that this will precipitate a move away from cognitive versus behavioral clinical research to genuine cognitive-behavioral programs evaluated in an empirical fashion.

For cognitive-behavioral intervention with young offenders, clinicians must be sensitive to advances in criminological research and theory. A number of developments in criminological research await integration into clinical programs in a systematic fashion. The data on delinquency cessation with maturity through adolescence (Mulvey & LaRosa, 1986) await a full theoretical account, but the case can be made that developmental trends should be used to inform clinical practice with young offenders, perhaps with the aim of reinforcing such developmental trends. Hawkins and Weis (1985) have made suggestions that might assist in making progress toward this end. They propose that during normal development three types of factors—opportunities for social involvement, skills, and reinforcement—are crucial to socialization. The focus for prevention should therefore be on the agents of socialization, parents, schools, and peers, together with life and employment skills training and community development. Individually these are familiar, but they are brought together by Hawkins and Weis in a coherent model to inform practice.

Although research on sex differences and rational choice strategies increasingly presses home the point that young offenders are a heterogeneous group, the research on subgroups and typologies of young offenders (e.g., Quay, 1987) may inform clinical practice. It is not difficult to see that a young offender of the "undersocialized aggression" type might require a different emphasis in clinical work than a young offender categorized as being of the "attention deficit" type. My opinion is that typologies can be helpful, but caution needs to be exercised lest assessment become an exercise focused exclusively on determining what type of young offender is being observed and, once the type is established, this then dictates the intervention and sight is lost of an individual analysis.

This, then, brings me to a list of recommendations culled from the text that seem to me to be crucial to informing the future practice of cognitive-behavioral work with young offenders:

Assess on an individual basis, using as many assessment methods as possible to maximize the chances of an accurate functional analysis.

Have clear criteria for acceptance for clinical intervention (e.g., motivation, willingness to discuss offense).

Make a clear distinction between criminological and clinical targets. For example, a young offender with social skills deficits qualifies, in a clinical sense, for intervention. Without clear evidence to the contrary there is no a priori justification for assuming that social skills training will modify criminal behavior.

Be prepared to design complex single-case studies using multiple baselines and a range of clinical techniques aimed at *both* cognition and behavior.

Pay attention to issues related to treatment integrity (e.g., training and motivation of any staff or family involved in the program).

Build strategies for generalization into program designs.

For professional interests and for the sake of future generations of young offenders be prepared to enter the social and/or political arena on behalf of a treatment and/or prevention philosophy.

At all levels be prepared to counter the "nothing works" myth (e.g., the meta-analyses findings).

In a perfect world all our efforts would be directed toward primary prevention and, indeed, a great deal of effort is being given to prevention programs (Burchard & Burchard, 1987; Johnson, 1987). However, we live in a far from perfect world and, like it or not, tertiary prevention in the form of clinical programs for young offenders is part of reality. So to answer the question posed at the beginning of this chapter, it is my conviction that when delivered properly, cognitive-behavioral procedures offer the most efficacious means for directing young people away from the penalties that will follow the transition from young offender to adult recidivist. This goal of turning young people back from a life of crime should guide all interventions with young offenders.

References

Achenbach, T. M. (1978). The child behavior profile: I. Boys aged 6–11. *Journal of Consulting and Clinical Psychology, 4,* 478–488.

Akers, R. L. (1977). *Deviant behavior: A social learning approach* (2nd ed.). Belmont, CA: Wadsworth.

Alexander, J. F. (1973). Defensive and supportive communication in normal and deviant families. *Journal of Consulting and Clinical Psychology, 40,* 223–231.

Alexander, J. F., Barton, C., Schiavo, R. S., & Parsons, B. V. (1976). Systems behavioral intervention with families of delinquents: Therapist characteristics, family behavior, and outcome. *Journal of Consulting and Clinical Psychology, 44,* 656–664.

Alexander, J. F., & Parsons, B. V. (1973). Short-term behavioral intervention with delinquent families: Impact on family processes and recidivism. *Journal of Abnormal Psychology, 81,* 219–225.

Alexander, J. F., & Parsons, B. V. (1982). *Functional family therapy.* Monterey, CA: Brooks/Cole.

Andrew, J. M. (1977). Delinquency: Intellectual imbalance? *Criminal Justice and Behavior, 4,* 99–104.

Arbuthnot, J., & Gordon, D. A. (1986). Behavioral and cognitive effects of a moral reasoning development intervention for high risk behavior-disordered adolescents. *Journal of Consulting and Clinical Psychology, 34,* 208–216.

Arbuthnot, J., Gordon, D. A., & Jurkovic, J. G. (1987). Personality. In H. C. Quay (Ed.), *Handbook of juvenile delinquency.* New York: Wiley.

Archer, D., & Akert, R. M. (1977). Words and everything else: Verbal and nonverbal cues in social interpretation. *Journal of Personality and Social Psychology, 35,* 443–449.

Arkowitz, H. (1981). Assessment of social skills. In M. Hersen & A. S. Bellack, (Eds.), *Behavioral assessment: A practical handbook* (2nd ed.). New York: Wiley.

Argyle, M. (1967). *The psychology of interpersonal behaviour.* Harmondsworth, Middlesex, England: Penguin Books.

Ausubel, D. (1958). *Theories and problems of child development.* New York: Grune & Stratton.

Ayala, H. E., Minkin, N., Phillips, E. L., Fixsen, D. L., & Wolf, M. M. (1973). *Achievement Place: The training and analysis of vocational behaviors.* Paper presented at the meeting of the American Psychological Association, Montréal.

Baars, B. J. (1986). *The cognitive revolution in psychology.* New York: Guilford Press.

Bailey, J. S., Timbers, G. D., Phillips, E. L., & Wolf, M. M. (1971). Modification of articulation of pre-delinquents by their peers. *Journal of Applied Behavior Analysis, 4,* 265–281.

153

Bailey, J. S., Wolf, M. M., & Phillips, E. L. (1970). Home-based reinforcement and the modification of pre-delinquents' classroom behavior. *Journal of Applied Behavior Analysis, 3,* 223–233.

Bailey, W. (1966). Correctional outcome: An evaluation of 100 reports. *Journal of Criminal Law, Criminology, and Police Science, 57,* 153–160.

Ball, R. A., & Lilly, J. R. (1988). Home incarceration with electronic monitoring. In J. E. Scott & T. Hirschi (Eds.), *Controversial issues in crime and justice.* Beverly Hills, CA: Sage Publications.

Bandura, A. (1973). *Aggression: A social learning analysis.* Englewood Cliffs, NJ: Prentice-Hall.

Bandura, A. (1977). *Social learning theory.* Englewood Cliffs, NJ: Prentice-Hall.

Bank, L., Patterson, G. R., & Reid, J. B. (1987). Delinquency prevention through training parents in family management. *The Behavior Analyst, 10,* 75–82.

Barlow, D. H., & Hersen, M. (1973). Single case experimental designs: Uses in applied clinical research. *Archives of General Psychiatry, 29,* 319–325.

Barlow, D. H., & Hersen, M. (1984). *Single case experimental designs: Strategies for studying behavior change* (2nd ed.). Elmsford, NY: Pergamon Press.

Barlow, G. (1979). Youth treatment centre. In C. Payne & K. J. White (Eds.), *Caring for deprived children.* London: Croom Helm.

Barrios, B. A. (1988). On the changing nature of behavioral assessment. In A. S. Bellack & M. Hersen (Eds.), *Behavioral assessment: A practical handbook* (3rd ed.). Elmsford, NY: Pergamon Press.

Barrios, B. A., & Hartmann, D. P. (1986). The contributions of traditional assessment: Concepts, issues and methodologies. In R. O. Nelson & S. C. Hayes (Eds.), *Conceptual foundations of behavioral assessment.* New York: Guilford Press.

Baxter, D. J., Barbaree, H. E., & Marshall, W. L. (1986). Sexual responses to consenting and forced sex in a large sample of rapists and nonrapists. *Behaviour Research and Therapy, 24,* 513–520.

Bayer, R. (1981). Crime, punishment and the decline of liberal optimism. *Crime and Delinquency, 27,* 169–190.

Beck, A. T. (1967). *Depression: Clinical, experimental, and theoretical aspects.* New York: Hoeber.

Beck, A. T., & Beck, R. W. (1972). Screening depressed patients in family practice: A rapid technique. *Postgraduate Medicine, 52,* 81–85.

Becker, R. E., & Heimberg, R. G. (1988). Assessment of social skills. In A. S. Bellack & M. Hersen (Eds.), *Behavioral assessment: A practical handbook* (3rd ed.). Elmsford, NY: Pergamon Press.

Bellack, A. S., & Hersen, M. (Eds.). (1988). *Behavioral assessment: A practical handbook* (3rd ed.). Elmsford, NY: Pergamon Press.

Bellack, A. S., Hersen, M., & Kazdin, A. E. (Eds.). (1982). *International handbook of behavior modification and therapy.* New York: Plenum Press.

Bellack, A. S., Hersen, M., & Lamparski, D. (1979). Role play tests for assessing social skills: Are they valid? Are they useful? *Journal of Consulting and Clinical Psychology, 47,* 335–342.

Belson, W. (1975). *Juvenile theft: The causal factors.* New York: Harper & Row.

Bippes, R., McLaughlin, T. F., & Williams, R. L. (1986). A classroom token system in a detention center: Effects for academic and social behavior. *Techniques: A Journal for Remedial Education and Counseling, 2,* 126–132.

Blackburn, R. (1983). Psychopathy, delinquency and crime. In A. Gale & J. A. Edwards (Eds.), *Physiological correlates of human behaviour: Vol. 3. Individual differences and psychopathology.* London: Academic Press.

Blackman, D. E. (1981). The experimental analysis of behaviour and its relevance to applied psychology. In G. Davey (Ed.), *Applications of conditioning theory*. London: Methuen.

Blackmore, J. (1974). The relationship between self-reported delinquency and official convictions among adolescent boys. *British Journal of Criminology, 14*, 172–176.

Blagg, H. (1985). Reparation and justice for juveniles. *British Journal of Criminology, 25*, 267–279.

Blakely, C. H., & Davidson, W. S. (1984). Behavioral approaches to delinquency: A review. In P. Karoly & J. J. Steffen (Eds.), *Adolescent behavior disorders: Foundations and contemporary concerns*. Lexington, MA: Lexington Books.

Blanchard, E. B., Andrasik, F., Evans, D. P., Neff, D. F., Appelbaum, D. A., & Rodichok, L. D. (1985). Behavioral treatment of 150 chronic headache patients: A clinical replication series. *Behavior Therapy, 16*, 308–327.

Blasi, A. (1980). Bridging moral cognition and moral action: A critical review of the literature. *Psychological Bulletin, 88*, 1–45.

Blumstein, A., Farrington, D. P., & Moitra, S. (1985). Delinquency careers: Innocents, desisters, and persisters. In *Crime and justice: An annual review of research* (Vol. 6). Chicago: University of Chicago Press.

Bootzin, R. R. (1975). *Behavior modification and therapy: An introduction*. Cambridge, MA: Winthrop.

Bornstein, P. H., Hamilton, S. B., & Bornstein, M. T. (1986). Self-monitoring procedures. In A. R. Ciminero, K. S., Calhoun, & H. E. Adams (Eds.), *Handbook of behavioral assessment* (2nd ed.). New York: Wiley.

Bowman, P. C., & Auerbach, S. M. (1982). Impulsive youthful offenders: A multimodal cognitive behavioral treatment program. *Criminal Justice and Behavior, 9*, 432–454.

Braukmann, C. J., Bedlington, M. M., Bedlen, B. D., Braukmann, P. D., Husted, J. J., Kirigin Ramp, K., & Wolf, M. M. (1985). The effects of community-based group-home treatment programs for male juvenile offenders on the use and abuse of drugs and alcohol. *The American Journal of Drug and Alcohol Abuse, 11*, 249–278.

Braukmann, C. J., & Fixsen, D. L. (1975). Behavior modification with delinquents. In M. Hersen, R. M. Eisler, & P. M. Miller (Eds.), *Progress in behavior modification* (Vol. 1). New York: Academic Press.

Braukmann, C. J., Fixsen, D. L., Phillips, E. L., Wolf, M. M., & Maloney, D. M. (1974). An analysis of a selection interview training package for predelinquents at Achievement Place. *Journal of Applied Behavior Analysis, 9*, 179–188.

Braukmann, C. J., Maloney, D. M., Fixsen, D. L., Phillips, E. L., & Wolf, M. M. (1974). An analysis of a selection interview training package for predelinquents at Achievement Place. *Criminal Justice and Behavior, 1*, 30–42.

Braukmann, C. J., & Wolf, M. M. (1987). Behaviorally based group homes for juvenile offenders. In E. K. Morris & C. J. Braukmann (Eds.), *Behavioral approaches to crime and delinquency: A handbook of application, research, and concepts*. New York: Plenum Press.

Braukmann, P. D., Kirigin Ramp, K., Braukmann, C. J., Willner, A. G., & Wolf, M. M. (1983). Analysis and training of rationales for child care workers. *Children and Youth Services Review, 5*, 177–194.

Brewin, C. R. (1988). *Cognitive foundations of clinical psychology*. London: Lawrence Erlbaum.

Brody, S. (1976). *The effectiveness of sentencing: A review of the literature*. London: HMSO.

Brown, B. J. (1975). An application of social learning methods in a residential programme for young offenders. *Journal of Adolescence, 8*, 321–331.

Brown, B. J. (1977). Gilbey House: A token economy management scheme in a residential school for boys in trouble. *British Association for Behavioural Psychotherapy Bulletin, 5*, 79–89.

Brown, M. (1982). Maintenance and generalization issues in skills training with chronic schizophrenics. In J. P. Curran & P. M. Monti (Eds.), *Social skills training: A practical handbook for assessment and treatment*. New York: Guilford Press.

Burchard, J. D. (1987a). Social policy and the role of the behavior analyst in the prevention of delinquent behavior. *The Behavior Analyst, 10,* 83–88.

Burchard, J. D. (1987b). Social and political challenges to behavioral programs with delinquents and criminals. In E. K. Morris & C. J. Braukmann (Eds.), *Behavioral approaches to crime and delinquency: A handbook of application, research, and concepts*. New York: Plenum Press.

Burchard, J. D., & Burchard, S. N. (1987). *Prevention of delinquent behavior*. Beverly Hills, CA: Sage Publications.

Burchard, J. D., & Harrington, W. A. (1986). Deinstitutionalization: Programmed transition from the institution to the community. *Child & Family Behavior Therapy, 7,* 17–32.

Burchard, J. D., & Lane, T. W. (1982). Crime and delinquency. In A. S. Bellack, M. Hersen, & A. E. Kazdin (Eds.), *International handbook of behavior modification and therapy*. New York: Plenum Press.

Cacioppo, J. T., & Petty, R. E. (1981). Social psychological procedures for cognitive response assessment: The thought-listing technique. In T. V. Merluzzi, C. R. Glass, & J. M. Genest (Eds.), *Cognitive assessment*. New York: Guilford Press.

Camp, B. W., & Bash, M. B. (1981). *Think aloud: Increasing social and cognitive skills—A problem-solving program for children*. Champaign, IL: Research Press.

Camp, B. W., Blom, G., Herbert, F., & Van Doornick, W. (1977). "Think aloud": A program for developing self-control in young aggressive boys. *Journal of Abnormal Psychology, 5,* 157–169.

Carpenter, P., & Sandberg, S. (1985). Further psychodrama with delinquent adolescents. *Adolescence, 20,* 599–604.

Carpenter, P., & Sugrue, D. P. (1984). Psychoeducation in an outpatient setting—designing a heterogeneous format for a heterogeneous population of juvenile delinquents. *Adolescence, 19,* 113–122.

Chamberlain, P., Patterson, G., Reid, J., Kavanagh, K., & Forgatch, M. (1984). Observation of client resistance. *Behavior Therapy, 15,* 133–155.

Chandler, M. J. (1973). Egocentrism and anti-social behavior: The assessment and training of social perspective-taking skills. *Developmental Psychology, 9,* 326–332.

Ciminero, A. R., Calhoun, K. S., & Adams, H. E. (Eds.) (1986). *Handbook of behavioral assessment* (2nd ed.). New York: Wiley.

Clarke, R. V. G. (1977). Psychology and crime. *Bulletin of The British Psychological Society, 30,* 280–283.

Clarke, R. V. G. (1983). Situational crime prevention: Its theoretical basis and practical scope. In N. Morris & M. Tonry (Eds.), *Crime and justice: An annual review of research* (Vol. 4). Chicago: University of Chicago Press.

Cohen, H. L. (1973). Motivationally-orientated designs for an ecology of learning. In A. R. Roberts (Ed.), *Readings in prison education*. Springfield, IL: C. C. Thomas.

Cohen, L. E., & Felson, M. (1979). Social change and crime rate trends: A routine activity approach. *American Sociological Review, 44,* 588–608.

Coles, M. H., Donchin, E., & Porges, S. W. (1986). *Psychophysiology: Systems, processes, and applications*. New York: Guilford Press.

Conners, C. K. (1969). A teacher rating scale for use in drug studies with children. *American Journal of Psychiatry, 126,* 884–888.

Cornish, D. B., & Clarke, R. V. G. (1986a). Introduction. In D. B. Cornish & R. V. G. Clarke (Eds.), *The reasoning criminal: Rational choice perspectives on offending*. New York: Springer-Verlag.

Cornish, D. B., & Clarke, R. V. G. (Eds.). (1986b). *The reasoning criminal: Rational choice perspectives on offending*. New York: Springer-Verlag.

Craighead, W. E., Kazdin, A. E., & Mahoney, M. J. (1976). *Behavior modification: Principles, issues and applications*. Boston: Houghton Mifflin.

Cullen, J. E. (1987). Group based treatment for institutional offending. In B. J. McGurk, D. M. Thornton, & M. Williams (Eds.), *Applying psychology to imprisonment: Theory & practice*. London: HMSO.

Cullen, J. E., & Seddon, J. W. (1981). The application of a behavioral regime to disturbed young offenders. *Personality and Individual Differences, 2*, 285–292.

Curran, J. P., & Monti, P. M. (Eds.). (1982). *Social skills training: A practical handbook for assessment and treatment*. New York: Guilford Press.

Daniel, C. J. (1987). A stimulus satiation treatment programme with a young male fireset-ter. In B. J. McGurk, D. M. Thornton, & M. Williams (Eds.), *Applying psychology to imprisonment: Theory & practice*. London: HMSO.

Davison, G. C., Robins, C., & Johnson, M. K. (1983). Articulated thoughts during simu-lated situations: A paradigm for studying cognition in emotion and behavior. *Cognitive Therapy and Research, 7*, 17–40.

Davidson, W. S., Redner, R., Blakely, C. H., Mitchell, C. M., & Emshoff, J. G. (1987). Diversion of juvenile offenders: An experimental comparison. *Journal of Consulting and Clinical Psychology, 55*, 68–75.

Davidson, W. S., Seidman, E., Rappaport, J., Berck, P., Rapp, N., Rhodes, W., & Herring, J. (1977). Diversion programs for juvenile offenders. *Social Work Research and Abstracts, 13*, 40–49.

DeLange, J. M., Barton, J. A., & Lanham, S. L. (1981). The WISER way: A cognitive-behavioral model for group social skills training with juvenile delinquents. *Social Work With Groups, 4*, 37–48.

DeLange, J. M., Lanham, S. L., & Barton, J. A. (1981). Social skills training for juvenile delinquents: Behavioral skill training and cognitive techniques. In D. Upper & S. Ross (Eds.), *Behavior group therapy, 1981: An annual review* (Vol. 3). Champaign, IL: Research Press.

Dishion, T. J., Loeber, R., Stouthamer-Loeber, M., & Patterson, G. R. (1984). Skill deficits and male adolescent delinquency. *Journal of Abnormal Child Psychology, 12*, 37–54.

Dumas, J. E., & Wahler, R. G. (1983). Predictors of treatment outcome in parent training: Mother insularity and socioeconomic disadvantage. *Behavioral Assessment, 5*, 301–313.

Dunford, F. W., & Elliott, D. S. (1984). Identifying career criminals using self-reported data. *Journal of Research in Crime and Delinquency, 21*, 57–86.

Eisler, R. M., Hersen, M., Miller, P. M., & Blanchard, E. B. (1975). Situational determi-nants of assertive behavior. *Journal of Consulting and Clinical Psychology, 43*, 330–340.

Elliot, D., & Voss, H. (1974). *Delinquency and dropout*. Lexington, MA: Lexington Books.

Ellis, A. (1962). *Reason and emotion in psychotherapy*. New York: Lyle Stuart.

Emery, R. E., & Marholin, D. (1977). An applied behavior analysis of delinquency: The irrelevancy of relevant behavior. *American Psychologist, 6*, 860–873.

Emshoff, J. G., Redd, W. H., & Davidson, W. S. (1976). Generalization training and the transfer of prosocial behavior in delinquent adolescents. *Journal of Behavior Therapy and Experimental Psychiatry, 7*, 141–144.

Eysenck, H. J. (1987). Personality theory and the problems of criminality. In B. J. McGurk, D. M. Thornton, & M. Williams (Eds.), *Applying psychology to imprisonment: Theory and practice*. London: HMSO.

Farrington, D. P. (1983). Offending from 10 to 25 years of age. In K. Teilmann Van Dusen & S. A. Mednick (Eds.), *Prospective studies of crime and delinquency*. The Hague: Kluwer-Nijhoff.

Farrington, D. P. (1986). Age and crime. In M. Tonry & N. Morris (Eds.), *Crime and justice: An annual review of research* (Vol. 7). Chicago: University of Chicago Press.

Feindler, E. L., & Ecton, R. B. (1986). *Adolescent anger control: Cognitive-behavioral techniques.* Elmsford, NY: Pergamon Press.

Feindler, E. L., Marriott, S. A., & Iwata, M. (1984). Group anger control training for junior high school delinquents. *Cognitive Therapy and Research, 8,* 299–311.

Feldman, M. P., & Peay, J. (1982). Ethical and legal issues. In A. S. Bellack, M. Hersen, & A. E. Kazdin (Eds.), *International handbook of behavior modification and therapy.* New York: Plenum Press.

Filipczak, J., & Friedman, R. M. (1978). Some controls on applied research in a public secondary school: Project PREP. In A. C. Catania & A. T. Brigham (Eds.), *Handbook of applied behavior analysis: Social and instructional processes.* New York: Irvington.

Filipczak, J., & Wodarski, J. S. (1982). Behavioral intervention in public schools: I. Short-term results. In D. J. Safer (Ed.), *School programs for disruptive adolescents.* Baltimore: University Park Press.

Finch, A. J., & Eastman, E. S. (1983). A multi-method approach to measuring anger in children. *Journal of Psychology, 115,* 55–60.

Fishman, D. B., Rotgers, F., & Franks, C. M. (Eds.). (1988). *Paradigms in behavior therapy: Present and promise.* New York: Springer.

Fixsen, D. L., Phillips, E. L., & Wolf, M. M. (1973). Experiments in self government with predelinquents. *Journal of Applied Behavior Analysis, 6,* 31–47.

Fo, W. S. O., & O'Donnell, C. R. (1974). The buddy system: Relationship and contingency conditions in a community intervention program for youth and non-professionals as behavior change agents. *Journal of Consulting and Clinical Psychology, 42,* 163–168.

Fo, W. S. O., & O'Donnell, C. R. (1975). The buddy system: Effect of community intervention on delinquent offences. *Behavior Therapy, 6,* 522–524.

Försterling, F. (1986). Attributional conceptions in clinical psychology. *American Psychologist, 41,* 275–285.

Foster, S. L., Bell-Dolan, D. J., & Burge, D. A. (1988). Behavioral observation. In A. S. Bellack & M. Hersen (Eds.), *Behavioral assessment: A practical handbook* (3rd ed.). Elmsford, NY: Pergamon Press.

Foster, S. L., & Cane, J. D. (1986). Design and use of direct observation. In A. R. Ciminero, K. S. Calhoun, & H. E. Adams (Eds.), *Handbook of behavioral assessment* (2nd ed.). New York: Wiley.

Freedman, B. J., Rosenthal, L., Donahue, C. P., Schlundt, D. G., & McFall, R. M. (1978). A social-behavioral analysis of skill deficits in delinquent and non-delinquent adolescent boys. *Journal of Consulting and Clinical Psychology, 46,* 1448–1462.

Friedman, R. M., Filipczak, J., & Fiordaliso, R. (1977). Within-school generalization of the Preparation through Responsive Education Programs (PREP) academic project. *Behavior Therapy, 8,* 986–995.

Gaffney, L. R., & McFall, R. M. (1981). A comparison of social skills in delinquent and nondelinquent adolescent girls using a behavioral role-playing inventory. *Journal of Counsulting and Clinical Psychology, 49,* 959–967.

Garrett, C. J. (1985). Effects of residential treatment on adjudicated delinquents: A meta-analysis. *Journal of Research in Crime and Delinquency, 22,* 287–308.

Geller, E. S., Johnson, D. F., Hamlin, P. H., & Kennedy, T. D. (1977). Behavior modification in prisons: Issues, problems, and compromises. *Criminal Justice and Behavior, 4,* 11–43.

Gendreau, P., & Ross, B. (1979). Effective correctional treatment: Bibliotherapy for cynics. *Crime and Delinquency, 25,* 463–489.

Gentry, M., & Ostapiuk, E. B. (1988). Management of violence in a youth treatment centre. In K. Howells & C. Hollin (Eds.), *Clinical approaches to aggression and violence. Issues in Criminological and Legal Psychology,* No. 12. Leicester: The British Psychological Society.

Gibbs, J. C., Arnold, K. D., Cheesman, F. L., & Ahlborn, H. H. (1984). Facilitation of sociomoral reasoning in delinquents. *Journal of Consulting and Clinical Psychology, 52,* 37–45.

Glaser, D. (1977). The compatibility of free will and determinism in criminology: Comments on an alleged problem. *Journal of Criminal Law and Criminology, 67,* 486–490.

Glass, G. V., McGaw, G., & Smith, M. L. (1981). *Meta-analysis in social research.* Beverly Hills, CA: Sage Publications.

Glick, B., & Goldstein, A. P. (1987). Aggression replacement training. *Journal of Counseling and Development, 65,* 356–367.

Glueck, S., & Glueck, E. (1950). *Unraveling juvenile delinquency.* New York: Harper & Row.

Goff, C. (1986). Criminological appraisals of psychiatric explanations of crime: 1936–1950. *International Journal of Law and Psychiatry, 9,* 245–260.

Goldfried, M. R. (1971). Systematic desensitization as training in self-control. *Journal of Consulting and Clinical Psychology, 37,* 228–234.

Goldsmith, J. B., & McFall, R. M. (1975). Development and evaluation of an interpersonal skill-training program for psychiatric inpatients. *Journal of Abnormal Psychology, 84,* 51–58.

Goldstein, A. P., & Keller, H. (1987). *Aggressive behavior: Assessment and intervention.* Elmsford, NY: Pergamon Press.

Gordon, D. A., & Arbuthnot, J. (1987). Individual, group and family interventions. In H. C. Quay (Ed.), *Handbook of juvenile delinquency.* New York: Wiley.

Gottschalk, R., Davidson, W. S., Gensheimer, L. K., & Mayer, J. P. (1987). Community-based interventions. In H. C. Quay (Ed.), *Handbook of juvenile delinquency.* New York: Wiley.

Groh, T. R., & Goldenberg, E. E. (1976). Locus of control with subgroups in a correctional population. *Criminal Justice and Behavior, 3,* 169–179.

Gross, A. M., Brigham, T. A., Hopper, C., & Bologna, N. C. (1980). Self-management and social skills training: A study with pre-delinquent and delinquent youth. *Criminal Justice and Behavior, 7,* 161–184.

Gunn, J. (1977). Criminal behaviour and mental disorder. *British Journal of Psychiatry, 130,* 317–329.

Gutride, M. E., Goldstein, A. P., & Hunter, G. F. (1973). The use of modeling and role playing to increase social interaction among psychiatric patients. *Journal of Consulting and Clinical Psychology, 40,* 408–415.

Hains, A. A. (1984). A preliminary attempt to teach the use of social problem-solving skills to delinquents. *Child Study Journal, 14,* 271–285.

Hains, A. A., & Ryan, E. B. (1983). The development of social cognitive processes among juvenile delinquents and nondelinquent peers. *Child Development, 54,* 1536–1544.

Hartmann, D. P., & Wood, D. D. (1982). Observational methods. In A. S. Bellack, M. Hersen, & A. E. Kazdin (Eds.), *International handbook of behavior modification and therapy.* New York: Plenum Press.

Hawkins, J. D., & Lishner, D. M. (1987). Schooling and delinquency. In E. H. Johnson (Ed.), *Handbook on crime and delinquency prevention.* New York: Greenwood Press.

Hawkins, J. D., & Weis, J. G. (1985). The social development model: An integrated approach to delinquency prevention. *Journal of Primary Prevention, 6,* 73–97.

Hawkins, R. P. (1982). Developing a behavior code. In D. P. Hartmann (Ed.), *New directions for methodology of social and behavioral science: Using observers to study behavior.* San Francisco: Jossey-Bass.

Haynes, S. N., & Horn, W. F. (1982). Reactivity in behavioral observations: A methodology and conceptual critique. *Behavioral Assessment, 4,* 369–385.

Hazel, J. S., Schumaker, J. B., Sherman, J. A., & Sheldon-Wildgen, J. (1981). The development and evaluation of a group skills program for court-adjudicated youth. In D. Upper & S. M. Ross (Eds.), *Behavioral group therapy, 1981: An annual review*. Champaign, IL: Research Press.

Hazel, J. S., Schumaker, J. B., Sherman, J. A., & Sheldon-Wildgen, J. (1982). Group training for social skills: A program for court-adjudicated probationary youth. *Criminal Justice and Behavior, 9*, 35–53.

Heal, K., & Laycock, G. (Eds.), (1986). *Situational crime prevention: From theory into practice*. London: HMSO.

Heaton, R. C., Safer, D. J., Allen, R. P., Spinnato, N. C., & Prumo, F. M. (1976). A motivational environment for behaviorally deviant junior high school students. *Journal of Abnormal Child Psychology, 4*, 263–275.

Henderson, J. Q. (1981). A behavioral approach to stealing: A proposal for treatment based on ten cases. *Journal of Behavior Therapy and Experimental Psychiatry, 12*, 231–236.

Henderson, M., & Hollin, C. (1983). A critical review of social skills training with young offenders. *Criminal Justice and Behavior, 10*, 316–341.

Henderson, M., & Hollin, C. R. (1986). Social skills training and delinquency. In C. R. Hollin & P. Trower (Eds.), *Handbook of social skills training, Vol. 1: Applications across the life span*. Oxford: Pergamon Press.

Heppner, P. P. (1982). Utilizing a personal problem-solving inventory. *Journal of Counseling Psychology, 29*, 66–75.

Herbert, M. (1987). *Behavioural treatment of children with problems: A practice manual* (2nd ed.). London: Academic Press.

Hersen, M., & Bellack, A. S. (1977). Assessment of social skills. In A. R. Ciminero, K. S. Calhoun, & H. E. Adams (Eds.), *Handbook of behavioral assessment*. New York: Wiley.

Hersen, M., & Turner, S. M. (Eds.). (1985). *Diagnostic interviewing*. New York: Plenum Press.

Higgins, J. P., & Thies, A. P. (1981). Social effectiveness and problem-solving thinking of reformatory inmates. *Journal of Offender Counseling, Services and Rehabilitation, 5*, 93–98.

Hindelang, M. J., Hirschi, T., & Weis, J. G. (1981). *Measuring delinquency*. Beverly Hills, CA: Sage Publications.

Hoghughi, M. S. (1979). The Aycliffe token economy. *British Journal of Criminology, 19*, 384–399.

Hollin, C. R. (1983). Young offenders and alcohol: A survey of the drinking behaviour of a Borstal population. *Journal of Adolescence, 6*, 161–174.

Hollin, C. R. (1989). *Psychology and crime: An introduction to criminological psychology*. London: Routledge.

Hollin, C. R., & Courtney, S. A. (1983). A skills training approach to the reduction of institutional offending. *Personality and Individual Differences, 4*, 257–264.

Hollin, C. R., & Henderson, M. (1981). The effects of social skills training on incarcerated delinquent adolescents. *International Journal of Behavioural Social Work and Abstracts, 1*, 145–155.

Hollin, C. R., & Henderson, M. (1984). Social skills training with young offenders: False expectations and the "failure of treatment." *Behavioural Psychotherapy, 12*, 331–341.

Hollin, C. R., Huff, G. J., Clarkson, F., & Edmondson, A. C. (1986). Social skills training with young offenders in a Borstal: An evaluative study. *Journal of Community Psychology, 14*, 289–299.

Hollin, C. R., & Trower, P. (Eds.). (1986a). *Handbook of social skills training, Vol. 1: Applications across the lifespan*. Oxford: Pergamon Press.

Hollin, C. R., & Trower, P. (Eds.). (1986b). *Handbook of social skills training, Vol. 2: Clinical applications and new directions*. Oxford: Pergamon Press.

Hollin, C. R., & Trower, P. (1988). Development and applications of social skills training:

A review and critique. In M. Hersen, R. M. Eisler, & P. M. Miller (Eds.), *Progress in behavior modification* (Vol. 22). Beverly Hills, CA: Sage Publications.

Hollin, C. R., & Wheeler, H. M. (1982). The violent young offender: A small group study of a Borstal population. *Journal of Adolescence, 5,* 247–257.

Howells, K. (1987). Forensic problems: Investigation. In S. J. E. Lindsay & G. E. Powell (Eds.), *Handbook of clinical psychology.* London: Gower.

Hudson, B. (1987). *Justice through punishment: A critique of the "justice" model of corrections.* London: Macmillan.

Hudson, B. L. (1986). Community applications of social skills training. In C. R. Hollin & P. Trower (Eds.), *Handbook of social skills training, Vol. 1: Applications across the life span.* Oxford: Pergamon Press.

Huff, G. (1987). Social skills training. In B. J. McGurk, D. M. Thornton, & M. Williams (Eds.), *Applying psychology to imprisonment: Theory & practice.* London: HMSO.

Huizinga, D., & Elliott, D. S. (1986). Reassessing the reliability and validity of self-report delinquency measures. *Journal of Quantitative Criminology, 2,* 293–327.

Hunter, J., Schmidt, F., & Jackson, G. (1982). *Meta-analysis: Cumulating research findings across studies.* Beverly Hills, CA: Sage Publications.

Hunter, N., & Kelley, C. K. (1986). Examination of the validity of the Adolescent Problems Inventory among incarcerated juvenile delinquents. *Journal of Consulting and Clinical Psychology, 54,* 301–302.

Jacob, T. (1975). Family interaction in disturbed and normal families: A methodological and substantive review. *Psychological Bulletin, 82,* 33–65.

Jacobson, N. S. (1985a). The role of observational measures in behavior therapy. *Behavioral Assessment, 7,* 297–308.

Jacobson, N. S. (1985b). Uses versus abuses of observational measures. *Behavioral Assessment, 7,* 323–330.

James, I. L., Beier, C. H., Maloney, D. M., Thompson, L., Collins, L. B., & Collins, S. R. (1983). *1983 directory of the National Teaching-Family Association.* Boys Town, NE: Father Flanagan's Boys' Home.

Jeffery, C. R. (1965). Criminal behavior and learning theory. *Journal of Criminal Law, Criminology and Police Science, 56,* 294–300.

Jennings, W. S., Kilkenny, R., & Kohlberg, L. (1983). Moral development theory and practice for youthful and adult offenders. In W. S. Laufer & J. M. Day (Eds.), *Personality theory, moral development, and criminal behavior.* Toronto: Lexington Books.

Jesness, C. F., Allison, T. F., McCormick, P. M., Wedge, R. F., & Young, M. L. (1975). *The Cooperative Behavior Demonstration Project.* Sacramento, CA: California Youth Authority.

Jesness, C. F., & DeRisi, W. M. (1973). Some variations in techniques of contingency management in a school for delinquents. In J. S. Stumphauzer (Ed.), *Behavior therapy with delinquents.* Springfield, IL: C. C. Thomas.

Johnson, E. H. (Ed.). (1987). *Handbook on crime and delinquency prevention.* New York: Greenwood Press.

Jurkovic, G. J. (1980). The juvenile delinquent as moral philosopher: A structural-developmental approach. *Psychological Bulletin, 88,* 709–727.

Kagan, C. (1984). Social problem solving and social skills training. *British Journal of Clinical Psychology, 23,* 161–173.

Kallman, W. M., & Feuerstein, M. J. (1986). Psychophysiological procedures. In A. R. Ciminero, K. S. Calhoun, & H. E. Adams (Eds.), *Handbook of behavioral assessment.* New York: Wiley.

Kanfer, F. H. (1975). Self-management methods. In F. H. Kanfer & A. P. Goldstein (Eds.), *Helping people change: A textbook of methods.* Elmsford, NY: Pergamon Press.

Kanfer, F. H. (1985). Target selection for clinical change programs. *Behavioral Assessment, 7,* 7–20.

Kanfer, F. H., & Grimm, L. G. (1977). Behavioral analysis: Selecting target behaviors in the interview. *Behavior Modification, 4,* 419–444.

Kaplan, P. J., & Arbuthnot, J. (1985). Affective empathy and cognitive role-taking in delinquent and nondelinquent youth. *Adolescence, 20,* 323–333.

Karacki, L., & Levinson, R. B. (1970). A token economy in a correctional institution for youthful offenders. *Howard Journal of Penology and Crime Prevention, 13,* 20–30.

Katkin, E. S., & Hastrup, J. L. (1982). Psychophysiological methods in clinical research. In P. C. Kendall & J. B. Butcher (Eds.), *Handbook of research methods in clinical psychology.* New York: Wiley.

Kauffman, J., & Nelson, M. (1977). Educational programming for secondary school age delinquent and maladjusted pupils. *Behavioral Disorders, 2,* 29–37.

Kazdin, A. E. (1982). The token economy: A decade later. *Journal of Applied Behavior Analysis, 15,* 431–445.

Kazdin, A. E. (1987). Treatment of antisocial behavior in children: Current status and future directions. *Psychological Bulletin, 102,* 187–203.

Kazdin, A. E., & Bootzin, R. R. (1972). The token economy: An evaluative review. *Journal of Applied Behavior Analysis, 5,* 343–372.

Kendall, P. C., & Bacon, S. F. (1988). Cognitive behavior therapy. In D. B. Fishman, F. Rotgers, & C. M. Franks (Eds.), *Paradigms in behavior therapy: Present and promise.* New York: Springer.

Kendall, P. C., & Hollon, S. D. (Eds.). (1981). *Assessment strategies for cognitive-behavioral interventions.* New York: Academic Press.

Kiesler, D. J. (1966). Some myths of psychotherapy research and the search for a paradigm. *Psychological Bulletin, 65,* 110–136.

Kifer, R. E., Lewis, M. A., Green, D. R., & Phillips, E. L. (1974). Training pre-delinquent youths and their families to negotiate conflict situations. *Journal of Applied Behavior Analysis, 7,* 357–364.

Kirigin, K. A., Braukmann, C. J., Atwater, J., & Wolf, M. M. (1982). An evaluation of Achievement Place (Teaching-Family) group homes for juvenile offenders. *Journal of Applied Behavior Analysis, 15,* 1–16.

Kirigin, K. A., Phillips, E. L., Timbers, G. D., Fixsen, D. L., & Wolf, M. M. (1975). The modification of academic behavior problems of youths in a group home setting. In B. C. Etzel, J. M. LeBlanc, & D. M. Baer (Eds.), *New developments in behavioral research: Theory, method and application.* Hillsdale, NJ: Lawrence Erlbaum.

Kirigin, K. A., Wolf, M. M., Braukmann, C. J., Fixsen D. L., & Phillips, E. L. (1979). Achievement Place: A preliminary outcome evaluation. In J. S. Stumphauzer (Ed.), *Progress in behavior therapy with delinquents.* Springfield, IL: C. C. Thomas.

Klein, N. C., Alexander, J. F., & Parsons, B. V. (1977). Impact of family systems intervention on recidivism and sibling delinquency: A model of primary prevention and program evaluation. *Journal of Consulting and Clinical Psychology, 45,* 469–474.

Klinger, E. (1978). Modes of normal consciousness flow. In K. S. Pope & J. L. Singer (Eds.), *The stream of consciousness: Scientific investigations into the flow of human experience.* New York: Plenum Press.

Krohn, M. D., Massey, J. L., & Skinner, W. F. (1987). A sociological theory of crime and delinquency: Social learning theory. In E. K. Morris & C. J. Braukmann (Eds.), *Behavioral approaches to crime and delinquency: A handbook of application, research, and concepts.* New York: Plenum Press.

Kumchy, C., & Sayer, L. A. (1980). Locus of control and delinquent adolescent populations. *Psychological Reports, 46,* 1307–1310.

L'Abate, L., & Milan, M. A. (1985). *Handbook of social skills training and research.* New York: Wiley.

Lane, T. W., & Murakami, J. (1987). School programs for delinquency prevention and intervention. In E. K. Morris & C. J. Braukmann (Eds.), *Behavioral approaches to crime and delinquency: A handbook of application, research, and concepts.* New York: Plenum Press.

Laws, D. R. (1974). The failure of a token economy. *Federal Probation, 38,* 33–38.

Ledwidge, B. (1978). Cognitive-behavior modification: A step in the wrong direction? *Psychological Bulletin, 95,* 353–375.

Ledwidge, B. (1979). Cognitive-behavior modification: A rejoinder to Locke and Meichenbaum. *Cognitive Therapy and Research, 3,* 133–139.

Lefcourt, H. M., & Ladwig, G. W. (1965). The American Negro: A problem in expectancies. *Journal of Personality and Social Psychology, 1,* 377–380.

Levitt, E. E., & Lubin, B. (1975). *Depression: Concepts, controversies and some new facts.* New York: Springer-Verlag.

Liberman, K. P., King, L. W., DeRisi, W. J., & McCann, M. (1975). *Personal effectiveness: Guiding people to assert themselves and improve their personal skills.* Champaign, IL: Research Press.

Liberman, R. P., Ferris, C., Salgado, P., & Salgado, J. (1975). Replication of Achievement Place model in California. *Journal of Applied Behavior Analysis, 8,* 287–299.

Lipton, D., Martinson, R., & Wilks, D. (1975). *The effectiveness of correctional treatment.* New York: Praeger.

Locke, E. A. (1979). Behavior modification is not cognitive and other myths: A reply to Ledwidge. *Cognitive Therapy and Research, 3,* 119–125.

Loeber, R., & Dishion, T. (1983). Early predictors of male delinquency: A review. *Psychological Bulletin, 94,* 168–199.

Long, S. J., & Sherer, M. (1984). Social skills training with juvenile offenders. *Child and Family Behavior Therapy, 6,* 1–11.

Lowe, C. F. (1983). Radical behaviourism and human psychology. In G. C. L. Davey (Ed.), *Animal models of human behaviour.* Chichester, England: Wiley.

Lowe, C. F., & Higson, P. J. (1981). Self-instructional training and cognitive behaviour modification: A behavioural analysis. In G. Davey (Ed.), *Applications of conditioning theory.* London: Methuen.

Luria, A. R. (1961). *The role of speech in the regulation of normal and abnormal behavior.* New York: Liveright.

Maloney, D. M., Harper, T. M., Braukmann, C. J., Fixsen, D. L., Phillips, E. L., & Wolf, M. M. (1976). Teaching conversation skills to predelinquent girls. *Journal of Applied Behavior Analysis, 9,* 371.

Martinson, R. (1974). What works? Questions and answers about prison reform. *The Public Interest, 35,* 22–54.

Masters, J. C., Burish, T. G., Hollon, S. D., & Rimm, D. C. (1987). *Behavior therapy: Techniques and empirical findings* (3rd ed.). Orlando, FL: Harcourt Brace Jovanovich.

Mathews, A., & MacLeod, C. (1986). Discimination of threat cues without awareness in anxiety states. *Journal of Abnormal Psychology, 95,* 131–138.

McClannahan, L. E., Krantz, P. J., McGee, G. G., & MacDuff, G. S. (1984). Teaching-family model for autistic children. In W. P. Christian, G. T. Hannah, & T. J. Glahn (Eds.), *Programming effective human services.* New York: Plenum Press.

McCord, J. (1978). A thirty-year follow-up of treatment effects. *American Psychologist, 33,* 284–289.

McCown, W., Johnson, J., & Austin, S. (1986). Inability of delinquents to recognise facial affects. *Journal of Social Behavior and Personality, 1,* 489–496.

McDougall, C., Barnett, R. M., Ashurst, B., & Willis, B. (1987). Cognitive control of anger. In B. J. McGurk, D. M. Thornton, & M. Williams (Eds.), *Applying psychology to imprisonment: Theory & practice.* London: HMSO.

McDougall, C., Thomas, M., & Wilson, J. (1987). Attitude change and the violent football supporter. In B. J. McGurk, D. M. Thornton, & M. Williams (Eds.), *Applying psychology to imprisonment: Theory & practice*. London: HMSO.

McFall, R. M. (1982). A review and reformulation of the concept of social skills. *Behavioral Assessment, 4*, 1–33.

McGurk, B. J. (1979). Megargee's theory of control and development of the Undercontrolled Personality Scale. *Directorate of Psychological Services Report*, Series II, No. 68. London: Home Office.

McGurk, B. J., & Newell, T. C. (1981). Social skills training with a sex offender. *The Psychological Record, 31*, 277–283.

McGurk, B. J., & Newell, T. C. (1987). Social skills training: Case study with a sex offender. In B. J. McGurk, D. M. Thornton, & M. Williams (Eds.), *Applying psychology to imprisonment: Theory & practice*. London: HMSO.

McNeil, J. K., & Hart, D. S. (1986). The effect of self-government on the aggressive behavior of institutionalized delinquent adolescents. *Criminal Justice and Behavior, 13*, 430–445.

Meichenbaum, D. H. (1971). Examination of model characteristics in reducing avoidance behavior. *Journal of Personality and Social Psychology, 17*, 298–307.

Meichenbaum, D. M. (1977). *Cognitive behavior modification*. New York: Plenum Press.

Meichenbaum, D., & Goodman, J. (1971). Training impulsive children to talk to themselves: A means of developing self-control. *Journal of Abnormal Psychology, 77*, 115–126.

Milan, M. A. (1987). Basic behavioral procedures in closed institutions. In E. K. Morris & C. J. Braukmann (Eds.), *Behavioral approaches to crime and delinquency: A handbook of application, research, and concepts*. New York: Plenum Press.

Miller, A. D., Ohlin, L. E., & Coates, R. B. (1977). *A theory of social reform: Correctional change processes in two states*. Cambridge, MA: Ballinger.

Miller, N. E. (1960). Learning resistence to pain and fear: Effects of overlearning, exposure, and rewarded exposure in context. *Journal of Experimental Psychology, 60*, 137–145.

Milne, J., & Spence, S. H. (1987). Training social perception skills with primary school children: A cautionary note. *Behavioural Psychotherapy, 15*, 144–157.

Modgil, S., & Modgil, C. (Eds.). (1987). *B. F. Skinner: Consensus and controversy*. New York: Falmer Press.

Monahan, J., & Steadman, H. J. (Eds.). (1983). *Mentally disordered offenders: Perspectives from law and social science*. New York: Plenum Press.

Morganstern, K. P. (1988). Behavioral interviewing. In A. S. Bellack & M. Hersen (Eds.), *Behavioral assessment: A practical handbook* (3rd ed.). Elmsford, NY: Pergamon Press.

Morris, E. K. (1987). Introductory comments: Applied behavior analysis in crime and delinency: Focus on prevention. *The Behavior Analyst, 10*, 67–68.

Morton, T. L., & Ewald, L. S. (1987). Family-based interventions for crime and delinquency. In E. K. Morris & C. J. Braukmann (Eds.), *Behavioral approaches to crime and delinquency: A handbook of application, research, and concepts*. New York: Plenum Press.

Mulvey, E. P., & LaRosa, J. F. (1986). Delinquency cessation and adolescent development: Preliminary data. *American Journal of Orthopsychiatry, 56*, 212–224.

Murphy, G. C., Hudson, A. M., King, N. J., & Remenyi, A. (1985). An interview schedule for use in the behavioural assessment of children's problems. *Behaviour Change, 2*, 6–12.

Nelson, R. O., & Barlow, D. H. (1981). Behavioral assessment: Basic strategies and initial procedures. In D. H. Barlow (Ed.), *Behavioral assessment of adult disorders*. New York: Guilford Press.

Nettleback, T., & Kirby, N. H. (1976). A comparison of part and whole training methods with mildly mentally retarded workers. *Journal of Occupational Psychology, 49*, 115–120.

Nietzel, M. T. (1979). *Crime and its modification: A social learning perspective*. Elmsford, NY: Pergamon Press.

Nietzel, M. T., & Himelein, M. J. (1986). Prevention of crime and delinquency. In B. A. Edelstein & L. Michelson (Eds.), *Handbook of prevention*. New York: Plenum Press.

Nietzel, M. T., & Himelein, M. J. (1987). Probation and parole. In E. K. Morris & C. J. Braukmann (Eds.), *Behavioral approaches to crime and delinquency: A handbook of application, research, and concepts*. New York: Plenum Press.

Novaco, R. W. (1975). *Anger control: The development and evaluation of an experimental treatment*. Lexington, MA: D. C. Heath.

Novaco, R. W. (1978). Anger and coping with stress. In J. P. Foreyt & D. P. Rathjen (Eds.), *Cognitive behavior therapy*. Lexington, MA: Heath.

Novaco, R. W. (1979). The cognitive regulation of anger and stress. In P. Kendall & S. Hollon (Eds.), *Cognitive-behavioral interventions: Theory, research and procedures*. New York: Academic Press.

Novaco, R. W. (1980). Training of probation counsellors for anger problems. *Journal of Counselling Psychology, 27,* 385–390.

Novaco, R. W. (1985). Anger and its therapeutic regulation. In M. A. Chesney & R. H. Rosenman (Eds.), *Anger and hostility in cardiovascular and behavioral disorders*. New York: Hemisphere.

O'Donnell, C. R., Lydgate, T., & Fo, W. S. O. (1979). The buddy system: Review and follow-up. *Child Behavior Therapy, 1,* 161–169.

Ollendick, T. H., & Hersen, M. (1979). Social skills training for juvenile delinquents. *Behaviour Research and Therapy, 17,* 547–554.

Ostapiuk, E. B., & Westwood, S. (1986). Glenthorne Youth Treatment Centre: Working with adolescents in gradations of security. In C. Hollin & K. Howells (Eds.), *Clinical approaches to criminal behaviour. Issues in Criminological and Legal Psychology, No. 9.* Leicester, England: The British Psychological Society.

Ostrom, T., Steele, C., Rosenblood, L. K., & Mirels, H. (1971). Modification of delinquent behavior. *Journal of Applied Social Psychology, 1,* 118–136.

Overall, J. E., & Gorham, D. R. (1962). The Brief Psychiatric Rating Scale. *Psychological Reports, 10,* 799–812.

Palamara, F., Cullen, F. T., & Gersten, J. C. (1986). The effect of police and mental health intervention on juvenile deviance: Specifying contingencies in the impact of formal reaction. *Journal of Health and Social Behavior, 27,* 90–105.

Parks, C. W., & Hollon, S. D. (1988). Cognitive assessment. In A. S. Bellack & M. Hersen (Eds.), *Behavioral assessment: A practical handbook* (3rd ed.). Elmsford, NY: Pergamon Press.

Parsons, B. V., & Alexander, J. F. (1973). Short-term family intervention: A therapy outcome study. *Journal of Consulting and Clinical Psychology, 41,* 195–201.

Patterson, G. R. (1985). Beyond technology: The next stage in developing an empirical base for training. In L. L'Abate (Ed.), *Handbook of family psychology and therapy* (Vol. 2). Homewood, IL: Dorsey.

Patterson, G. R. (1986). Performance models for antisocial boys. *American Psychologist, 41,* 432–444.

Patterson G. R., & Stouthamer-Loeber, M. (1984). The correlation of family management practices and delinquency. *Child Development, 55,* 1299–1307.

Perkins, D. E. (1987). A psychological treatment programme for sex offenders. In B. J. McGurk, D. M. Thornton, & M. Williams (Eds)., *Applying psychology to imprisonment: Theory & practice*. London: HMSO.

Peterson, D. R. (1968). *The clinical study of social behavior*. New York: Appleton-Century-Crofts.

Phillips, E. L. (1978). *Progress report: A 1977 evaluation of Boys Town Youth Care Department program*. Monograph Series, Boys' Town Community-Based Programs, Omaha, Neb.

Phillips, E. L., Phillips, E. A., Fixsen, D. L., & Wolf, M. M. (1971). Achievement Place: The modification of the behaviors of pre-delinquent boys with a token economy. *Journal of Applied Behavior Analysis, 4,* 45–59.

Phillips, E. L., Phillips, E. A., Fixsen, D. L., & Wolf, M. M. (1974). *The teaching-family handbook* (rev. ed.). Lawrence, KS: University of Kansas Printing Service.

Platt, J. J., Perry, G., & Metzger, D. (1980). The evaluation of a heroin addiction treatment program within a correctional setting. In R. Ross & P. Gendreau (Eds.), *Effective correctional treatment.* Toronto: Butterworths.

Pope, K. S. (1978). How gender, solitude, and posture influence the stream of consciousness. In K. S. Pope & J. L. Singer (Eds.), *The stream of consciousness: Scientific investigation into the flow of human experience.* New York: Plenum Press.

Powers, E., & Witmar, H. (1951). *An experiment in the prevention of delinquency: The Cambridge-Somerville youth study.* New York: Columbia University Press.

Preston, M. A. (1982). Intermediate treatment: A new approach to community care. In M. P. Feldman (Ed.), *Developments in the study of criminal behaviour, Vol. 1: The prevention and control of offending.* Chichester, England: Wiley.

Prins, H. (1982). *Criminal behaviour: An introduction to criminology and the penal system* (2nd ed.). London: Tavistock Publications.

Quay, H. C. (1977). The three faces of evaluation: What can be expected to work? *Criminal Justice and Behavior, 4,* 341–354.

Quay, H. C. (1987). Institutional treatment. In H. C. Quay (Ed.), *Handbook of juvenile delinquency.* New York: Wiley.

Quinsey, V. L., Chaplin, T. C., & Upfold, D. (1984). Sexual arousal to nonsexual violence and sadomasochistic themes among rapists and non-sex offenders. *Journal of Consulting and Clinical Psychology, 52,* 651–657.

Quinsey, V. L., Chaplin, T. C., & Varney, G. (1981). A comparison of rapists' and non-sex offenders' sexual preferences for mutually consenting sex, rape, and physical abuse of women. *Behavioral Assessment, 3,* 127–135.

Reid, I. (1982). The development and maintenance of a behavioural regime in a Youth Treatment Centre. In M. P. Feldman (Ed.), *Developments in the study of criminal behaviour, Vol. 1: The prevention and control of offending.* Chichester, England: Wiley.

Reid, I. D., Feldman, M. P., & Ostapiuk, E. B. (1980). The Shape Project for young offenders: Introduction and overview. *Journal of Offender Counseling, Services and Rehabilitation, 4,* 233–246.

Remington, B., & Remington, M. (1987). Behavior modification in probation work: A review and evaluation. *Criminal Justice and Behavior, 14,* 156–174.

Reppetto, T. A. (1976). Crime prevention and the displacement phenomenon. *Crime and Delinquency, 22,* 166–177.

Repucci, N. D., & Saunders, J. T. (1974). Social psychology of behavior modification: Problems of implementation in natural settings. *American Psychologist, 29,* 649–660.

Roberts, A. R. (1987). National survey and assessment of 66 treatment programs for juvenile offenders: Model programs and pseudomodels. *Juvenile and Family Court Journal, 38,* 39–45.

Roberts, R. N., & Tharp, R. G. (1980). A naturalistic study of school children's private speech in an academic problem-solving task. *Cognitive Therapy and Research, 4,* 341–352.

Romero, J. J., & Williams, L. M. (1983). Group psychotherapy and intensive probation supervision with sex offenders: A comparative study. *Federal Probation, 41,* 36–42.

Rosen, R. C., & Keefe, R. J. (1978). The measurement of human penile tumescence. *Psychophysiology, 15,* 366–376.

Rosenbaum, M. (1980). A schedule for assessing self-control behaviors: Preliminary findings. *Behavior Therapy, 11,* 109–121.

Ross, R. R., & Fabiano, E. A. (1985). *Time to think: A cognitive model of delinquency prevention and offender rehabilitation.* Johnson City, TN: Institute of Social Sciences and Arts.

Ross, R. R., Fabiano, E. A., & Ewles, C. D. (1988). Reasoning and rehabilitation. *International Journal of Offender Therapy and Comparative Criminology, 32,* 29–35.

Ross, R. R., & McKay, H. B. (1976). A study of institutional treatment programs. *International Journal of Offender Therapy and Comparative Criminology, 20,* 165–173.

Rotenberg, M. (1974). Conceptual and methodological notes on affective and cognitive role taking (sympathy and empathy): An illustrative experiment of delinquent and non-delinquent boys. *Journal of Genetic Psychology, 125,* 177–185.

Rotenberg, M., & Nachshon, I. (1979). Impulsiveness and aggression among Israeli delinquents. *British Journal of Social and Clinical Psychology, 18,* 59–63.

Rotter, J. B. (1954). *Social learning and clinical psychology.* Englewood Cliffs, NJ: Prentice-Hall.

Rotter, J. B. (1966). Generalized expectancies for internal versus external control of reinforcement. *Psychological Monographs, 80,* (Whole No. 609).

Rotton, J., & Frey, J. (1985). Air pollution, weather, and violent crime: Concomitant time-series analysis of archival data. *Journal of Personality and Social Psychology, 49,* 1207–1220.

Rutherford, A. (1986). *Growing out of crime: Society and young people in trouble.* Harmondsworth, Middlesex, England: Penguin Books.

Rutter, M., & Giller, H. (1983). *Juvenile delinquency: Trends and perspectives.* Harmondsworth, Middlesex, England: Penguin Books.

Safer, D. J., Heaton, R. C., & Parker, F. C. (1981). A behavioral program for disruptive junior high school students: Results and follow-up. *Journal of Abnormal Child Psychology, 9,* 483–494.

Sarason, I. G., & Ganzer, V. J. (1973). Modeling and group discussion in the rehabilitation of juvenile delinquents. *American Psychologist, 23,* 254–266.

Saunders, J. T., Reppucci, N. D., & Sarata, B. P. (1973). An examination of impulsivity as a trait characterizing delinquent youth. *American Journal of Orthopsychiatry, 43,* 789–795.

Schafer, S. (1977). The problem of free will in criminology. *Journal of Criminal Law and Criminology, 67,* 481–485.

Schlichter, K. J., & Horan, J. J. (1981). Effects of stress innoculation on the anger and aggression management skills of institutionalized juvenile delinquents. *Cognitive Therapy and Research, 5,* 359–365.

Schneider, P. R., Griffith, W. R., & Schneider, A. L. (1982). Juvenile restitution as a sole sanction or condition of probation: An empirical analysis. *Journal of Research in Crime and Delinquency, 19,* 47–65.

Schrest, L., & Rosenblatt, A. (1987). Research methods. In H. C. Quay (Ed.), *Handbook of juvenile delinquency.* New York: Wiley.

Schwartz, A., & Goldiamond, I. (1975). *Social casework: A behavioral approach.* New York: Columbia University Press.

Serna, L. A., Schumaker, J. B., Hazel, J. S., & Sheldon, J. B. (1986). Teaching reciprocal social skills to delinquents and their parents. *Journal of Clinical Child Psychology, 15,* 64–77.

Shapland, J. (1978). Self-reported delinquency in boys aged 11 to 14. *British Journal of Criminology, 18,* 255–266.

Shepherd, G. (1980). The treatment of social difficulties in special environments. In P. Feldman & J. Orford (Eds.), *Psychological problems: The social context.* Chichester, England: Wiley.

Shepherd, G. (1983). Social skills training with adults. In S. Spence & G. Shepherd (Eds.), *Developments in social skills training.* London: Academic Press.

Shepherd, G. (1984). Assessment of cognitions in social skills training. In P. Trower (Ed.), *Radical approaches to social skills training*. London: Croom Helm.

Siegal, L. J. (1986). *Criminology* (2nd ed.). St. Paul, MN: West Publishing.

Sinclair, I., & Clarke, R. (1982). Predicting, treating, and explaining delinquency: The lessons from research on institutions. In M. P. Feldman (Ed.), *Developments in the study of criminal behaviour, Vol. 1: The prevention and control of offending*. Chichester, England: Wiley.

Skinner, B. F. (1938). *The behavior of organisms*. New York: Appleton-Century-Crofts.

Skinner, B. F. (1953). *Science and human behavior*. New York: Macmillan.

Skinner, B. F. (1974). *About behaviorism*. London: Cape.

Skinner, B. F. (1986a). Is it behaviorism? *Behavioral and Brain Sciences, 9*, 716.

Skinner, B. F. (1986b). What is wrong with daily life in the western world? *American Psychologist, 41*, 568–574.

Sloane, H. N., & Ralph, J. L. (1973). A behavior modification program in Nevada. *International Journal of Offender Therapy and Comparative Criminology, 17*, 290–296.

Snyder, J., & Patterson, G. R. (1987). Family interaction and delinquent behavior. In H. C. Quay (Ed.), *Handbook of juvenile delinquency*. New York: Wiley.

Snyder, J. J., & White, M. J. (1979). The use of cognitive self-instruction in the treatment of behaviorally disturbed adolescents. *Behavior Therapy, 10*, 227–235.

Sobell, L. C., & Sobell, M. B. (1978). Validity of self-reports in three populations of alcoholics. *Journal of Consulting and Clinical Psychology, 46*, 901–907.

Spence, A. J., & Spence, S. H. (1980). Cognitive changes associated with social skills training. *Behaviour Research and Therapy, 18*, 265–272.

Spence, S. H. (1979). Social skills training with adolescent offenders: A review. *Behavioural Psychotherapy, 7*, 49–56.

Spence, S. H. (1981a). Validation of social skills of adolescent males in an interview conversation with a previously unknown adult. *Journal of Applied Behavior Analysis, 14*, 159–168.

Spence, S. H. (1981b). Differences in social skills performance between institutionalized male offenders and a comparable group of boys without offence records. *British Journal of Clinical Psychology, 20*, 163–171.

Spence, S. H. (1982). Social skills training with young offenders. In M. P. Feldman (Ed.), *Developments in the study of criminal behaviour, Vol. 1: The prevention and control of offending*. Chichester, England: Wiley.

Spence, S. H., & Marzillier, J. S. (1979). Social skills training with adolescent male offenders: I. Short-term effects. *Behaviour Research and Therapy, 17*, 7–16.

Spence, S. H., & Marzillier, J. S. (1981). Social skills training with adolescent male offenders: II. Short-term, long-term and generalized effects. *Behaviour Research and Therapy, 19*, 349–368.

Spivack, G., Platt, J. J., & Shure, M. B. (1976). *The problem-solving approach to adjustment: A guide to research and intervention*. San Francisco: Jossey-Bass.

Stefanek, M. E., Ollendick, T. H., Baldock, W. P., Francis, G., & Yaeger, N. J. (1987). Self-statements in aggressive, withdrawn, and popular children. *Cognitive Research and Therapy, 11*, 229–239.

Stravynski, A., & Shahar, A. (1983). The treatment of social dysfunction in non-psychotic outpatients: A review. *Journal of Nervous and Mental Diseases, 171*, 721–728.

Strosahl, K. D., & Ascough, J. C. (1981). Clinical uses of mental imagery: Experimental foundations, theoretical misconceptions, and research issues. *Psychological Bulletin, 89*, 422–438.

Stuart, R. B. (1971). Behavioral contracting with the families of delinquents. *Journal of Behavior Therapy and Experimental Psychiatry, 2* 1–11.

Stumphauzer, J. S. (1976). Elimination of stealing by self-reinforcement of alternative behavior and family contracting. *Journal of Behavior Therapy and Experimental Psychiatry, 7*,
265–268.

Sutherland, E. H. (1924). *Principles of criminology*. Philadelphia: Lippincott.

Sutherland, E. H. (1947). *Principles of criminology* (4th ed.). Philadelphia: Lippincott.

Sutherland, E. H., & Cressey, D. R. (1970). *Criminology* (8th ed.). Philadelphia: Lippincott.

Sutherland, E. H., & Cressey, D. R. (1974). *Criminology* (9th ed.). Philadelphia: Lippincott.

Taylor, L. (1984). *In the underworld*. London: Guild Publishing.

Thelen, M. H., Fry, R. A., Dollinger, S. J., & Paul, S. C. (1976). Use of videotaped models
to improve the interpersonal adjustment of delinquents. *Journal of Consulting and Clinical
Psychology, 44*, 492.

Thornberry, T., Moore, M., & Christenson, R. (1985). The effect of dropping out of high
school on subsequent criminal behavior. *Criminology, 23*, 3–18.

Thornton, D., Curran, L., Grayson, D., & Holloway, V. (1984). *Tougher regimes in detention
centres: Report of an evaluation by the Young Offender Psychology Unit*. London: HMSO.

Thornton, D. M. (1987). Treatment effects on recidivism: A reappraisal of the "nothing
works" doctrine. In B. J. McGurk, D. M. Thornton, & M. Williams (Eds.), *Applying
psychology to imprisonment: Theory & practice*. London: HMSO.

Thorpe, D. (1978). Intermediate treatment. In N. Tutt (Ed.), *Alternative strategies for coping
with crime*. Oxford: Blackwell.

Trasler, G. (1986). Situational crime control and rational choice: A critique. In K. Heal &
G. Laycock (Eds.), *Situational crime prevention: From theory into practice*. London: HMSO.

Trasler, G. (1987). Biogenetic factors. In H. C. Quay (Ed.), *Handbook of juvenile delinquency*.
New York: Wiley.

Trower, P., Bryant, B., & Argyle, M. (1978). *Social skills and mental health*. London:
Methuen.

Truax, C. B. (1966). Reinforcement and non-reinforcement in Rogerian psychotherapy.
Journal of Abnormal Psychology, 71, 1–9.

Twentyman, G. T., & Zimmering, R. T. (1979). Behavioral training of social skills: A critical
review. In M. Hersen, R. M. Eisler, & P. M. Miller (Eds.), *Progress in behavior modification*
(Vol. 7). New York: Academic Press.

Tyler, V. O., & Brown, G. D. (1968). Token reinforcement of academic performance with
institutionalized delinquent boys. *Journal of Educational Psychology, 59*, 164–168.

Tyron, W. W. (1982). A simplified time-series analysis for evaluating treatment interventions. *Journal of Applied Behavior Analysis, 15*, 423–429.

Van Den Haag, E. (1982). Could successful rehabilitation reduce the crime rate? *Journal of
Criminal Law and Criminology, 73*, 1022–1035.

Ward, C. I., & McFall, R. M. (1986). Further validation of the Problem Inventory for Adolescent Girls: Comparing Caucasian and black delinquents and nondelinquents. *Journal
of Consulting and Clinical Psychology, 54*, 732–733.

Weber, D. E., & Burke, W. H. (1986). An alternative approach to treating delinquent
youth. *Residential Group Care and Treatment, 3*, 65–85.

Weinrott, M. R., Jones, R. R., & Howard, J. R. (1982). Cost effectiveness of teaching family
programs for delinquents: Results of a national evaluation. *Evaluation Review, 6*, 173–
201.

Welch, G. J. (1985). Contingency contracting with a delinquent and his family. *Journal of
Behavior Therapy and Experimental Psychiatry, 16*, 253–259.

Wells, R. A., & Dezen, A. E. (1978). The results of family therapy revisited: The non-
behavioral methods. *Family Process, 17*, 251–274.

Welsh, R. S. (1971). The use of stimulus satiation in the elimination of juvenile firesetting
behavior. In A. M. Grazians (Ed.), *Behavior therapy and children*. Chicago: Aldine.

Werner, J. S., Minkin, N., Minkin, B. L., Fixsen, D. L., Phillips, E. L., & Wolf, M. M. (1975). "Intervention package": An analysis to prepare juvenile delinquents for encounters with police officers. *Criminal Justice and Behavior, 2,* 55–84.

West, D. J. (1980). The clinical approach to criminology. *Psychological Medicine, 10,* 619–631.

West, D. J. (1982). *Delinquency: Its roots, careers and prospects.* London: Heinemann.

West, D. J., & Farrington, D. P. (1977). *The delinquent way of life.* London: Heinemann.

Williams, D. Y., & Akamatso, T. J. (1978). Cognitive self-guidance training with juvenile delinquents: Applicability and generalization. *Cognitive Therapy and Research, 2,* 285–288.

Williams, G. (1975). The definition of crime. In J. Smith & B. Hogan (Eds.), *Criminal law* (2nd ed.). London: Butterworths.

Willis, A. (1986). Help and control in probation: An empirical assessment of probation practice. In J. Pointing (Ed.), *Alternatives to custody.* Oxford: Blackwell.

Wodarski, J. S., & Filipczak, J. (1982). Behavioral intervention in public schools: II. Long-term follow-up. In D. J. Safer (Ed.), *School programs for disruptive adolescents.* Baltimore, MD: University Park Press.

Wolery, M., & Billingsley, F. F. (1982). The application of Revasky's R_n test to slope and level changes. *Behavioral Assessment, 4,* 93–103.

Wolfgang, M. E., Thornberry, T. P., & Figlio, R. M. (1987). *From boy to man, from delinquency to crime.* Chicago: University of Chicago Press.

Wolpe, J. (1983). *The practice of behavior therapy* (3rd ed.). Elmsford, NY: Pergamon Press.

Wood, G., Green, L., & Bry, B. H. (1982). The input of behavioral training upon the knowledge and effectiveness of juvenile probation officers and volunteers. *Journal of Community Psychology, 10,* 133–141.

Yochelson, S., & Samenow, S. E. (1976). *The criminal personality, Vol. 1: A profile for change.* New York: Jason Aronsen.

Yule, W., & Brown, B. J. (1987). Some behavioral applications with juvenile offenders outside North America. In E. K. Morris & C. J. Braukmann (Eds.), *Behavioral approaches to crime and delinquency: A handbook of application, research, and concepts.* New York: Plenum Press.

Zuriff, G. E. (1985). *Behaviorism: A conceptual reconstruction.* New York: Columbia University Press.

Author Index

Subject Index

Functional analysis, 26–29, 48–49
  antecedents, 26–27
  behavior, 27–28
  consequences, 28–29
Functional family therapy (FFT), 95–98
  contingency contracting and, 95–97
  definition of, 95

"Getting It Together" (GIT) program, 73
Glenthorne Youth Treatment Centre, 86–87, 138–40
Goal stage, of social skills model, 54

Homework, social skills training (SST), 56

Impulsivity, 11–12
Individual programs, 51–78
  behavior therapy, 51–54
  cognitive-behavioral programs, 65–71
  multimodal programs, 71–73
  social skills training, 54–65
Institutional behavior, 60
Institutional reparation, definition of, 53
Institutional structure, improving intervention success and, 135–38
Institutions:
  types of, 79–89
    residential establishments, 84–89
    secure institutions, 79–84
Instruction technique, social skills training (SST), 56
Intervention:
  case study, 73–78
  failure, 133–35
    client resistance, 134–35
    how to minimize, 135–43
    institutional resistance, 133–34
  outcome studies, 119–20
    community-based treatment, 123–25

potential negative outcomes, 125–26
residential treatment, 121–23
success, 129–33
  assessment, 129–30
  improvement of, 135–143
  program design/delivery, 131–33
See also Family-based intervention; School-based intervention
Interviewing, 40–41
  assessment and, 32–34, 46–49
  goals of, 32–33
  interview schedule, 33

Justice model, 127–28
Juvenile crime, 1–23
  definition of, 1–2
  self-report studies, 2–4
See also Young offenders

Learning theories, 5–10
  differential association theory, 5–7
  operant learning, 7–9
  social learning theory, 9–10
Locus of control, 12

Macro skills training, 58–59
Meta-analysis technique, 120–21
  effect size (ES), 120
    in community-based interventions, 124
    for contingency management/cognitive behavioral studies, 123
Micro skills training, 57–58
Modeling, social skills training (SST), 56
Moral education, 72
Moral reasoning, 12–13
  development of, 70–71
Multimodal programs, 71–73
  aggression replacement training (ART), 72–73
  "Getting It Together" (GIT) program, 73
  WISER program, 71

About the Author

Clive Hollin, formerly a Senior Psychologist in the English prison system, is a Lecturer in Psychology at the University of Leicester, where he teaches the psychology of criminal behavior to both undergraduates and professionals training at postgraduate level. He has published widely in the field of criminological psychology, including the recent text *Psychology and Crime: An Introduction to Criminological Psychology*, and has chaired the Training Committee of the Division of Criminological and Legal Psychology of The British Psychological Society.

Psychology Practitioner Guidebooks

Editors

Arnold P. Goldstein, Syracuse University
Leonard Krasner, Stanford University & SUNY at Stony Brook
Sol L. Garfield, Washington University in St. Louis

William L. Golden, E. Thomas Dowd & Fred Friedberg—
HYPNOTHERAPY: A Modern Approach

Patricia Lacks—BEHAVIORAL TREATMENT FOR PERSISTENT
INSOMNIA

Arnold P. Goldstein & Harold Keller—AGGRESSIVE BEHAVIOR:
Assessment and Intervention

C. Eugene Walker, Barbara L. Bonner & Keith L. Kaufman—
THE PHYSICALLY AND SEXUALLY ABUSED CHILD: Evaluation and
Treatment

Robert E. Becker, Richard G. Heimberg & Alan S. Bellack—SOCIAL
SKILLS TRAINING TREATMENT FOR DEPRESSION

Richard F. Dangel & Richard A. Polster—TEACHING CHILD
MANAGEMENT SKILLS

Albert Ellis, John F. McInerney, Raymond DiGiuseppe & Raymond
Yeager—RATIONAL-EMOTIVE THERAPY WITH ALCOHOLICS AND
SUBSTANCE ABUSERS

Johnny L. Matson & Thomas H. Ollendick—ENHANCING CHILDREN'S
SOCIAL SKILLS: Assessment and Training

Edward B. Blanchard, John E. Martin & Patricia M. Dubbert—NON-DRUG
TREATMENTS FOR ESSENTIAL HYPERTENSION

Samuel M. Turner & Deborah C. Beidel—TREATING OBSESSIVE-
COMPULSIVE DISORDER

Alice W. Pope, Susan M. McHale & W. Edward Craighead—SELF-ESTEEM
ENHANCEMENT WITH CHILDREN AND ADOLESCENTS

Jean E. Rhodes & Leonard A. Jason—PREVENTING SUBSTANCE
ABUSE AMONG CHILDREN AND ADOLESCENTS

Gerald D. Oster, Janice E. Caro, Daniel R. Eagen & Margaret A. Lillo—
ASSESSING ADOLESCENTS

Robin C. Winkler, Dirck W. Brown, Margaret van Keppel & Amy
Blanchard—CLINICAL PRACTICE IN ADOPTION

Roger Poppen—BEHAVIORAL RELAXATION TRAINING AND
ASSESSMENT

Michael D. LeBow—ADULT OBESITY THERAPY

Robert Paul Liberman, William J. DeRisi & Kim T. Mueser—SOCIAL
SKILLS TRAINING FOR PSYCHIATRIC PATIENTS

Johnny L. Matson—TREATING DEPRESSION IN CHILDREN AND
ADOLESCENTS

Sol L. Garfield—THE PRACTICE OF BRIEF PSYCHOTHERAPY

Arnold P. Goldstein, Barry Glick, Mary Jane Irwin,
Claudia Pask-McCartney & Ibrahim Rubama—REDUCING
DELINQUENCY: Intervention in the Community

Albert Ellis, Joyce L. Sichel, Raymond J. Yeager, Dominic J. DiMattia,
Raymond DiGiuseppe—RATIONAL-EMOTIVE COUPLES THERAPY

Clive R. Hollin—COGNITIVE-BEHAVIORAL INTERVENTIONS WITH
YOUNG OFFENDERS